THE PLANTFINDER'S GUIDE TO

TENDER PERENNIALS

THE PLANTFINDER'S GUIDE TO

TENDER
PERENNIALS

Ian Cooke

DAVID & CHARLES
Newton Abbot

TIMBER PRESS
Portland, Oregon

Dedicated to
Joy, Hannah, Josh, Sam and Tom

'If you would be happy for a week, take a wife;
If you would be happy for a month, kill a pig;
If you would be happy all your life, plant a garden.'

Attributed to T. Fuller

ACKNOWLEDGEMENTS

I wish to thank my wife, Joy, for her patience and encouragement, and also for stoically looking after all my plants, while I wrote this book. A reluctant convert! I also acknowledge the assistance of friends and colleagues who have supplied me with information, in particular the valuable help given by Brian Halliwell in painstakingly checking my text for technical and botanical accuracy. Thanks also to my friend Philip who gave me house space and tolerated my moodiness as I worked on the manuscript.

The publishers would like to acknowledge the kind cooperation of the following who gave permission to photograph in their gardens: Angus White of Architectural Plants, Cooks Farm, Nuthurst, Horsham, West Sussex, RH13 6LH; Will Giles at Oak Tree House, 6 Cotman Road, Thorpe, Norwich, Norfolk; the Director at The Royal Botanic Gardens, Kew, London; Mr and Mrs R. Paice at Bourton House, Bourton-on-the-Hill, Gloucestershire; Colegrave Seeds, West Adderbury, Banbury, Oxfordshire, OX17 3EY; Mr and Mrs D. Ward of 53 Ladywood, Eastleigh, Hampshire; Lynn and Peter Prior, The Little Cottage, Southampton Road, Lymington, Hampshire; Mr and Mrs Ian Pasley-Tyler of Coton Manor, Northamptonshire, NN6 8RQ; John Coke of Green Farm Plants, Bentley, Farnham, Surrey, GU10 5JX

PICTURE ACKNOWLEDGEMENTS

Karl Adamson 24, 32, 42, 48, 56, 64, 76, 88, 92, 96, 104, 112 Ian Cooke 23, 31BR, 52, 54, 81, 91, 114, 121BR, 154TR, 161, 172, 173 Marie O'Hara 2, 3, 6, 8, 10, 11, 12, 15TR, 16, 18, 26TR, 26BL, 27, 28TR, 29, 31TL, 34, 36, 37, 39, 40, 41, 45, 46, 47, 51, 58, 59, 60, 61, 62, 66, 67, 69, 70, 72, 73, 75, 79, 80, 82TR, 82TL, 83, 84, 85, 86, 94, 98, 99 100, 103, 106TL, 106BR, 108, 109, 110, 111, 115, 116, 121TL, 124, 129, 130, 131, 132BR, 132TL, 134, 136, 137, 138, 140, 141, 142, 143, 144, 146, 147, 149, 151, 152, 153TL, 153BR, 154BL, 156, 158, 159, 160, 162, 166, 170, 177, 179TL, 179TR Nigel Temple 13, BL15, Royal Horticultural Society, Lindley Library 14, Steven Wooster/Christopher Lloyd's garden 20

Illustrations on pages 36, 143, 153, 164, 165, 168, 169, 171, 173 by Coral Mula
Illustrations on pages 118, 119, 120, 123, 125, 126, 127, 128, 131, 133, 148 by Alison Hoblyn

First published in the UK in 1998 by David & Charles Publishers, Brunel House, Newton Abbot, Devon
ISBN 0 7153 0635 9
A catalogue record for this book is available from the British Library.

First published in North America in 1998 by Timber Press Inc., 133 SW Second Avenue, Suite 450, Portland, Oregon 97204, USA
ISBN 0 88192 450 4
Cataloguing-in-Publication Data is on file with the Library of Congress

Printed in France by Imprimerie Pollina S.A.

Photographs page 1 Exotic planting at Will Giles' Garden
page 2 *Rhodochiton atrosanguineus*; page 3 *Arctotis × hybrida* 'Flame'

Contents

Preface

It all began at a Chelsea Flower Show some years ago. I was struggling through the jostling crowds for a glimpse of parading flowers and pattern book gardens with that sinking, cynical feeling that so often mars 'Chelsea' for the perennial visitor. Then it happened. There before me was something quite different! It was love at first sight!

The exhibit was a sea of colour – nothing sophisticated, no props, just plants. It was a display of tender perennials grown and mounted by the apprentices of the Royal Parks. Here were the pastel daisies of argyranthemums in a dozen different varieties, the brilliantly coloured catherine wheels of gazanias, spires of penstemons and carpets of verbena. Among the feast of flowers ran silvery threads of helichrysum foliage, fountains of stripy arundo and filigree euryops. Never before had I seen this range of plants displayed together. Gathered from the corners of the world, all they had in common was their intolerance of frost. I fell in love with tender perennials. It was a memorable Chelsea, for from that whirlwind romance there has developed a deep passion which looks set to become a lifelong devotion.

After that Chelsea I started collecting tender perennials with the fervour of the newly converted and planted them in bedding displays in the gardens of Reading University, where I then worked. Plants were garnered from many sources. Some were unexpected, such as Bristol Zoological Gardens, that unique Victorian time capsule. Here gardening is still practised as the art and craft it used to be a hundred years ago, with standard lantanas, old named heliotropes, cannas and coloured-leaf geraniums.

Then I met Ivan Dickings, another professional but with a private passion for tender perennials. In his beautiful garden in Suffolk he showed me displays of hundreds of tender perennials among shrubs and other plants, demonstrating their garden versatility. Letters and visits to Kew Botanic Gardens, the Royal Horticultural Society at Wisley, Probus, Beth Chatto's garden in Essex and so many others resulted in generous packages of carefully wrapped cuttings.

As time went on and I became acquainted with others with a similar interest, the idea arose of a society of some sort. Feeling like a publican suggesting a wine tasting for a temperance group, I approached the Hardy Plant Society with the proposal of starting a group for aficionados of tender perennials. The Half-Hardy Group was born. Repeated enquiries for a nursery that supplied a range of tender perennials led to the setting up of my own specialist nursery, Brockings Exotics. Then came the request for a book on the subject. That has taken a little longer, but here it is!

The recently introduced *Dahlia* 'Moonfire' grows to around 45 cm (18 in) and has rich bronze foliage.

Part One Introducing Tender Perennials

I What Is a Tender Perennial?

There can be no concise definition of what a tender perennial is that would satisfy a botanist without boring most gardeners and readers. For the purposes of this book it will be assumed to mean 'any perennial plant that will grow outside successfully in temperate climates during the summer months, but requires some winter protection'. The latter is normally a frost-protected glasshouse, but the ingenious gardener will undoubtedly find other ways of overwintering those plants on the borderlines of hardiness.

Such a statement is of course incomplete; not only do plants vary considerably in their cold tolerance but the individual microclimates of gardens are very different. A gardener who is lucky enough to cultivate a garden on a sheltered south-facing slope in Cornwall, the southern states of the USA or the Mediterranean areas of Europe may well regard argyranthemums, verbenas and cannas as totally hardy. By contrast, a gardener struggling on a bleak site in the north of England or Canada may consider such plants as pansies and wallflowers to be tender. This book is generally written for those climates where

A luxuriant mix of tender perennials complemented by an old terracotta rhubarb-forcing pot.

winter frosts would prevent such tender plants from remaining outside during the winter.

The term 'tender perennial' is a catch-all phrase that covers a wide group of plants that share a method of culture. Specialist plant books such as this often include a section on the botany of the plants under discussion. In this case, as the plants come from many genera, it is difficult to find common ground for discussion. Many families, including Compositae, Solanaceae, Labiatae, Malvaceae, Cannaceae and a host of others are represented, and the taxonomic features of such a range of plants are quite diverse.

Horticulturally the range is wide and includes shrubs, sub-shrubs and herbaceous, bulbous and tuberous plants. In stature they encompass everything between diminutive dwarfs such as *Sutera cordata* 'Snowflake' at a mere 5 cm (2 in) and giants such as *Canna musifolia* at 2.5 m (8¼ ft). In temperate climates, where such plants must be propagated annually or returned to glasshouses for the winter, their ultimate potential is rarely appreciated; given ideal conditions in their native homes, without the intrusion of winter frost, many ultimately become trees or large shrubs. For example, *Jacaranda mimosifolia*, which is normally seen as a small foliage plant, will in its native Bolivia ultimately grow into a 10 m (30 ft) tree with beautiful blue flowers.

The visual attractions of such a dissimilar group of plants are predictably extensive. As well as variously formed flowers in every imaginable colour, there are plants with beautiful foliage, with interesting outlines (often described as architectural plants), and with perfumed flowers or aromatic leaves. Their uses within the garden are equally diverse, with plants for formal beds and borders as well as planters and hanging baskets.

Among the tender perennials there are many robust, brightly coloured and even brash plants that will appeal to those of us with a penchant for gardening in the bold style. By contrast there are many others with more graceful outlines, diminutive flowers and softer colourings that will be acceptable to those with a gentler taste. Tender perennials descend from many different families native to many parts of the world, and this makes them a most diverse group of plants.

Tender perennials are also sometimes described as half-hardy perennials because they spend half of the year under glasshouse protection and the other half outside. Both terms are equally acceptable. Garden centres and other commercial sources sometimes coin various phrases such

A hot colour combination using the free-flowering *Cuphea cyanea*, with the foliage of *Pelargonium* 'Vancouver Centennial' and a double red begonia with bronze leaves.

as 'patio plants', 'summer shiners' and 'inside – outside plants', and plants offered as 'conservatory plants' will also often include tender perennials.

Occasionally tender perennials are dismissed as being poor value or as difficult plants requiring a great deal of extra attention, though gardeners who make such accusations will often be found spending tedious hours tying up soaring delphiniums, disbudding chrysanthemums and painstakingly handpicking caterpillars from their brassicas. They are of course not plants that can be totally neglected from year to year, but if they are considered as a bunch of flowers with roots that will last for four or five months, their value can be easily appreciated.

2 History, Habitat & Hardiness

For centuries gardeners and botanists have collected plants from far-flung regions of the world and brought them back to their homelands to cultivate in their gardens. Plants are very adaptable and many grow and thrive in conditions quite unlike their native climates. Others struggle, but such is the nature of the gardener that these plants are seen as a challenge rather than rejected as failures.

Despite the amazing range of garden plants now available, the desire for the new and unusual is ever-increasing. Tender perennials have in recent years been one of the popular groups of plants that have met this request for something different. As garden plants, most tender perennials are very rewarding, giving interest and colour from the moment they are planted. Most are quite easy to grow and make satisfying plants for new and young gardeners, offering rapid results. Most continue growing

The feathery foliage of *Arundo donax* 'Variegata' contrasted with the rich foliage of *Iresine herbstii* 'Brilliantissima' and the dwarf *Dahlia* 'Bednall Beauty'.

and flowering throughout the summer months until an abrupt end with the first frost.

THE HISTORY OF TENDER PERENNIALS

To trace the origins of this group of plants we need to go back at least to the early 19th century. In the 1820s and 1830s, there was a move away from 'cottage gardening' towards the display of plants *en masse*, later known as bedding out. Many of the plants used for this type of display had already arrived or were soon to be introduced. The blue *Lobelia erinus* had been introduced from the Cape of Good Hope before 1700 and sweet-scented *Heliotropium peruvianum* from Peru in 1757. The striking red *Salvia splendens* and yellow *Calceolaria rugosa* both arrived from Chile in 1822 and *Begonia semperflorens* from Brazil in 1829. *Petunia violacea*, the forerunner of many of our modern petunias, was introduced in 1831.

All of these plants came from warm temperate or subtropical regions and were originally grown under glass in the UK. As time progressed it was discovered that these plants would survive and even thrive outside in the British summer, although they needed glasshouse protection over winter. In this way the whole concept of bedding out, which was to become the overriding garden style for most of the 19th century, had its inception. It was also soon discovered that these plants had a longer flowering season than many traditional cottage-garden plants and were still colourful in late summer. Undoubtedly the repeal of the glass tax in 1845, which meant that sheet glass dropped in price from 1s 2d to a mere 2d, had a great deal to do with the sudden increase in the popularity of glasshouses. In turn, this encouraged the popularity of tender plants.

In the same year 'Tom Thumb', the first dwarf red bedding pelargonium, was introduced and the Royal Horticultural Society arranged a competition for colour schemes for flowerbeds. As the bedding movement gained momentum, arguments developed first over the basic issue of 'mixing versus massing', referring to the older cottage style of display versus the newer bedding style. Then the debate moved on to the theory of colour schemes. Such eminent gardeners as John Lindley, who was responsible for the Royal Horticultural Society

Victorian conservatories such as this one at Finsbury Park in North London would probably have grown many tender perennials as newly introduced novelties in the 19th century.

gardens (then at Chiswick), James Donald, who designed the Hampton Court displays, and Donald Beaton, bedding advisor to the Royal Botanic Gardens at Kew, all hotly debated what was at the time a key issue.

Propagation in the 19th century

It must be remembered that many of the plants used for bedding displays today are in fact perennial and could last from year to year. Even such familiar plants as the red *Salvia splendens*, multicoloured petunias and blue lobelia, which are now almost solely produced each year from seed, will grow on to subsequent years given suitable conditions. A mild winter and a particularly sheltered spot will allow a number of bedding plants left in from the previous season to sprout into growth and early flower, proving the perennial nature of the plant. Under normal circumstances, however, we do not now make any effort to keep those plants which can be so easily propagated from seed.

Back in the 19th century, however, the majority of bedding plants were propagated in vast numbers by cuttings. The quantities involved for some of the large gardens were on a vast scale; the great Italianate gardens at Shrubland Park in Suffolk and Trentham Park in

Staffordshire each used over 100,000 plants annually and in 1880 the gardeners at Drumlanrig raised 300,000 plants for bedding out. Glasshouse facilities were rarely geared to production on such a scale and many makeshift arrangements were used. Plants such as verbenas were rooted with as many as 20 cuttings in a 7.5 cm (3 in) pot. In some cases they were overwintered in unheated pits and frames, the latter being insulated with dry litter or covered with sacking in cold weather. Damp and subsequent disease was a problem and some gardeners would use quicklime in the frame to absorb excess moisture. Pest and disease control was by means of simple remedies such as tobacco or laurel water. Rooted cuttings were often not potted until the spring, when a further batch of cuttings was taken, a practice which is quite the norm today. Plants were also often grown under the vines in a vinery until the leaves eventually obliterated the light. They did not always fare well and disasters from both cold and pest damage are recorded. That the gardeners were even partially successful attests to their skill.

The fountain garden at Shrubland Park, pictured in 1856, shows the formal style used to display bedding plants in the 19th century.

Some curious techniques were developed, one being the practice of mossing plants. This took place in late spring, when the plants were being hardened off. Each plant was tipped from its pot, wrapped in a small nest of moss and bedded back into the frame. It is said that watering was then quicker and easier. When planting time came, such plants were lighter than those in heavy clay pots and could be instantly planted, rather like those in the biodegradable pots we have today.

Plant hybridization was in its infancy and when new cultivars were produced they were subsequently propagated by cuttings, as there was no knowledge of how to perpetuate them by pure breeding strains or by modern F_1 hybrid techniques. Such a tedious and labour-intensive system did not deter our Victorian forebears and nurseries offered myriad varieties of verbena and other favourite plants.

One of the popular bedding schemes in the 1850s used *Verbena venosa* with variegated pelargoniums, which produced an effect resembling shot silk. The promotion of this idea in the gardening press of the day led to an unprecedented demand on nurserymen for variegated pelargoniums, making the writer of the feature most out of favour with the trade.

The fashion spreads

Eventually the fashion for bedding made its way from the vast gardens of the rich to the more modest plots of the cottager. In the September issue of the *Gardener's Chronicle* for 1852 there is an account of Mr Bellenden Ker's 'little flower garden' at his cottage near Cheshunt: 'Among bedding plants the following are still gay, viz.- Tom Thumb, Ivy-leaved, Ayre's Gem, Huntsman, Lady Mary Fox, Mangle variegated and Compactum pelargoniums; Kentish Hero, Amplexicaulis and Kayii Calceolarias; a semi-double purple petunia, Robinson's Defiance and other Verbenas, *Lantana delicatissima*, *Bouvardia triphylla*, *Salvia patens*, *Cuphea platycentra*, the white-flowered variegated alyssum and *Isotoma axilliaris*, which is the only annual Mr Wooley [the gardener] has retained.' One wonders at the scale of a cottage garden that requires a gardener! Some of these plants are still available today and it is particularly interesting to read of

Isotoma, which has recently been rediscovered and widely promoted as new.

One of the arguments against bedding out was the short life of the display and as a result of this there developed the greater use of foliage plants such as cannas, coleus, palms, yuccas, bananas and many others, including caladium, maranta, croton and philodendron, which we would think of as hothouse plants. Cannabis was even grown for its attractive foliage! One of the earliest proponents of this style was John Gibson, who produced foliage displays at Battersea Park in London in 1864. As well as beds filled with such exotics, individual tree ferns or bananas would be dotted across lawns or through glades to create a 'cool and tropical forest scene'. We would now describe this style as subtropical bedding and it is once again becoming popular. Even William Robinson, an opponent of bedding in general, took up this style and in 1871 wrote a book on the subject called *The Subtropical Garden*.

The final Victorian refinement of the bedding system was the use of dwarf foliage plants to produce intricate designs and patterns. Plants such as *Alternanthera*, *Iresine* and various succulents together with some alpine plants had a long season of display and could be clipped into tight shapes. The first real exponent was John Fleming, head gardener at Cliveden in Berkshire, who laid out a bed in 1868 with the monogram 'HS' for Harriet, Duchess of Sutherland. After this followed coats of arms, mottoes, emblems, dragons and a host of other patterns. The style became known as carpet bedding or mosaiculture.

The first floral clock was created by John Hattie, superintendent of the parks in Edinburgh, in the 1890s. The idea had come from Paris and was described as a floral

Exotic foliage plants growing as specimens in grass show the subtropical style favoured by William Robinson.

freak. A further dimension was added, literally, with the creation of sculptural beds where crowns, vases, baskets and cushions complete with tassels were all produced from plant material.

Decline and renaissance

By the late 19th century the fashion for bedding had started to wane. Writers such as Gertrude Jekyll were proposing a return to English cottage-garden style. Bedding plants fell from favour and in the 20th century two world wars caused the demise of many of the big estates, along with the loss of skills, glasshouses and the vast range of plants they contained. At the same time, the science of plant breeding developed and it became possible to produce bedding plants reliably from seed each year. Eventually F_1 hybrid seed strains were developed and we can now produce predictable results from a packet of seed. Seed also gives the convenience of starting afresh each year with vigorous stock free from pests and disease, and avoids the high cost of overwintering under heated glass. Consequently, many of the older-style bedding plants have all but disappeared. Fortunately, a fair number have survived in private gardens, small nurseries and parks departments and have now reappeared from their exile.

Many long-forgotten treasures such as scented heliotropes, double nasturtiums, bronze calceolarias,

Carpet-bedding displays such as this at Saltburn-by-the-Sea, North Yorkshire, were very elaborate, highly formal and used many thousands of plants.

double blue lobelias and pink and yellow marguerites have been rediscovered. Hailed as new and promoted as patio or basket plants, they have soft colours and graceful habits that have proved instantly acceptable both to the average gardener and the plant collector in search of something different.

BREEDERS AND COLLECTORS

Back in the 19th century many new cultivars were produced in the great gardens of the aristocracy and named by the head gardeners after the estate or its owner. Consequently, we have heliotropes such as *Heliotropium* 'Chatsworth' and 'Lord Roberts'; *Pelargonium* 'Lady Plymouth'; *Coleus* (*Solenostemon*) 'Lord Falmouth' and *Verbena* 'Sissinghurst' and 'Lawrence Johnson'. Sadly this traditional habit has disappeared and plants are often now renamed purely for commercial purposes. The recently raised *Helichrysum petiolare* 'Goring Silver', named by its raiser after the local village, is now being offered under many names. Although it is possible to register names and protect plants with propagation rights, the process is complicated and really only for the serious nurseryperson.

While much attention is devoted to popular groups of plants such as roses and dahlias, there are few breeders working specifically to produce new cultivars of tender perennials today. In the UK, the most spectacular work has been done by Hector Harrison, who has produced an amazing range of hybrid diascias with an abundance of flowers and a long display season. However, the colour range remains strictly within the pinks, apricots and lavender pinks and it will require a genetic breakthrough to expand beyond this range. In the 1960s and 1970s Roy and Kenneth Pedley did much work on the improvement of coleus and many of the good cultivars grown today were raised and selected by them. Since then no one has done any serious work on this genus.

Many of the holders of the National Collections are serious collectors acquiring plants from diverse sources, although few actually hybridize them. Various commercial growers are also serious plant collectors and particular mention should be made of Derry Watkins and her passion for South African plants. Following her trips to South Africa many new plants have entered cultivation through her nursery, Special Plants. A link has also recently been established between Pershore College in Worcestershire

Coleus 'Coppersmith', a lovely cultivar raised by the Pedley brothers, who specialized in coleus for many years.

and Kirstenbosch Botanical Gardens in South Africa. It is to be hoped that, after trials, many new plants will become available in the UK and elsewhere.

For some years, work on osteospermums, abutilons and argyranthemums has been undertaken at Cannington College in Somerset, originally under the guidance of Roy Cheek. Argyranthemums such as *A.* 'Mary Cheek' and 'Cheek's Peach', *Osteospermum* 'Cannington Roy' and 'James Elliman' and *Abutilon* 'Cannington Peter' and 'Cannington Sally', plus many others, bear witness to the work of this institution. The college has also imported a whole new range of argyranthemums from Australia and it will be interesting to see how many of these thrive in the more moderate temperate climate of the UK.

NATIVE HABITATS

The popularity of travel abroad has whetted the appetite of many otherwise conservative gardeners. Returning home, they may not be able to garden in a tropical country but there is the desire to create a tropical illusion by the use of 'exotic' looking plants. After groves of citrus, arching bougainvilleas, towering cannas and clouds of plumbago, the bedraggled roses and windswept lupins of a British summer look rather tame and lacklustre.

By far the majority of tender perennials come from areas with a Mediterranean-style climate, where summers are warm to hot and dry and winters are mild, with most of the annual rainfall. Sunshine levels are generally high. As well as areas around the Mediterranean Sea Basin, this classification includes South Africa, the southern USA, southern Japan, Chile, the North Island of New Zealand and the south-western regions of the British Isles (see page 188). All of these have a similar climate.

South Africa has an exceedingly rich flora which has attracted botanists and gardeners for hundreds of years. The climate is varied and habitats range from lush subtropical forests to arid deserts, and it is this variety that contributes to the richness of the plant life. Many South African plants have the specific name *capensis*, meaning from the Cape region, for example *Phygelius capensis*. Well-known tender perennials include subjects such as *Anisodontea, Arctotis, Diascia, Euryops, Felicia, Gazania, Helichrysum, Pelargonium, Plumbago* and *Osteospermum*.

Then there are those plants from the Canary Isles and Madeira, including *Argyranthemum, Aeonium, Geranium palmatum* and *Lotus*. From Mexico and the southern USA come *Bidens, Lobelia, Salvia* and *Verbena*. Many of these plants show particular resistance to drought and revel in

These drifts of *Geranium maderense* and the towering blue echiums behind give a Mediterranean feel to the gardens at Tresco Abbey in the Scilly Isles.

hot dry summers. If the current British weather pattern of dry summers and mild winters persists, these may well be the plants of the future in the UK – though even in the best of British summers most will benefit from a little coddling in the form of some shelter from wind or a position against a warm wall.

Many New Zealand plants are suited to the British climate, as they come from a similar maritime location. *Senecio*, *Hebe*, *Olearia*, *Coprosma*, *Pittosporum*, sword-leaved *Phormium* and waxy-leaved *Griselinia* will all adapt to our tough conditions. Given a little shelter or a warm wall, many species will survive and even thrive here.

Some of these plants change their habit of growth in order to adapt to the variable British climate. For example, *Melianthus major*, which comes from South Africa, is really a large shrub and very impressive when fully mature. Under British conditions it often grows as a herbaceous perennial, producing a lush exuberance of silver foliage and then dying back to the ground each year. Many others grow with ease and vigour and some plants that flower for only a few weeks in spring in their homelands and become dormant in the hot dry summer will perform for many months in the constant 'spring' of a warm but often damp summer.

UNDERSTANDING HARDINESS

An understanding of hardiness is of primary importance to the growing of tender perennials, but there is in fact no precise definition of hardiness that is generally accepted. One standard student textbook comments that 'temperatures below 0°C (32°F) kill many plants but others are frost hardy'. It then dismisses the subject by concluding that 'we still do not know how it is that one plant can survive conditions that are lethal to another'. Not a promising explanation for this all-important term!

All plants have an individual range of favourable temperatures, sometimes referred to as optimum temperatures, for growth. Between these maximums and minimums, the fundamental plant processes can take place and growth occurs. Above, or more commonly below, these extremes they die. Commercial crops such as tomatoes, cucumbers and chrysanthemums have been the subject of considerable research, so that precise optimum temperatures can be given for various stages of growth and cropping.

The same cannot be said about the majority of garden plants grown outside and under glass. The rarer and newer the plant, probably the less we know about its ideal temperatures. It is often only as the result of the exchange of information between keen amateur gardeners as well as professional sources such as the botanic gardens that we learn about the hardiness of individual plants. Many of the garden plants that we now grow outside as hardy were considered tender when first collected and were accordingly often grown under protection.

It has been established that hardiness is a factor within individual plants, part of their genetic makeup, and it is consequently possible to breed plants for their hardiness. For example, *Grevillea* 'Canberra Gem' is the result of a cross between the hardy *G. juniperina* and the less hardy *G. rosmarinifolia*. The resulting interspecific hybrid is an excellent garden plant and fully frost-hardy down to −10°C (14°F).

The RHS Dictionary of Gardening defines hardiness as the 'capability [of a plant] to withstand all the year round climatic rigours of a certain area without glass'. The reference to 'glass' might be more correctly replaced with 'protection', as there are many materials other than glass that can be used to protect plants. Polythene, bubble film and fleece are the modern materials, with hessian, straw and bracken being their traditional counterparts.

Hardiness obviously relates not only to a specific plant but also to a climatic area – hence a plant that may be quite hardy in a mild climate will be considered tender in a colder area. Soil type and nutrition play a part in the equation as well. A poor, gravelly soil will only allow moderate growth, which will ripen adequately; it is less retentive of water during the winter months and therefore likely to be warmer. By contrast a heavy, rich soil will promote lush summer growth which may not ripen adequately, and in winter that soil will be colder when sub-zero temperatures persist.

Measuring hardiness

The variability of climate from one area to another and its effect on plant hardiness are seen to a marked degree in the USA. Plants that would be quite hardy in the mild climate of Florida would stand no chance of survival in the long, cold winters of New England. In order to address this problem of definition, a scale of climatic zones has been developed. This was first produced for horticultural purposes in 1927 and has been updated on various occasions, with the current scale of zones being produced by the United States Department of Agriculture. These zones are based on winter isotherms – lines drawn on a map linking together places with the same temperature at a given time.

Zone 1   below −46°C (−50°F)
Zone 2   −46 to −40°C (−50 to −40°F)
Zone 3   −40 to −34°C (−40 to −30°F)
Zone 4   −34 to −29°C (−30 to −20°F)
Zone 5   −29 to −23°C (20 to −10°F)
Zone 6   −23 to −18°C (−10 to 0°F)
Zone 7   −18 to −12°C (0 to 10°F)
Zone 8   −12 to −7°C (10 to 20°F)
Zone 9   −7 to −1°C (20 to 30°F)
Zone 10   -1 to 4°C (30 to 40°F)
Zone 11   above 4°C (above 40°F)

This scale is used in many gardening publications and catalogues, especially in the USA, for basic guidance on where to grow what. Such a scheme has its limitations, as it does not take into account other localized variables. Although it is occasionally used in the UK, the zone system is of limited value to British gardeners as the UK covers only climatic zones 6 to 9 (the tip of Cornwall is 9/10).

In the UK, the Consumer's Association prints a useful small map within its publication *Gardening from Which?* This divides the UK into four climatic zones referred to as regions 1 to 4, from coldest to warmest, and usually coloured for easy identification. It is interesting to see that London is designated as region 4, illustrating the fact that most cities have a microclimate somewhat warmer than their overall surroundings. Pelargoniums and other tender plants will often survive over winter in a city windowbox long after their country cousins have been frosted.

Such classifications can only be generalizations, and there will be gardens that have either unduly warm or cold conditions. A gardener in one well-known West Country garden told me that it was a cold garden, 'one extra coat down here compared to up in the town'! Such frost pockets are often the result of natural conditions, although they can be inadvertently created by badly placed windbreaks. Likewise there are many gardens that enjoy a milder climate, either because of some unique natural shelter or because windbreaks and shelterbelts have been carefully developed over the years, eventually creating a unique microclimate.

In the broadest of terms, hardy plants are those that we can grow outside in a certain area without winter protection. Half-hardy perennials, or tender perennials, do require winter protection of some sort but will thrive outside in the summer months, provided temperatures are high enough and there is no danger of frost. For the purpose of this book, I have devised a unique star rating system appropriate to the consideration of tender plants. On a scale of one to five stars it indicates the lowest winter temperature a plant is generally able to withstand (see page 22).

Part Two A Selection of the Best

3 A–Z of Tender Perennials

The following list encompasses a wide range of tender perennial genera. Inevitably personal choice has influenced the selections, especially of cultivars, which in some cases are too numerous to be included in their entirety. A few hardy plants that fit in well with these tender perennials for one reason or another are also included. Most tender perennials flower from early summer to autumn, so the flowering season is not specified except in those that differ from the norm.

HEIGHTS

The figure at the end of the entry gives approximate height. It is difficult to give accurate heights for many tender perennials as they are rarely allowed to grow to their full maturity even under conservatory conditions. The heights listed here can be assumed to be the predictable height achieved in a single growing season, though even that is very uncertain, given the vagaries of a temperate climate. A '+' sign indicates that under conservatory conditions or when grown on from year to year the plant will achieve a greater height.

PLANT NAMES

In addition to botanical names, commonly used nursery names are sometimes given for ease of identification. With tender perennials there does seem to be a particular trend to popularize them by the use of gimmicky names. For example, *Sutera cordata* 'Snowflake' is better known as *Bacopa*; it is said that a nurseryman thought it would never sell under its correct name, so he rechristened it. With some genera such as *Verbena* it is almost impossible to list all the names that are sometimes used.

HARDINESS

For guidance each plant is classified in one of the following groups, although many other cultural factors will also determine their actual response.

★★★★★ **Fully hardy** Plants will withstand temperatures down to around −15°C (5°F) and can therefore be generally regarded as hardy down to zone 7.

★★★★ **Hardy** Plants will withstand temperatures down to around −5°C (23°F) when established and can be regarded as hardy down to zone 9.

★★★ **Almost hardy** Plants are able to withstand occasional light frost down to −1°C (30°F). Hardy to zone 10.

★★ **Half hardy** Plants will withstand no frost but require only cool overwintering temperatures of around 5–10°C (41–50°F) – zone 11 plants.

★ **Tender** Plants will withstand no frost and require to be kept warm over winter at around 12–15°C (54–59°F) – zone 11 plants.

AWARD OF GARDEN MERIT

The Award of Garden Merit (AGM) is awarded by the Royal Horticultural Society to plants of outstanding excellence for garden use or decoration. The award is given either following trial at the Society's garden at Wisley or submission to one of the society's committees. In this book it is denoted by the symbol ♔.

DESCRIPTIONS

In general I have chosen to describe the plants featured here in an informal rather than botanical style. Where there is no description of flowers, the plant is grown for its foliage and flowers are insignificant or rarely produced. Likewise, foliage is only described where it is a distinct feature of the plant. By far the majority of tender perennials are propagated by tip cuttings and only where propagation is different is it specifically described.

ABUTILON
Malvaceae

This is a genus of over 100 fast-growing shrubby plants. Some are annuals but most are perennial and tender or on the borderline of hardiness, requiring the protection of a warm wall or other shelter. Many are from South or Central America, although the genus is found throughout temperate areas.

Most of those that interest us here are hybrids, used for summer garden display. Ultimately some will make small trees and as such are valuable as centrepieces for patio planters, or as highlight plants among other lower-growing tender perennials. They are useful additions to the cool conservatory, where you can look up into the bell-like flowers of larger mature plants, which are produced throughout the year.

A range of colours is available from white through yellow and orange to pink and red within the tender species and lavender/blues in the hardier ones. Many cultivars have attractive contrasting veining within the flowers. A number have variegated foliage, but in some the effects are caused by abutilon mosaic virus and some people regard the effect as too close to the appearance of a sick plant. The habits of growth vary from vigorous, sturdy types which make small trees 2–3 m (6½–10 ft) tall to the more stocky types which remain bushes of no more than 60 cm (2 ft). Others have a lax habit of growth and can be trained as climbers or grown in baskets and allowed to trail.

Hardiness varies between species and cultivars. Basically, *A. vitifolium*, together with its hybrids and cultivars, and *A. megapotamicum* are the only ones that are likely to survive outside in sheltered spots in temperate areas. Most of the others need to be kept frost-free but prefer a temperature of 10°C (50°F) over winter to grow comfortably. Plants of the tender types left outside may survive mild winters, often dying back to the ground but then slowly regrowing into presentable plants the next season.

BOTANY

Most abutilons are shrubs or small trees. The leaves are petiolate, cordate, ovate or elliptic and often palmately lobed into three, five or seven sections; the margins are often dentate or serrate. The flowers are often solitary but sometimes grouped into racemes or panicles. They are bell-shaped and pendant and consist of five petals, often conspicuously veined. The calyx is often prominent and in species such as *A. megapotamicum* forms a major part of the plant's display.

HISTORY

Abutilons were recognized as valuable conservatory and bedding plants in the 19th century. Most of the cultivars are derived from *A. striatum*, which was introduced in 1837, and *A. darwinii*, introduced in 1871, both from Brazil. Of the many cultivars that appear in the 19th-century lists, 'Louise Marignac', 'Boule de Neige', 'Thompsonii' and 'Canary Bird' are probably the only ones still grown today.

PROPAGATION

Abutilons are propagated by short tip cuttings, the most suitable material coming from stocky side-shoots. They can be taken in early autumn or in early spring, although the best displays are produced from the autumn-rooted batch as they take a fair time to reach sizeable flowering plants. As the leaves are often quite large, it may be necessary to reduce the leaf area by trimming large leaves with a sharp knife.

After rooting, the young plants are grown on in a good potting compost under glass, tying the main stem to a cane as it grows. Most abutilons look more natural when the main stem (leader) is left unpinched, so that in time the plant will have a natural pyramidal habit. Usually sideshoots form quite naturally as the plant grows, but if this does not happen some growers prefer to pinch the leader.

CULTIVATION

Some of the more lax growers such as *A. megapotamicum* and *A. × millerii* do make better plants when pinched early. The mass of whippy shoots can be tied to a cane while in the greenhouse and when planted out can be spread and tied to a trellis. Older plants of most tender types can be pruned quite hard in late winter or early spring and the bushy new growths will soon produce flower buds, as most abutilons flower on young wood.

When planted in the garden, all abutilons need full sun to thrive and a well-drained fertile soil. It is difficult to quantify the heights of most abutilons as they are rarely allowed to grow to their full heights. In a heated conservatory many of the hybrids will make small trees 3 m (10 ft) or more in height but when abutilons are grown as a bedding or patio plant 1.5 m (5 ft) or less is the average achievement in a single season. Exceptions are noted.

The pale foliage of *Abutilon* 'Savitzii' contrasts with the vivid pink of *Verbena* 'Sissinghurst', McGregor's Ornamental beet and seed-raised pelargoniums.

PLATE I
Abutilon
All plants at shown approximately ½ size

A. 'Ashford Red'

A. 'Cannington Peter'

A. *pictum* 'Thompsonii'

A. 'Savitzii'

A. 'Cerise Queen'

A. 'Souvenir de Bonn'

A. 'Canary Bird'

A. megapotamicum 'Variegatum'

A. 'Boule de Neige'

A. 'Rotterdam'

PLANT LIST

A. **'Ashford Red'** A soft red. ★★ ♈

A. **'Boule de Neige'** Snowy white bells, set off by dark arrowhead foliage and almost black stems. Originally raised in the 19th century, it is still the best white cultivar. ★★

A. **'Canary Bird'** Produces lovely yellow bells, held clear of fresh green foliage, on almost black stems. Another 19th-century introduction. 'Golden Fleece' is similar. ★★ ♈

A. **'Cannington Carol'** A compact cultivar with small soft red flowers and small yellow variegated leaves. 90 cm (3 ft) ★ ♈

A. **'Cannington Peter'** Produces splendid crimson flowers over spotty yellow and green vine-shaped leaves. Young leaves are predominantly green and older ones almost pure gold. It is quite compact and stocky and has been known to overwinter outside in a mild winter. It is the variegated form of 'Nabob', originally produced by the transfer of virus to that cultivar. 1.2 m (4 ft) ★★ ♈

A. **'Cannington Sally'** Bright gold variegation with orange-red flowers. ★★

A. **'Cannington Sonia'** Large yellow bells over dark variegated foliage. ★★

Abutilon 'Canary Bird' is one of the few remaining 19th-century cultivars, still as good today as it was 100 years ago.

A. **'Cerise Queen'** Rich cerise-rose flowers and green foliage. ★★

A. **'Fireball'** One of the most compact growers, with small, finely pointed leaves and soft orange-red bells. 75 cm (2½ ft) ★★

A. **'Hinton Seedling'** Lovely clear orange bells and soft green foliage. Its lax habit makes it suitable for training to a trellis or over an arch. ★★★

A. **'Louise Marignac'** A lovely old Victorian cultivar that makes a vigorous plant with enormous green leaves and delicate pale satin-pink flowers. ★★

A. **'Master Michael'** Vermilion red flowers and green foliage. ★★★

A. megapotamicum **'Variegatum'** Yellow arrowhead foliage and flowers like small red balloons with yellow skirts and protruding purple stamens. The slender arching growth makes it well suited to hanging baskets. ★★

A. × *millerii* **'Variegata'** Another lax grower with small leaves and yellow variegation. The flowers are flared apricot 'skirts' with brown calyces. The variegated form is more commonly grown than the type, which is probably a hybrid between *A. megapotamicum* and *A. pictum.* 1.8 m (6 ft) ★★

A. **'Nabob'** The darkest of all abutilons, with striking

Abutilon 'Ashford Red', a good reliable soft red for bedding or conservatory display.

dark maroon bells with almost black stems. It is sturdy, with strong green foliage. ★★ ♛

A. **'Patrick Synge'** A vigorous, slender habit. Flowers are a rusty orange with maroon shading, shaped like the lanterns of *A. megapotamicum*. It is almost hardy on a warm wall. ★★★

A. pictum **'Thompsonii'** An old Victorian cultivar, vigorous and easy to grow, probably the most commonly seen of all abutilons. It was introduced from Jamaica by Messrs Veitch & Sons, the noted Victorian nursery firm. It has mottled yellow leaves and orange flowers. ★★

A. **'Pink Lady'** A lovely deep smoky pink. ★★

A. **'Rotterdam'** Bright orange-red open bells of an attractive shape with very dark green foliage. Slow-growing. ★★

A. **'Savitzii'** Almost white leaves with irregular green swathes. Flowers are often not produced until late in the season or on older plants and are pale orange/brown bells with purple veins. It is still well worth growing as a foliage plant. It is a somewhat tender cultivar and needs to be kept warmer than the others during the winter to grow well. 75 cm (2½ ft) ★

A. **'Souvenir de Bonn'** Makes a very tall plant with large green leaves, broadly margined with white. The orange bells are distinctly marked with darker veining. It is often confused with *A.* 'Savitzii'. ★★ ♛

A few more abutilons that can be regarded as hardy garden plants are listed on page 156.

ACALYPHA

Euphorbiaceae

A genus of about 430 species of evergreen shrubs, trees and annuals from tropical and subtropical regions. A few are occasionally grown for greenhouse display, while the following is a tender perennial.

A. hispaniolae A trailing version of the red-hot cat's tail, so called because of the trailing furry flowers in bright scarlet. Compact and floriferous, good in baskets. Rather tender and performs best in a very sheltered site or conservatory. 10 cm (4 in) ★

AEONIUM

Crassulaceae

A genus of about 30 species of succulent perennials mainly from Madeira, the Canary Isles, the Cape Verde Isles, North Africa and the Mediterranean. Many are grown for glasshouse display or as houseplants. In frost-free climates they make striking border plants. From the

An arrangement of potted plants, including *Aeonium arboreum* 'Atropurpureum', offset by smooth round pebbles.

many available, just one is listed here for its striking appearance.

A. arboreum Erect succulent sub-shrub like a small succulent tree, with chunky branches topped with rosettes of succulent foliage. Frost tender. Very effective in groups of succulents. 2 m (6½ ft) + under conservatory conditions. ★ ♛ Most commonly seen as the purple-leaved form, **'Atropurpureum'** ♛.

AGASTACHE

Labiatae

A genus of 30 species of aromatic perennials from hilly habitats in China, Japan, the USA and Mexico. A few make good garden plants.

A. **'Firebird'** Coppery-orange spikes over aromatic minty foliage. Grown in a dry spot, it should be hardy. 60 cm (2 ft) ★★★

A. mexicana An aromatic perennial, introduced from Mexico in 1938, bearing spikes of rose-red flowers in midsummer. 75 cm (2½ ft) ★★★

AGAVE

Agavaceae

This genus contains over 200 species of rosette-forming succulents from desert areas of North, Central and South America and the West Indies. Most have very sharp needle-like tips to the leaves, making them hazardous in family gardens. The tips can be removed, though purists would not approve.

A. americana Probably the most widely grown species, with rosettes of fat spiny grey-green leaves. Central leaves are upright, older leaves bend and trail. Makes an excellent specimen plant for a terrace planter on its own or with other succulents. Eventually becomes enormous. 3m (10 ft) ★★ ♔

A. a. 'Marginata' As above but bright yellow margins to the leaves. Can also achieve an immense size. ★★

A. a. 'Mediopicta' Similar but with pale yellow central band. Highly desirable plant, often in short supply. ★★ ♔

ALONSOA
Scrophulariaceae

A genus of about 12 species of evergreen shrubs, sub-shrubs and perennials from tropical and subtropical South America. Many are nowadays grown from seed as annuals.

A. warscewiczii Small bushy sub-shrub with dark stems and scarlet flowers throughout summer. Grow from cuttings or seed. Various peach-coloured selections such as **'Peachy-Keen'**. 45 cm (18 in) ★★★ ♔

ALOYSIA
Verbenaceae

There are 37 species in this genus of deciduous and evergreen shrubs from warm areas of North and South America. Most are aromatic.

A. triphylla (syn. *Lippia citriodora*) Small, wiry shrub from Chile and Argentina with sparse growth and narrow soft green leaves richly scented with citrus. Tiny off-white flowers in late summer. Needs a warm, sheltered situation outside; mulch well in the autumn and prune back frost-damaged growth in mid-spring. Alternatively, can be tub-grown for conservatory and patio display. Not a dominant plant but worth growing for its scent. 90 cm (3 ft) ★★★★ ♔

ALTERNANTHERA
Amaranthaceae

Perennials from tropical regions of mainly the USA and Africa, the main constituent of most carpet displays because of their attractive vibrant foliage and tolerance of clipping. Nomenclature is very confused but most are variants of *A. amoena* and *A. bettzichiana*. Colours range from green and yellow through to reds, purples and bronzes and the small leaves vary considerably in shape. A silvery-white variegated form is grown in the USA. They are usually sold by colour descriptions. 10 cm (4 in) ★

The diminutive pink foliage of alternanthera contrasted with the rich pink of iresine and the dark-leaved aeonium.

ANISODONTEA
Malvaceae

A genus of 19 species of woody perennials and shrubs from various parts of southern Africa.

A. capensis Delicate open shrub-like habit, profusion of tiny mallow-like flowers, rich pink with maroon centres. Excellent, eye-catching conservatory plant. Can be trained as a small standard. 1 m (3¼ ft) ★

A. malvastroides Similar to the above but with paler pink flowers and soft pale green leaves. Pleasant but somehow not quite as eye-catching. 1.2 m (4 ft) ★

ANTIRRHINUM
Scrophulariaceae

This genus of 30–40 species of annuals, perennials and sub-shrubs is found in Europe, North Africa and the USA. Most of the popular types widely grown for bedding today have been bred from *A. majus* and are grown annually from seed. The selections given here are relatively new and propagated vegetatively.

A range of prostrate shrubby antirrhinums suitable for baskets and planters includes **'Rose Pink'**, **'Primrose Vein'**, **'Deep Pink'** and **'Lemon Blush'**. All are said to be scented and rust-resistant. Trailing to 20 cm (8 in) ★★

Arctotis × *hybrida* 'Rosita', a cultivar raised early in the 20th century and still worth growing for its distinctive pale pink flowers.

APTENIA
Alizoaceae

A genus of two species of prostrate succulents from South Africa.

A. cordifolia 'Variegata' Succulent foliage with pale green and cream variegation, tiny fluffy pink mesembryanthemum flowers. Trailer, so good for baskets. Trailing to 10 cm (4 in) ★

ARCTOTIS
Compositae

The plants in this group of hybrids, sometimes called Zulu daisies, were for many years botanically classified as × *Venidio-Arctotis*, having been produced as bigeneric crosses between South African genera then named *Arctotis* and *Venidium*. They are now classed simply as *Arctotis*, probably hybrids between *A. venusta* and *A. fastuosa*.

The original crosses were made early in the 20th century and 13 named cultivars were produced. Most of the surviving cultivars are prostrate with silvery foliage and produce huge daisy-like flowers, many with dark centres. To perform well they need a warm, dry, sunny site. They are quite successful grown in containers, provided they are not overfed.

Although they propagate easily from cuttings they can be difficult to overwinter, damping off easily in the dull winters of the UK. Stock plants for overwintering should be grown in a well-drained compost and trimmed back in late summer to enable the plant to make fresh bushy growth before winter. Autumn-propagated cuttings become very leggy by spring and so it is best to use these as stock for a spring batch for planting. They do not look attractive as young potted plants but once planted establish quickly, producing a mat of foliage and a spectacular eye-catching display.

The original cultivars were bought and distributed by Suttons in the 1920s as 'Suttonflowers'. At some stage the stock and propagation rights were sold to a Sidney Lake, one time managing director of Jiffy pots. When he retired in the 1970s the stock was acquired by Allwood's, who until recently marketed them as the 'South African Sunshine Flower'. They are now more widely offered in garden centres, although not so often as many other tender perennials. Most grow to around 20 cm (8 in).

A. fastuosa One of the species that can be grown from seed as well as cuttings. Rich golden-yellow flowers. Taller than the others, growing to 30 cm (12 in) ★★

A. f. 'Zulu Prince' Enormous white flowers with orange and black markings at the base of the petals, creating a ring effect. This cultivar can be grown from seed. ★★

A. × hybrida 'African Sunrise' Rich orange with a dark centre. A new cultivar that is dwarf and compact. ★★

A. × h. 'Apricot' Soft creamy apricot deepening to almost orange centre with tiny black halo. Readily available. ★★

A. × h. 'Bacchus' Huge purple daisies, darker than 'Wine'. One of the originals. ★★

A. × h. 'Flame' Bright tangerine orange, with pewter grey centre. Amazingly weather-tolerant. ★★

A. × h. 'Rosita' Quite upright and slender, with very pale pink flowers. Worth growing only to complete the colour range. ★★

A. × h. 'Torch' An improvement on 'Flame' as it has a striking black centre. ★★

A. × h. 'White' Stocky white with a dark centre, better than the older cultivar 'Champagne', which lacks vigour. ★★

A. × h. 'Wine' A good cultivar but paler than the name suggests, somewhere between soft sugar pink and watery blackcurrant juice, with a dark central boss. ★★

A. × h. 'Yellow' Burnished golden yellow, old variety, true name unknown. ★★

ARGYRANTHEMUM
Compositae

Why such a delicate and graceful plant should be encumbered with such a leaden name defies understanding, although no doubt the botanists have a reason. These plants, commonly known as marguerites, Paris daisies or Atlantic Island daisies, used to be members of either the genus *Chrysanthemum* or *Leucanthemum* and are not surprisingly within the family Compositae.

There are many species, most of which are native to the Canary Isles and Madeira. Few typical species are available in commerce and in general the most garden-worthy plants are cultivars. Given suitable conditions they are shrubby perennials, fairly upright in habit, with delicate leaves like a finely divided chrysanthemum. The leaves of many cultivars, particularly those with *A. foeniculaceum* within their parentage, are somewhat glaucous, providing a subtle foil to the flowers.

All the argyranthemums thrive in warm, sunny and somewhat dry positions. They are intolerant of frost, so in all but the mildest areas of the UK they must be considered as tender perennials and overwintered under

The bluish foliage of these argyranthemums is a perfect foil for the sugary-pink flowers.

frost-free glass. Because of their speed of growth and reliable flowering they make excellent dot plants in a summer bedding display or fine specimens in patio containers.

BOTANY

Argyranthemums are evergreen sub-shrubs with a procumbent or erect habit. The leaves are opposite or alternate and mostly finely dissected or lobed; some are glaucous in appearance. In the species *A. gracile* and the more widely known *A. g.* 'Chelsea Girl', leaves are reduced to thread-like lobes. The flower form that is widely found in this family is correctly called a capitulum. It is variable, being single like a simple daisy, double with many petals or anemone-centred, which is similar to a single flower but with enlarged disc-florets giving a dome-shaped centre. The flowers may be solitary or more commonly grouped in a loose corymb.

HISTORY

Although *A. frutescens* was introduced back in 1699 its near relative *A. foeniculaceum* was not introduced until 1890, and there are few published references to either until the 1900s when they became popular as windowsill plants and for summer bedding. As well as these two species, old periodicals have references to a cultivar of *A. frutescens* known as 'Grandiflora', yellows called 'Etoile d'Or' and 'Golden Sun', and anemone-centred varieties called 'Coronation', 'Queen Alexandra' and 'Perfection'.

Both of the latter were white but had pink counterparts.

A delightful account in the *Gardeners' Chronicle* of 15 September 1900 describes the use of the cultivar 'Flor d'Or' for a fancy dress costume for the daughter of a Bognor nurseryman. The young lady was entirely covered with flowers in a design of lovers' knots and hearts with a crown of the same in the cultivar 'Grandiflora'.

The cultivar 'Mrs F. Sander', with large cushion-like flowers resembling a double pyrethrum, was said to be valuable as a cut flower, despite a tendency to weak stems. It was given an Award of Merit in 1910 but proved to be a controversial plant. By 1912 it was being widely grown at Hampton Court, with a report in a *Gardeners' Chronicle* article in 1913 that the criticism of weak stems was unfounded. A subsequent article by another contributor criticizes the plant for being prone to aphids, leafminer and reversion but argues that its weak stems are not noticed when it is planted in masses.

PROPAGATION AND CULTIVATION

Propagation is by tip cuttings in autumn or spring and they grow easily in most potting composts. Young plants should be pinched regularly to produce bushy specimens or, in the case of some cultivars, can be trained into standards. Over winter they like a temperature around 10°C (50°F). Spring-raised plants can be finished in 9 or 10 cm (3½ or 4 in) pots and autumn-rooted plants in 15 cm (6 in) pots as good-sized specimens. Some can be trained into short standards. They may be attacked by aphids and leaf miner and occasionally produce a gall-like growth

The compact habit and copious flowering of *Argyranthemum maderense* make it a valuable summer bedding plant.

PLATE II
Argyranthemum
All plants shown approximately ⅔ size

A. *foeniculaceum*
'Royal Haze'

A. 'Pink Australian'

A. 'Petite Pink'

A. 'Blizzard'

A. 'Yellow Australian'

A. 'Powder Puff Pink'

A. *maderense*

A. 'Cornish Gold'

A. 'Peach Cheeks'

A. 'Mary Wootton'

A. gracile 'Chelsea Girl'

A. 'Mrs F. Sander'

at ground level. Ideally such diseased plants should be destroyed, although propagating material taken from higher up the same plant does not seem to be affected and healthy plants can be produced. None will tolerate frost but they require only cool winter temperatures of about 5–10°C (41–50°F).

Being tender, argyranthemums should not be planted out until all danger of frost has passed in late spring or the beginning of summer. Many cultivars make large plants up to 1 m (3¼ ft) across by the end of the summer, so a generous space should be allowed. Like most summer bedding subjects, they appreciate a well-cultivated soil and adequate moisture for establishment, after which they will tolerate considerable dryness which often increases flowering. Specimens planted in containers will need a balanced liquid feed to prolong growth and flowering. In most cases the new flowers mask the old dying heads, although in a wet summer and in prime positions some deadheading may be needed. Some cultivars tend to 'flush' and can be trimmed over with shears after each burst of flower to encourage a later display.

In mild areas, especially in sheltered sites against warm walls, they can make sizeable shrubs lasting a number of years. If you are leaving plants outside try mulching the bases thickly with a loose strawy compost so that even if the tops are killed by frost there is a chance the bases will survive and regrow the next season.

PLANT LIST

Unfortunately there is a proliferation of names and synonyms within the trade, which was simplified, at least in part, by a trial of argyranthemums by the Royal Horticultural Society in 1993, held at Wisley. Sadly, garden centres still tend to sell them under all sorts of confusing names. Good collections can be seen at Brockings Exotics and at Cannington College in Somerset, which holds the National Collection. Regrettably most garden centres stock a very limited range, often consisting only of 'Vancouver', 'Jamaica Primrose' and unnamed whites. Most of the following are excellent garden plants and would be more widely grown if available.

A. **'Blizzard'** Small tufty double white flowers with crinkly petals make a tight rounded bun shape. 30 cm (12 in) ★★

A. callichrysum **'Etoile d'Or'** (syn. Yellow Star) Single buttercup-yellow daisies, over compact, clear green foliage. Probably an old variety. Tends to be weak in winter with some foliage bronzing but recovers and performs well in summer. 45 cm (18 in) ★★

A. c. **'Penny'** Small single yellow flowers, loose habit, prodigious flowering. Because of the rate of flowering can be difficult to find propagation material but seems to root and grow from almost any material. Introduced from Guernsey in 1988 by Ivan Dickings and named after his wife. 75 cm (2½ ft) ★★

A. c. **'Prado'** The deepest yellow of all. 45 cm (18 in) ★★

A. **'Cornish Gold'** A good large single yellow, basically an improved form of 'Jamaica Primrose' with finer foliage and a denser habit. Very free-flowering. 60 cm (2 ft) ★★ ♓

A. **'Edelweiss'** White anemone-centred flowers, sturdy habit. Very similar to 'Quinta White' but much more compact. 45 cm (18 in) ★★

A. foeniculaceum **'Royal Haze'** Icy blue-green finely cut foliage, white daisies and upright, open habit. Collected by Roy Cheek in northwest Tenerife in 1987. 75 cm (2½ ft) ★★ ♓

A. frutescens **ssp.** *canariensis* Vigorous, reliable plant making good standards, with chalk-white flowers freely produced. One of the tallest. The slightly odd habit of

Argyranthemums such as *A. callichrysum* 'Penny' provide a long-lasting display in urns and planters.

growth gives blind shoots higher up near flowering shoots. 1 m (3¼ ft) ★★ ♔

A. 'Gill's Pink' Good reliable single pink, larger than 'Petite Pink' and more reliable than 'Wellwood Park'. 45 cm (18 in) ★★

A. gracile 'Chelsea Girl' Finest thread-like silver foliage with small white daisies. Good foliage plant which is quite upright and makes a good standard. Collected in Tenerife in 1981 by James Compton. 60 cm (2 ft) ★★ ♔

A. 'Jamaica Primrose' An old favourite, with large yellow single daisies and vigorous dark foliage. Introduced by Geoffrey C. Herklots and brought to Wisley by Graham Stuart Thomas. It was the first argyranthemum to receive an Award of Merit in 1953. Probably superseded now by 'Cornish Gold'. 75 cm (2½ ft) ★★ ♔

A. 'Lemon Meringue' A weak lemon yellow, anemone-centred with a ragged outer ring. A very poor variety. 45 cm (18 in) ★★

A. 'Levada Cream' Long-stemmed single primrose flowers fading to cream and rich green leaves. Spreading habit. Introduced from garden sources from south-east Madeira by Mr and Mrs Salt. 60 cm (2 ft) ★★ ♔

A. 'Leyton Treasure' Curious tufted ivory/beige flowers, nearly all centre and with no real ray petals. 45 cm (18 in) ★★

A. maderense (syn. *A. ochroleucum*) This species is native to Lanzarote and grows on rocky outcrops. It has blue/green foliage with pale primrose daisies, giving a very soft effect and associating well with blues or dark maroon. Quite distinct. A paler, almost white form is sometimes offered. 45 cm (18 in) ★★ ♔

A. 'Margaret Lynch' A compact plant with pale lime-green leaves and white close-petalled flowers. Collected in Tenerife in the 1980s and named after the collector. 45 cm (18 in) ★★

A. 'Mary Cheek' A compact plant with shell pink, double-quilled flowers, giving a very delicate effect. Raised by Roy Cheek and named after his wife. It should be more widely grown. 45 cm (18 in) ★★ ♔

A. 'Mary Wootton' Pale 'hint-of-pink' double flowers with anemone centres, lax habit. Tends to be shy-flowering. Probably a short-day plant, so flowers best in the autumn and spring. Named after Miss New Zealand 1948. 75 cm (2½ ft) ★★

A. 'Mrs F. Sander' A very old Victorian variety with shaggy white flowers which gained an Award of Merit in the 19th century. Sometimes offered under the name 'Snowflake'. Tends to flower in flushes. 75 cm (2½ ft) ★★

A. 'Peach Cheeks' Lovely soft orange/apricot flowers with darker centres fading to pale biscuit colour. Variability means that as well as single flowers, double anemone-centred flowers are produced as occasional bonus. It has a gently sprawling habit. Sent by Gordon Rollason from South Africa in 1989. 45 cm (18 in) ★★

A. 'Petite Pink' (previously 'Pink Delight') Small single pink daisies, free-flowering, perfect compact habit, silvery foliage, a very desirable plant. It makes a good small standard. 30 cm (12 in) ★★ ♔

A. 'Pink Australian' Sugar-pink double, similar to 'Vancouver' and in my experience better, with a nicer habit and tidier flower. 60 cm (2 ft) ★★

A. 'Powder Puff Pink' Pale pink double flowers with quilled petals and very tight centre, compact, curious. 30 cm (12 in) ★★

A. 'Quinta White' (syn. 'Sark') Another double white with anemone centres, larger flowers than 'Edelweiss' and more lax in habit. Discovered in Madeira by Mr and Mrs Salt. Subsequently introduced by Ivan Dickings from the garden of La Seignerie as 'Sark'. The earlier name of 'Quinta White' takes precedence. 75 cm (2½ ft) ★★ ♔

A. 'Rollason's Red' Bright magenta red single flowers, with a yellow halo around a dark centre – grow in light shade for intense colour. Loose habit. Introduced to the UK from South Africa and named after George Rollason, who sent the cuttings. Not an easy cultivar but the deepest and nearest to red. 45 cm (18 in) ★★

A. 'Snowflake' Pewter grey foliage with profusion of white daisy flowers. Very reliable. Makes a good standard. 75 cm (2½ ft) ★★ ♔

A. 'Tony Holmes' Enormous white single flowers, yellow centres, the largest of the argyranthemums. Difficult to grow as shoots tend to go blind. 45 cm (18 in) ★★

A. 'Vancouver' Bright sugar pink, fading with age to pale pink. Fully double flowers with anemone centres. Vigorous and will make a standard. Goes well with *Verbena* 'Sissinghurst' but screams at salmon pinks. 75 cm (2½ ft) ★★ ♔

A. 'Wellwood Park' Single pink, vigorous habit. Shy-flowering. 75 cm (2½ ft) ★★

A. 'Whiteknights' (formerly *A. frutescens* ssp. *frutescens*) Good, compact, single white cultivar, very floriferous. 30 cm (12 in) ★★ ♔

A. 'Yellow Australian' A recent introduction available in the trade under several names. Large, well-formed anemone-centred flowers with broad outer ring. A really good double yellow at last. Upright and vigorous. 75 cm (2½ ft) ★★

ARUNDO
Poaceae/Graminae

A genus of two or three species of rhizomatous perennial grasses from warm temperate regions of the northern hemisphere.

A. donax Known sometimes as the great reed, this is a veritable giant of a plant which is of value only in the back of the border in gardens, where there is space to appreciate its towering stems with big floppy bluish leaves. Great for the back of a sub-tropical display. 3 m (10 ft) ★★★

A. d. 'Variegata' This refined and variegated version of the above was much revered by the Victorians. The effect is like a huge white-striped bamboo. It prefers a moist, sheltered spot and does not overwinter well unless the site is very sheltered. A real aristocrat. In most situations grow as a summer plant, lift and return to the greenhouse for winter. It can be pruned to the ground each year, which will result in lush compact foliage, or

Much loved by the Victorians, *Arundo donax* 'Variegata' is quite rightly regarded as a choice and valuable garden plant.

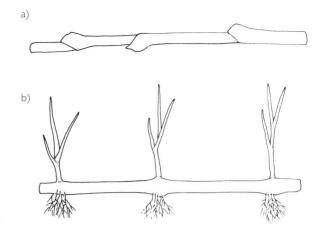

Fig. 1 a) Shoot of arundo trimmed to about 20cm (8in) and prepared for propagation by removing all leaves. b) After rooting and shooting, the new plantlets are ready for separating and potting.

alternatively left unpruned, when it will ultimately reach 1.8 m (6 ft) + ★★★

PROPAGATION

The propagation of *Arundo donax* 'Variegata' is traditionally by division but as it does not make many offsets only a few new ones can be separated each year. Its rootstock is amazingly tough so it may be necessary to use a serrated kitchen knife or secateurs to separate the divisions. The woody stems must be shortened to about 20 cm (8 in) before potting in a 12 or 15 cm (4½ or 6 in) pot. New shoots will usually come from beneath the soil, although sometimes they appear from the leaf axils of the remaining stem.

For the adventurous there is an alternative way of propagating arundos which seems to break many of the rules of propagation. At the end of the season in early autumn, remove a few mature stems of the arundo. Prepare them by removing all the foliage, which will leave a stick like a bamboo cane (Fig. 1). Then find a shallow watertight tray – the type sold as cat litter trays are ideal – or alternatively line a seed tray with plastic. Fill the tray with 5 cm (2 in) of water, then cut the prepared stems into sections a little shorter than the tray length and float them in the tray. The tray must be placed in a warm greenhouse, preferably with bottom heat to keep the water constantly warm. A warm windowsill in the house will probably suffice.

Within a few weeks, shoots will appear at most of the axils where the leaves were removed. Soon after this, roots will develop into the water. Top up the water from time to time and replace it altogether if it becomes green and stagnant.

The young plants should be well rooted by late winter, when you can gently remove them from the water. Carefully cut up the old stems to separate the young plants and pot into small pots of potting compost. This is the tricky stage, as roots formed in water do not acclimatize to terrestrial culture with ease. Water carefully and keep warm and humid. You can expect to lose as many as 50 per cent of those that initially root but this is still a very effective way to propagate this choice plant.

ASTERISCUS

Asteraceae/Compositae

A genus of four species originating in the Mediterranean, Cape Verde Isles and Canary Isles. The name means 'little star'.

A. maritimus (syn. *A.* 'Gold Coin') Disc-shaped, daisy flowers with truncated chunky petals in buttercup yellow produced over slender green leaves. Loose habit makes it suitable for baskets and edges of planters. 30 cm (12 in) ★★

BEGONIA

Begoniaceae

This large genus contains over 900 species and numerous cultivars originating in widespread tropical and subtropical regions. They are widely cultivated as greenhouse and house plants and include the well-known bedding begonias. Many are succulent and prefer light shade and a moist site. The leaves easily scorch if watered in hot sun. A few are recognized as patio plants but probably far more could be used outside in the summer.

B. fuchsioides Produces slender arching branches with tiny, shiny green leaves and clusters of soft pink fuchsia-like flowers. It originates from Venezuela and needs to be kept at around 10°C (50°F) during the winter. It has a long season of flowering and makes a good conservatory plant as well as a specimen for a planter. 75 cm (2½ ft) ★ ♛ There is a red form with sealing-wax red flowers, more correctly known as ***B. foliosa* var. *miniata* 'Rosea'**, which is in many ways a better garden plant than the type; a mature plant in full flower is a striking sight.

B. grandis* var. *evansiana An almost hardy species introduced in 1812 from northern China. It has lopsided green leaves with red veins and red stems. The flowers are pink and the whole plant has the typical succulence of the

The buttercup yellow of *Bidens ferulifolia* offset by the sombre tones of an ivy-leaved pelargonium.

begonias. Personally I find it disappointing, although this may be because it is so rarely given the right spot. 45 cm (18 in) ★★★

***B.* 'Gustav Lind'** Naming of this lovely old-fashioned windowsill plant is variable. It is a Semperflorens type but with double cerise-pink pom-poms over polished bronze, almost red, foliage. As it does not set seed it has to be propagated from cuttings, which root easily. Select material from lower shoots on the plant as these will branch easily and make an attractive plant. Cuttings rooted from top growth make a tall single-stemmed plant that will not produce side shoots. There are also white and red forms of the same plant and some with green leaves. All need to be kept warm over winter at around 10°C (50°F) and suffer from powdery mildew if too dry. 20 cm (8 in) ★

B. sutherlandii A diminutive tuberous species bearing masses of small orange flowers. It originates from South Africa and Tanzania but is virtually hardy. Its trailing habit makes it of particular use in baskets. 30 cm (12 in) ★★★ ♛

BIDENS
Asteraceae/Compositae

This genus contains some 200 species of annuals and perennials, relatively few of which are generally cultivated.

B. aurea Small dark leaves, yellow star-like flowers and a wiry, sprawling habit. It is good in planters or as an interplant among other species. 45 cm (18 in) ★★

B. ferulifolia The most widely cultivated species and quite rightly so as it is a splendid plant. Its delicate, finely cut, ferny foliage sets off a profusion of yellow five-petalled flowers. It is free-flowering, producing its first buds almost as soon as the cuttings are rooted. It is a good constituent for baskets and planters, its only fault being its quite strong yellow colouring and frequent usage, which can become too much. There are some recently introduced strains of this plant, such as the cultivar 'Goldie', which are said to be improvements on the species. 30 cm (12 in) ★★ ♆

B. ostruthioides The aristocrat of the group, with flowers like small yellow dahlias. It has an upright habit and coarsely fingered leaves. More difficult to overwinter than the others. A plant for curiosity value rather than splendour. 45 cm (18 in) ★★

BOUGAINVILLEA
Nyctaginaceae

Genus of 14 species of evergreen or partly deciduous shrubs, trees and thorny climbers. They originate from South America and are grown for their colourful bracts, which are available in a wide range of colours. Although frost tender, they do not need especially high temperatures to overwinter: at 7°C (45°F) they will survive quite successfully but will lose their leaves and become dormant. Above 10°C (50°F) they will continue to grow and may flower throughout the winter.

Propagation is by semi-ripe cuttings in late summer or by hardwood cuttings in late winter. The latter will be leafless stems, about 15 cm (6 in) long, and do not require a tip so can be made from prunings. The use of a hormone rooting powder is desirable as the percentage take of cuttings can be low.

Bougainvilleas make good conservatory plants or specimens to stand outside in the summer. As they can be slow-growing, it is normal to keep plants for several seasons to build up a good-sized regular-flowering specimen. They can be grown in loamless or soil-based compost and will require progressively larger pots as they grow. For tidiness, they generally require a small trellis or tripod of canes for support, or within a conservatory can be trained up a series of permanent wires. During the summer months water them quite copiously but in winter keep them almost dry. In late winter prune them quite hard, retaining a framework of branches and trimming side-shoots back to two or three buds. Bougainvilleas readily produce sports, which has led to a wide range of cultivars being available. Under conservatory conditions they eventually make large plants many metres tall, the height depending upon age, pruning and size of conservatory.

B. × buttiana 'Golden Glow' Pale yellow to rich gold. ★★

B. × b. 'Mrs Butt' (syn. 'Crimson Lake') Rich crimson shaded magenta. The first hybrid produced between B. peruviana and B. glabra in 1910. It originated in a Mrs Butt's garden in Columbia. ★★ ♆

B. glabra This classic bougainvillea can have white through to magenta bracts. Cultivars are more often seen than the species. ★★ ♆

B. g. 'Snow Queen' A pure white. ★★

B. g. 'Variegata' Purple bracts and green leaves edged in a narrow white margin. ★★

B. 'Killie Campbell' Bronze-orange bracts. ★★ ♆

B. 'Raspberry Ice' (syn. 'Tropical Rainbow') Almost white leaves with a green central splash and rich cerise-pink flowers. ★★

B. 'Scarlett O'Hara' Brilliant scarlet/cerise bracts. Vigorous. ★★

BOUVARDIA
Rubiaceae

This genus of around 30 species occurs naturally in tropical and subtropical areas of the southern USA to South America. They were very popular in the 19th century for conservatory display but are almost unknown today. Propagation is by softwood tip cuttings or root cuttings. Keep at a minimum of 5°C (41°F) over winter and grow on for several seasons to achieve a well-clothed plant. Can be pruned quite hard in early spring.

B. longiflora Well-branched shrubby habit, with long, tubular, white flowers, through from late summer to winter. Sweetly scented. 1 m (3¼ ft) ★★

B. ternifolia Small shrub bearing brilliant scarlet flowers. 75 cm (2½ ft) ★★

BRACHYSCOME
Asteraceae/Compositae

A genus containing many annuals as well as perennials.

The straggly habit of *Brachyscome multifida* 'Lemon Mist' is used to advantage by growing it in a hanging basket.

They are natives of Australia, Tasmania, New Zealand and New Guinea.

B. *multifida* Delicate feathery green foliage, covered throughout the summer in masses of small daisies. Semi-trailing, therefore good in baskets or as a filler in patio planters. Several cultivars such as **'Pink Mist'**, **'Lemon Mist'** and **'Blue Mist'**. Propagated from tip cuttings in autumn or spring. 20 cm (8 in) ★★

B. 'Strawberry Mousse' Small fingered leaves, bright sugar-pink daisies, with 'laid-back' petals and golden centres. Floriferous. Relatively new and as yet untested. 20 cm (8 in) ★★

BRACTEANTHA
Compositae

Previously part of the genus *Helichrysum*, most of the straw flowers are better known for their value as flowers for drying. Most are grown from seed, although these selections are vegetatively propagated. Cuttings root easily and should not be taken until mid-spring or plants become too large before planting.

B. 'Gold Ball' A compact plant with tiny golden-orange balls over grey/green foliage. Flowers open eventually like miniature straw flowers. 30 cm (12 in) ★★

B. *bracteata* 'Dargan Hill Monarch' Bright orange/yellow everlasting straw flowers, slightly silvery foliage. Good chunky border plant. 45 cm (18 in) ★★

B. *b.* 'Skynet' Similar to the above, but with pink flowers tinged sunrise orange. A cut above the average. 45 cm (18 in) ★★

BRUGMANSIA
Solanaceae

The 'angels' trumpets' used to be classified as *Datura* and are still often found under this name. The five species originate from the southern USA down to South America. All are large shrubs or small trees and bear enormous flowers with long spidery tips to the ends of the fluted trumpet. Many have a rich heady scent but all parts of the plant are toxic.

Propagation is by cuttings rooted in spring or autumn, which grow exceedingly fast. They respond well to a rich compost and generous feeding, although they will not flower freely until well-established and pot-bound. To achieve the best effect, they should be grown as conservatory plants or kept in a pot or planter from year to year; they are only seen at their best when plants are of a stature to enable the trumpets to be viewed at eye level or above. The main drawback with plants grown under glass is red spider mite, although this is less of a problem when plants are stood outside for the summer. There are a number of species and cultivars available, although their naming is generally very muddled in commerce.

B. *arborea* The simple pure white angels' trumpet with single, sweetly scented flowers. 1.8 m (6 ft)+ ★★

B. *aurea* Produces enormous soft yellow trumpets, lovely satin texture, hint of apricot. It is strongly scented at night. Often sold as 'Golden Queen'. 1.8–4 m (6–13 ft) ★

B. × *candida* 'Grand Marnier' Voluptuous single trumpets in lovely soft apricot pink. Various pink cultivars are sold under this name. 1.8 m (6 ft) ★ ♛

B. × *c.* 'Knightii' One of the most commonly seen cultivars, with long soft leaves and dramatic double white trumpet flowers with rich scent. 1.8 m (6 ft)+ ★ ♛

B. × *c.* 'Variegata' (syn. 'Sunset') Probably the variegated form of 'Grand Marnier', with two-tone green leaves with white splashes around the margins. Highly scented apricot flowers. Slow-growing. 1.2 m (4 ft) ★

B. *sanguinea* The hardiest of the genus and will sometimes survive outside, although it dies back to the ground and shoots again each spring. Flowers are more cylindrical in a rich tomato red with soft sea-green foliage. Free-flowering and easy to grow. 1.8 m (6 ft)+ ★★ ♛

B. *suaveolens* White with a heavy night perfume. 1.8 m (6 ft)+ ★ ♛

CALCEOLARIA
Scrophulariaceae

Within this genus there are hardy plants, the well-known

greenhouse calceolarias with their huge gaudy bubble-like pouches and a number of tender perennials that can be used outside in the summer. They occur in temperate and tropical areas of Mexico and Central and South America. Those listed here are almost hardy and may survive in favoured positions. All are shrubby and root easily from cuttings. Occasionally they show chlorosis, which may indicate iron deficiency and should be treated with a proprietary chelated iron product.

C. **'Camden Hero'** Big round burnt orange pouches, almost terracotta, over sturdy plants with quite large soft greyish-green leaves. Often confused with the better-known and probably better cultivar 'Kentish Hero'. 30 cm (12 in) ★★

C. × *clibranii* Green leaves, topped with slender stems carrying bunches of large, pendant, sun-yellow pouches. Needs some support with split canes and twine, but quite exquisite and worth the effort. 45 cm (18 in) ★★

C. integrifolia Very tough, almost hardy and will make a small shrub after a few years. In summer it is covered with huge bunches of small bobbly yellow pouches. It is the main parent of some of the modern cultivars such as 'Sunshine' which are generally raised from seed. 60 cm (2 ft) ★★★ ♔

C. **'Kentish Hero'** A small wiry plant smothered with clusters of bright orange pouches deepening to a rusty colour with age. An old plant recently rediscovered. Very easy to grow, although it can be brittle to handle. 30 cm (12 in) ★★

CANARINA
Campanulaceae

C. canariensis Herbaceous climber growing from tuberous roots. In its native home in the Canary Islands it will grow to enormous proportions but under conservatory conditions it makes a good manageable climber. Flowers are orange-red and bell-shaped, produced between late winter and mid-spring. It is frost tender and should be kept overwinter at around 5°C (41°F). It may be possible to overwinter the tubers outside in a sheltered position but growth may be too slow to allow flowering outside. 1–1.5 m (3¼–5 ft) ★★ ♔

CANNA
Cannaceae

This is a genus of fast-growing rhizomatous perennials, grown for their huge exotic leaves and flamboyant flowers. They are sometimes called Indian shot plants because

Cannas as part of an exuberant bedding display with cleome, iresine and spiky-leaved cordyline.

of their hard, round seeds. One journalist described cannas as 'gladiolus-gone-bananas', an apt description for their banana-like leaves and flamboyant gladiolus-like flowers. The foliage is generally either green or bronzy-purple, although there are yellow-variegated forms, silvery glaucous types and even one with pink- and purple-striped leaves. The flowers come in every colour combination except blues and purples, varying in size from the tiny flowers of many of the species to the huge floppy blooms of the modern hybrids. They may be spotted or pencilled with a second colour. Flowering of most cannas will commence in early to midsummer and continue to early autumn or later if the weather is mild.

BOTANY

Cannas are herbaceous perennials with a rhizomatous rootstock. The large leaves which are such a feature of this plant are oblong to broadly elliptical and spirally arranged. The petiole sheathes the stem. The flowers are large, showy and irregular, with a calyx comprising three sepals. There are three united petals and between two and five petaloid stamens. One bears the fertile anther cells, while the others are infertile and often appear as petals. One of these infertile staminodes is reflexed and is known as the lip or labellum. When there are two others present they are often called wings. In the garden

The vibrant foliage colours of *Canna* 'Durban' make it worth growing for its leaves alone.

PLATE III *Canna*

All plants shown at approximately ⅓ size

C. 'Rosemond Coles'

C. 'En Avant'

C. 'Intrigue'

C. 'Durban'

C. 'Reine Charlotte'

C. 'Talisman'

C. 'Picadore'

C. indica

C. 'King Midas'

C. 'Roi Soleil'

C. 'Taney'

C. 'Striata'

C. glauca

hybrids, the lip and the wings are often quite large, wavy and brightly coloured. The fruit is a warty capsule.

HISTORY

Although *Canna indica* has been cultivated since 1570, it was not until the 19th century that cannas really became popular. Hybridization started in France in the mid-19th century, when Monsieur Thré Année, who had collected plants during his travels in South America, bred on his return to Paris a race of early hybrids that rapidly became popular for their exotic foliage.

By 1870, Monsieur Crozy of Lyons was working on cannas and he produced some of the earliest large-flowered forms. By 1895 his catalogue listed over 240 different cultivars. Other familiar names such as Sprenger, Vilmorin, Lemoine, Paul & Son and Rollason were also associated with canna breeding. In 1893 the RHS held at least one trial of cannas, with some 45 cultivars entered, 11 of which received Awards of Merit. These were the 'novelty' plants of the late 19th century.

Cannas were used in formal bedding, particularly to create the jungle-like subtropical effect that was so fashionable at the time. William Robinson lists many in his classic book *The Subtropical Garden*, while Gertrude Jekyll, who often used them in her colour borders, preferred simple descriptions such as 'tall red canna' rather than naming cultivars. Around the 1920s, cannas lost their popularity in the UK and except in surviving traditional bedding schemes were rarely seen until quite recently.

Cannas have remained popular in warmer climates and are commonly grown in Australia, India, South Africa, southern states of the USA and the warmer parts of Europe. Good collections are to be found in the Botanic Gardens at Melbourne and Durban and the Brooklyn Botanics in New York. Nearer to the UK there are collections at Lyons and Munich. A good display may be seen most years in a long border near the greenhouses at the RHS gardens at Wisley.

PROPAGATION

Cannas grow from swollen roots, correctly known as rhizomes but often called tubers in nurserymen's catalogues. These are easily divided to produce new plants. The rhizomes are frost-tender and it is necessary to lift them from their display beds at the end of each season and store them under frost-free conditions over winter. In early spring, shake or wash excess soil from the rhizomes, then cut them up into smaller sections. They can be divided into many pieces provided each section has a shoot or bud, though for most garden purposes a larger section with 3–5 growing points will make a more substantial plant. Put each clump into a 15 or 20 cm (6 or 8 in) pot in a good open potting compost and water them sparingly until root and shoot growth has started. Most books suggest that they need a temperature of 16°C (60°F) but much lower temperatures are quite adequate as long as they do not get frosted. Unless high temperatures can be provided, division should wait until early to mid-spring.

Growing from seed

Canna cultivars can only be propagated reliably by division but growing from seed may provide a reasonable range of colours and types. File the seed gently until the pale inner layers are just visible, then soak it in warm water for 48 hours. By this time the seed will have swollen and be ready for sowing in the normal way. If a temperature of 21°C (70°F) can be maintained, germination will be rapid. As soon as the small seedlings are big enough to handle, separate them and grow them individually in small pots as the young roots are fragile.

Sometimes seed is available on specialist lists for canna species which will often come true from seed. Most of these are small-flowered and of limited garden value. The exception is *C. warscewiczii*, which has a pretty cherry red flower and purple-tinted foliage. It grows easily from seed and will flower within the first year. Be sure to save some seed for future years as the rhizomes of this one do not overwinter well.

CULTIVATION

Cannas are easy and rewarding plants to grow provided they are planted in a warm sunny site after all danger of frost is past. They are not fussy about soil types, but respond to a soil that has been well cultivated and enriched with compost or manure. As they are vigorous plants, space them generously, leaving at least 75 cm (2½ ft) between them. Feed generously and water copiously in dry spells. As soon as autumn frosts blacken the foliage, dig up the fleshy rhizomes and store them in frost-free conditions such as a dry shed or cellar. Check the roots over winter and dampen them lightly if necessary to avoid total drying out. This should be done sparingly as excess moisture may cause the roots to start into growth or rot. In a sheltered site in milder parts of the UK the rhizomes can be left in position permanently as long as they are covered with a thick mulch in autumn to protect them from frost.

All cannas can be grown in pots or tubs for patio or conservatory display. Use a good potting compost in a generous-sized container, preferably 30 cm (12 in) or more in diameter. Water frequently and liquid feed. All will withstand an occasional light frost down to −1°C (30°F) as dormant tubers, but require minimum temperatures of about 5–10°C (41–50°F) as growing plants.

NAMING

The naming of cannas is very muddled. Although they are included in the International Register of Tulips, Hyacinths and Other Bulbs, the list is incomplete. Nevertheless, it makes interesting reading, with the origin of many old cultivars listed. The National Collection of Canna, comprising about 100 species and cultivars, is held by Brockings Exotics. Most grow to 1.5–2 m (5–6½ ft) tall, depending on site and season. Exceptions are noted.

CANNA SPECIES

C. glauca Slender habit with narrow glaucous leaves, and delicate lemon-yellow upright flowers. It has a spreading rhizome. ★★

C. indica Produces small green leaves topped with small flowers, orange/red with a yellow mark on lower petals. It is doubtful that the plant generally offered under this name is the true wild species. This species is quite short, growing to around 1.2 m (4 ft). ★★

C. i. '**Purpurea**' Widely grown and makes a good background display. It is slender of habit with rich purple leaves and small upright orange flowers. The name of this is also doubtful, but the plant is well worth growing. There is also a red-flowered form. ★★

C. iridiflora Makes a huge plant with green leaves and pendulous bright pink flowers. Splendid when grown well but because of its late flowering is often grown in a conservatory. The stock generally offered is probably a cultivar correctly known as *C.* × *ehemanii*. ★★

C. musifolia A must for the back of a display. It is a strong grower producing immense dark green leaves with red veining and red stems, but does not generally flower in the UK. When conditions are right, the flower is a deep orange but small. This is one of the tallest and will make 2.4 m (8 ft) in a good year, more in a hot climate. ★★

C. warscewiczii Can be grown from seed and will flower in the same season at around 60 cm (2 ft). Having green leaves with dark veins and black stems topped with small bright cherry red flowers, it looks good with *Dahlia* 'Bishop of Llandaff'. ★★

The fickle *Canna* 'Cleopatra' is capable of producing red flowers and purple foliage as well as these yellow flowers.

CANNA CULTIVARS

Some of these date from the 19th century, while others are more recent. All have relatively large flowers compared to the species. Many other cultivars are in existence but they are not generally available.

C. '**Angele Martin**' Pale pewter-bronze foliage, flowers soft apricot suffused rose. ★★

C. '**Assaut**' Dates from around 1920 and has dark leaves with bronze veins and large dark imperial red flowers. ★★

C. '**Australia**' Very deep rich, glossy, purple foliage and large orange-red flowers. Any exceptional cultivar but rather difficult to overwinter. 2 m (6½ ft) + ★★

C. '**Black Knight**' Said to be the darkest of all the red-flowered cultivars. The real thing is a choice plant with lovely bronze leaves, although there are some very poor and incorrect stocks offered by some nurseries. ★★

C. '**Cleopatra**' (syn. 'Yellow Humbert') Green foliage with irregular purple streaks. Flowers yellow, red or mixed. No two flowers or leaves the same. High curiosity value. ★★

C. '**Di Bartolo**' Purple foliage and large deep pink flowers. ★★

C. '**Durban**' Probably the gaudiest of all cannas, with rich purple leaves, striped and feathered with soft strawberry pink. The pink stems are topped in late summer with bright mandarin orange flowers, making a bold and striking if garish effect. ★★

C. **'En Avant'** Also sometimes offered as 'Golden Bird' and was raised in 1914. The golden-yellow flowers are beautifully sprinkled with red dots. It has green leaves. ★★

C. **'Etoile du Feu'** Purple foliage and shapely tomato-red blooms with yellow throats. ★★

C. **'Eureka'** One of the so-called white cannas, in reality a pale primrose yellow with red peppering fading to off white. Bluish leaves. ★★

C. **'Extase'** Large wavy-petalled flowers in a lovely shade of pale pink, creating an exquisite overall effect. A little shorter than others, flowering at around 1 m (3¼ ft). ★★

C. **'Fireside'** Makes a compact stocky plant, with large, paddle-like green leaves. The big open red flowers have a small yellow throat. A very good reliable grower. ★★

C. **'Gnom'** Very compact, large pale salmon flowers and green leaves. 45 cm (18 in) ★★

C. **'Hercule'** Bronze foliage, huge scarlet flowers. Very similar to 'Assaut'. ★★

C. **'Horn'** True dwarf growing to just over 30 cm

C. 'Panache' is one of the more delicate cannas, both in colouring and flower form, and is a valuable garden or conservatory plant.

(12 in). Cabbage-green leaves, huge gladiolus-like soft salmon pink flowers. ★★

C. **'Intrigue'** A recent introduction from the USA, grown mainly for its rich ruby lance-shaped foliage. Small orange flowers. 2 m (6½ ft) + ★★

C. **'King Humbert'** One of the most commonly used names, often ascribed to any bronze-leaved canna. The correct form, if it still exists, has deep red flowers. ★★

C. **'King Midas'** A reliable and free-flowering yellow cultivar with apple-green leaves. It is readily available and tough. ★★

C. **'La Gloire'** Raised in 1920. Bronze foliage, pale apricot flowers. ★★

C. **'Louis Cayeux'** Another classic registered in 1924. Produces green leaves and large orchid-shaped flowers in a bright salmon pink. It is very floriferous. ★★

C. **'Lucifer'** One of the best. The habit is very short, with green leaves and masses of red/yellow bicolour flowers. Often sold as 'Dwarf Lucifer', it grows to only 60 cm (2 ft). ★★

C. **'Melanie'** Name is doubtful, but a beautiful cultivar with huge cerise-pink flowers. Early and very floriferous. ★★

C. **'Meyerbeer'** Green leaves and golden-yellow flowers freely bespeckled with large red spots, giving a striking effect. The gaudiest of the spotty ones. ★★

C. **'Orange Perfection'** Smallish orange flowers, early flowering and tough. Green leaves. Good background plant. ★★

C. **'Orchid'** Another freely available and reliable grower with green leaves. Bright salmon flowers with a yellow flushing and pencilled edge. It is free-flowering. ★★

C. **'Panache'** A recent introduction from the USA. It is a slender plant with narrow green foliage and small soft apricot flowers shading to pink, making a very delicate effect. Distinctly different and more sophisticated than many cannas. Flowers continuously from late spring to mid-autumn, making it ideal for conservatories. ★★

C. **'Perkeo'** Another oldie dating from 1949. The bright pink flowers are set over a compact clump of green foliage, no more than 90 cm (3 ft). ★★

C. **'Picadore'** Tomato-red flowers with yellow throat. Green leaves. ★★

C. **'Picasso'** Readily available yellow with faint red spots, but it is not so good as 'En Avant' or 'Meyerbeer'. Green leaves. ★★

C. **'Prince Charmant'** An old cultivar dating back to 1892 with dark strawberry-pink flowers and green leaves.

Brash-leaved *Canna* 'Striata' used as a foil for *Lobelia* 'Queen Victoria' and *Pelargonium* 'Happy Thought'.

Very rich, deep colouring. ★★

C. 'Professor Lorentz' Probably the most commonly seen canna, with orange flowers topping a vigorous clump of purple foliage. It is a good grower and very free-flowering but often sold under a variety of names. ★★

C. 'Reine Charlotte' An old and distinct cultivar raised in 1892. Flowers are a bright orient red boldly edged canary yellow; leaves are green. ★★

C. 'Richard Wallace' Green leaves and clear pale yellow flowers which are nicely shaped. It was raised in 1902. ★★

C. 'Roi Soleil' Crimson flowers with gold markings in the throat. Green leaves. ★★

C. 'Rosemond Coles' Enormous cabbage-green leaves. Flowers are tomato red with yellow margins, and spots in the throat. It is very big, bold and brash and not a plant for the faint-hearted. Often sold incorrectly as 'Lucifer'. ★★

C. 'Saladin' Dark sugar-pink flowers and bronze foliage. ★★

C. 'Semaphore' Raised in 1895. Bluish-bronze foliage and orange-apricot iris-shaped flowers. The nearest to a yellow flower with bronze foliage. ★★

C. 'Shenandoah' A lovely old variety dating back to 1894, with rich cerise-pink flowers over deep purple foliage on compact plants. The height is usually 90 cm (3 ft). ★★

C. 'Strasbourg' The green leaves are nicely pointed and have a faint dark margin. Flowers are cherry red and iris-shaped. Very compact and rarely grows above about 75 cm (2½ ft). ★★

C. 'Striata' Also known as *C. malawiensis* 'Variegata', 'Praetoria' and 'Kapit'. The green leaves have striking yellow veins and plum colouring to stems. The flowers are large and orange. ★★

C. 'Striped Beauty' Also variegated with delicate white splashes along veins of the green leaves. It has bright yellow flowers with a white blotch and mahogany throat. It is sometimes sold incorrectly as *C. indica* 'Variegata'. ★★

C. 'Stuttgart' Lovely foliage with irregular variegation, green, white and grey in sectors between veins. Small pale orange flowers. Amazingly vigorous but can scorch in bright sun. ★★

C. 'Talisman' Pale lemon yellow with pencilled red markings, quite distinct. Green leaves. ★★

C. 'Taroudant' A compact plant with green foliage. The yellow flowers are suffused and blotched with orange-red in a feathery pattern, giving a distinct effect. ★★

C. 'Tirol' Green leaves with purplish tinge. Large deep salmon flowers. ★★

C. 'Verdi' Bronze leaves with deeper veins. The vivid tangerine flowers are iris-shaped and have a yellow throat. ★★

C. 'Wyoming' Dates from 1906. It is very vigorous with huge dark leaves and large orange flowers, feathered with apricot. ★★

WATER CANNAS

These were bred by Robert J. Armstrong at the Longwood Gardens in the USA by crossing *Canna glauca* with hybrid cannas and were first registered in the 1970s. All are tall, growing to about 2 m (6½ ft), and freely produce delicate medium-sized upright flowers. The foliage is a glaucous blue-grey, slender and upright. The roots are thinner and longer than those of most cannas and must be handled with more care when dividing or lifting.

Grown as water plants, they need to be established in a rich soil in pots or baskets and then gradually submerged to give a maximum of 15 cm (6 in) of water above the roots. They will not tolerate frost so must be brought under cover for the winter and stored like any

PLATE IV
Canna

All plants shown at approximately ⅓ size

C. 'Endeavour'

C. 'Melanie'

C. 'King Humbert'

C. 'Australia'

C. 'Erebus'

C. 'Prince Charmant'

C. 'Shenandoah'

C. 'Stuttgart'

C. 'Tirol'

C. 'Panache'

C. 'Eureka'

C. indica

other canna. They will also grow in boggy soil at the side of a pool. When grown in pots, they can be permanently stood in deep saucers of water. They are very tolerant and in spite of their name will grow quite successfully in a flower bed with other cannas without excessively high levels of water.

C. 'Erebus' The shortest, with delicate pale salmon flowers over distinctly glaucous foliage. 90 cm (3 ft) ★★

C. 'Endeavour' Soft red flowers. 1.2 m (4 ft) ★★

C. 'Ra' The nearest to the parent species, with clear lemon yellow flowers. 1.5–2m (5–6½ ft) in a good season. ★★

C. 'Taney' Soft apricot-orange flowers. 1.2 m (4 ft) ★★

CENTAUREA
Asteraceae/Compositae

This large genus contains a wide range of annuals, perennials and sub-shrubs mainly found in dry sites in Europe and other countries bordering the Mediterranean.

C. cineraria ssp. cineraria Annoyingly renamed, it is better known by its old name of *C. gymnocarpa*. It is grown for its much dissected velvety silver foliage which makes a huge floppy cushion. It should be used as a specimen plant and associates well with most other colours, especially cannas where the finely cut centaurea foliage contrasts well with their fat paddle-like leaves. It is almost hardy and in a warm, well-drained site plants should be left in at the end of the season as a gamble. It can be tricky to propagate and is one of the few plants that is best propagated as a cutting with a heel. In order to stimulate the growth of suitable small side shoots it is worth pinching the tops of a few main shoots in midsummer. Like so many grey-leaved subjects, it prefers a closed propagating frame to mist, which tends to make the cuttings rot. 60 cm (2 ft) ★★★★

CESTRUM
Solanaceae

All members of this genus have quite scandent growth and need some trimming and training to keep in reasonable bounds. They can be grown outside in milder areas but are generally considered to be conservatory shrubs. They need an overwinter temperature of 5°C (41°F).

C. aurantiacum Vigorous shrubby conservatory plant with delicate yellow tubular flowers and narrow dark green leaves. Native to South and Central America from Venezuela to Guatemala. 2–3 m (6½–10 ft) ★★

C. elegans Vigorous evergreen shrub with arching habit.

Flowers are pink to crimson purple, borne throughout summer and autumn. A really lovely conservatory plant from Mexico. 3 m (10 ft) ★★ ♛

C. 'Newellii' Vigorous evergreen shrub with crimson flowers, raised in Norfolk around the 1880s. 3m (10 ft) ★★ ♛

C. parqui A deciduous shrub from Chile with narrow lance-shaped leaves, almost hardy so can be risked outside in mild areas in a sheltered spot. Huge heads of bright yellow-green night-scented flowers with a starry appearance throughout summer and autumn. 2 m (6½ ft) ★★★ ♛

CITRUS
Rutaceae

These evergreen trees and shrubs make excellent tub specimens for conservatory or summer patio display. Overwinter, temperatures should ideally be around 5°C (50°F) but they will tolerate short spells to near freezing point. Named cultivars are propagated from autumn cuttings, as plants raised from pips do not breed true. They prefer a loam-based compost. There are many different types of lemon, orange and grapefruit available, most of which have highly scented small white flowers. Fruit will often set and mature but don't expect a large crop. **C. × meyeri 'Meyer'** is probably one of the easiest and toughest, regularly producing flower and fruit. ★★

COLEUS
Labiatae/Lamiaceae

A genus of sub-shrubby exotics now correctly known as *Solenostemon*, a name that, although botanically accurate, is rarely used. Grown primarily for their brilliantly coloured and often curiously shaped leaves, they are mainly used for windowsill, conservatory and greenhouse display but also for bedding out in sheltered locations. Coleus are rewarding plants to grow because of their speed of growth and the amazing palette of colours they provide for many months. Provided a few basic principles are observed, they are also easy plants for beginners and children.

BOTANY

Solenostemon are closely related to *Plectranthus* and both were originally in the genus *Ocimum* until 1790, when they were separated. They are generally shrubby

The compact habit and clear colours of *Coleus* 'Walter Turner' make it a good cultivar for exhibition use.

perennials with stems that are square in cross-section. The leaves are simple, ovate, linear or lanceolate with incised or serrated margins and in some of the cultivars they may be grotesquely lobed. They are often brilliantly coloured.

The flowers are borne in terminal racemes, panicles or cymes. Each flower is a tiny two-lipped funnel-shaped tubular structure, usually in pale blue or white. In most coleus they are insignificant and are removed.

HISTORY

Few gardeners appreciate the heights of fame that the familiar coleus achieved in its brief heyday in the 1860s. Ornamental coleus were bred from four basic species. In 1853, *Coleus blumei*, with nettle-like leaves of purple, red and green, was introduced from Java, where it was widely cultivated. It was originally classified as a *Plectranthus*, a genus of plants to which the coleus are closely related. This was followed in 1861 by *Coleus verschaffeltii*, a species with heart-shaped leaves coloured in combinations of chocolate, ruby, violet and carmine. It was widely used for bedding displays at the time. Then in 1868, John G. Veitch brought back from the South Pacific *C. gibsonii*, a dwarf bushy type with green leaves blotched with dark

crimson, and *C. veitchii*, another with heart-shaped leaves in chocolate brown, edged in green. The stage was set for one of the most spectacular plant-breeding exercises of the time.

Using these four species, and with *C. verschaffeltii* as the seed parent, Mr F. Bause, the 'cross-breeder' for the RHS, worked at the Chiswick garden to produce new hybrids. Results were quickly achieved and plants were exhibited before the Floral Committee on Tuesday 7 April 1868. They attracted great interest and lists of names and descriptions appear in the subsequent issue of the *Gardeners' Chronicle*.

The council of the RHS decided to offer a collection of 12 hybrids for sale and an auction was arranged at New Steven's Rooms for 22 April 1868. On that day the figure of £390, in those days a considerable sum, was raised, the highest bid being 59 guineas for a plant of *C. bausei* from Messrs Veitch and Sons, who acquired six of the plants. Within a month, plants of these varieties were being advertised for sale priced at between 10/6d and 15/- (52p and 75p) each.

The Dutch Garden at Ascott, bedded out in Victorian style with coleus cultivars, cannas and silver foliage.

By 1869, at the peak of 'Coleus Fever', some of the new varieties were described by Shirley Hibberd in his book *New, Rare and Beautiful Leaved Plants*. His selections include plants from both the first and second RHS collections as well as *C. telfordii* 'Aurea', which had appeared as a golden-yellow sport from *C. blumei*. He nevertheless dismisses them as 'fashionable weeds' which would become unknown in a few years. Indeed most of the originals are unknown today, although 'Pineapple Beauty', which appeared in the 1877 catalogue of Messrs Rollison, is still available and one of the most reliable types. 'Kentish Fire', 'Display' and 'Crimson Ruffles' are other old names which are still available today.

During their peak of popularity in the 19th century coleus were regularly used as summer bedding plants, although the results were very dependent on the weather. The Victorian garden at Ascott, Buckinghamshire, now owned by the National Trust, regularly features large displays of coleus in the formal Dutch Garden, planted with canna, cordyline, silver foliage and heliotrope.

PROPAGATION

Coleus will root readily from cuttings at almost any season. For many growers, it is probably most convenient to root cuttings in late summer and then overwinter these small but well-established plants. If suitable greenhouse conditions are not available the plants can be overwintered on a sunny windowsill in a centrally heated room, but, as always, beware of drops in night-time temperature. They respond well to spring propagation, and cuttings rooted in mid-spring will often catch up on those rooted the previous season.

If possible, take cuttings from a non-flowering shoot that is representative of the plant. Coleus are very liable to produce sports and many new cultivars have been produced in this way, but it is easy to create an inferior strain by careless selection of propagation material. Take shoots about 5–7.5 cm (2–3 in) long, choosing ones on which the nodes are close together. Remove their lower leaves and trim below a node to make a classic nodal tip cutting. Hormone rooting powders are not necessary. A peat/sand mix is as good as any for a rooting medium and cuttings can be inserted in trays or pots according to quantity. A closed frame, plastic propagator or plastic bag is quite adequate for providing humidity. A steady temperature is required – ideally about 21°C (70°F). With a mist unit quite large cuttings can be rooted, produc-

ing an almost instant plant. Rooting will be complete in about two weeks.

Coleus is a good plant for children to propagate, because it withstands abuse, roots quickly and the results are immediately colourful. A further advantage is that any coleus shoot placed in water will root, making the rooting procedure visible.

CULTIVATION

When the cuttings have rooted, transfer them to 9 cm (3½ in) pots. A loamless compost gives good rapid growth, but many growers believe that in the long term the best-coloured plants are produced in one that is loam-based. As growth proceeds the plants can be potted on through consecutive sizes up to about 20 cm (8 in), which will give splendid specimen plants, although they need to be treated with care in the handling as the stems are brittle.

It must be remembered that coleus require quite high temperatures. Although they will thrive in a cool conservatory or outside on the patio in the summer, they require a steady 15°C (59°F) during the winter. Occasional drops to 10°C (50°F) can be tolerated but regular low temperatures will result in leaf-drop and root rots. They are very accommodating windowsill plants and will tolerate bright sun, producing excellent colouring. Plants will often survive throughout the winter, although the colours fade with the reduced light intensity. Remember not to leave them behind the curtains on a frosty night.

At all stages, coleus require good light conditions to produce the brightest leaf colour. This is especially so during the winter, when dirty glass or an excess of bubble film in a glasshouse will result in dull colours. Equally a light shading is necessary during the summer to prevent bleaching of the leaves and scorch on the more delicate cream and white-leaved cultivars.

Regular use of a balanced liquid feed according to the manufacturer's recommendations will encourage steady growth, especially with plants in loamless composts. Excess feeding will cause poor leaf colour and in particular feeding should be discontinued about four weeks before using plants for exhibition. The vivid colourings in coleus leaves are the result of a complex series of natural pigments, present in various patterns within the leaf. All leaves will also contain chlorophyll, the green pigment essential for photosynthesis and growth. When coleus are well grown this is often masked by the more

The old 19th-century cultivar *Coleus* 'Pineapple Beauty' trains well as a standard or, as here, as a fan.

brilliant colours, but an excess of nitrogenous feed will stimulate the production of chlorophyll, resulting in poor leaf colour.

Whitefly, aphids, red spider mite, mealy bug and scale insects are all known to affect coleus, but never to any great extent when the plants are well grown. Root rots and leaf-drop are more likely to be troublesome, but only when growing conditions are poor. Low temperatures and moving from one environment to another can cause this.

TRAINING

Coleus are also easily trained into a range of shapes. The most normal is the bush achieved by pinching the plants at about 7.5 cm (3 in) soon after potting and repeating this at frequent intervals, as soon as each new shoot is 5–7.5 cm (2–3 in) long. At no stage should coleus be allowed to flower unless seed is required, so all flower buds should be removed during the pinching process. This ensures that all the plant's energies are directed towards foliage production.

Fans can be produced by tying the sideshoots to a small semi-circular trellis and pinching any growths that protrude from the front or back. Short-jointed cultivars such as 'Beauty', 'Paisley Shawl' and 'Royal Scot' are suitable for this treatment.

To grow a standard, train the leader up a small cane until a leg of 60–90 cm (2–3 ft) is achieved. Pinch out the tip and allow the topmost sideshoots to develop to produce the head. 'Pineapple Beauty' is probably one of the best to grow as a standard. A variation on the standard is the pyramid, produced by allowing the main shoot to grow and then pinching out the sideshoots selectively to achieve

an inverted ice-cream cone shape. Pyramids are not easy to grow, but 'Glory of Luxembourg' is worth trying.

A few coleus, such as 'Lord Falmouth', 'Picturatum' and 'Blackheart' (syn. *C. rehneltianus*), have a prostrate habit and can be usefully displayed in hanging baskets. Three to five plants, preferably of the same type, make a splendid display in a 38 cm (15 in) basket.

COLEUS FOR EXHIBITING

Coleus respond well to good culture and can with some effort be grown into impressive plants that will often win top prizes in foliage plant classes at flower shows. The following tips are from one successful grower.

A good exhibition plant needs a long growing season. Ideally, autumn-rooted cuttings will be grown on, or those that have been rooted in late winter or early spring. If you buy in new plants each year, remember that there is no advantage in early purchase if an adequate temperature of at least 13°C (55°F) cannot be maintained at all times; a later-rooted plant will easily catch up an earlier one that has been stunted by cold.

Pot rooted cuttings into 9 cm (3½ in) pots using John Innes Potting Compost No. 1 or a loamless compost with additional grit or vermiculite. Water sparingly until the roots are well established. Place the pots in a good light and give them a quarter turn every day to encourage even growth. After three or four weeks, begin feeding plants in loamless composts with a general purpose balanced liquid fertilizer; plants in loam-based composts need considerably less feeding. As soon as the plants are about 7.5 cm (3 in) tall or have four pairs of leaves, pinch the growing tips if you wish to produce a bush shape.

Once the roots have totally surrounded the compost in the first pots, the plants can be potted on to 13 cm (5 in) pots using John Innes Potting Compost No. 2 or a similar loamless compost. Continue to water and turn regularly, and recommence feeding three or four weeks after potting according to the compost used. Growth should be vigorous. Pinch the side-shoots as soon as they have produced four pairs of leaves to encourage a many-stemmed, sturdy bush.

At some time in late spring it will be necessary to apply a light shading to the greenhouse glass to avoid excess sun scorching the plants. A light stipple with one of the proprietary greenhouse shading paints is adequate; avoid heavy shade as this will result in poor colours and leggy growth.

The next potting-on will be to a pot of either 18 or 20 cm (7 or 8 in) diameter. The actual pot size will depend on the requirements of the show schedules, which should always be consulted for serious exhibiting. John Innes Potting Compost No. 3 should be used at this stage. If you are using a loamless compost, put a small layer of pebbles in the base of the pot to provide stability for when the plant is fully grown, as loamless composts can be very light.

If there is any sign that the plant is opening out due to the weight of the branches, it can be staked by adding a series of 45 cm (18 in) canes around the perimeter of the pot, leaning slightly out. Using dark green twine, loop the stems in gently and support the growing plant. Tease out trapped leaves to leave the plant looking natural. It is far better to do this at this stage than to try to support a floppy plant just before a show.

By midsummer a fully grown coleus plant will need watering at least once on most bright days, possibly twice. The compost must be thoroughly wetted. During spring and summer regular feeding must take place, probably about twice a week, according to manufacturer's instructions. Some growers prefer to give a very weak feed at every watering so that the plant grows evenly.

Continue to pinch the plant regularly as well as turning it to encourage even growth. Throughout the growing period, it is essential that the plants always have adequate space to grow without their leaves touching those of neighbouring plants. This will mean progressive spacing as the plants grow.

The plants can be moved on eventually to 25 cm (10 in) pots to achieve massive specimens. If you are using loamless composts, adding pebbles to the base of the pot is now essential for stability. Such large plants can be exhibited at shows right through to late autumn, although heat will be required in the greenhouse from early autumn onwards and the leaf colour of coleus will fade as the autumn light levels drop.

The last pinching must always be made about four weeks before a show so that all the side shoots have a chance to grow out, but not to grow on to flower buds, which happens particularly at the end of the season. Stop feeding about two weeks before a show in order to slow growth and encourage the brightest leaf colour.

Fully grown coleus plants can be very brittle and great care must be taken in the transport to a show. Carefully dropping each plant into a plastic bin liner that just holds the plant firmly without crushing will give it consider-able support and also mean that it takes up less space in a car or van. On arrival, split the plastic open and shake the plant gently to allow displaced leaves to settle. Given a little time the plant will soon look natural again. Remember that coleus rapidly lose their colour under poor light conditions and even after two or three days in a hall or marquee they will look quite drab. Plants recover well when returned to the greenhouse but will need at least a week's rest before they can be shown again.

PLANT LIST

Apart from a few such as 'Pineapple Beauty', named vegetatively propagated coleus are only available from specialist nurseries. Most coleus are now grown from seed and indeed some excellent strains exist, though some of them run to flower before a sizeable plant is achieved and few are suitable for producing trained specimens. The National Collection of Named Coleus is held by Brockings Exotics and an excellent collection of some 60 or so cultivars is maintained at the RHS gardens at Wisley.

The great Victorian gardening writer Shirley Hibberd once described coleus as 'fashionable weeds' that would be unknown in a few years. It is true to say that they have never regained their peak of popularity but they are nevertheless still excellent garden plants for those willing to take the trouble to overwinter them.

Most well-grown coleus trained as bush specimens will achieve a height of 50–60 cm (1½–2 ft) in a single season. In the list of cultivars below, (Ex) signifies good for exhibiting, (St) good for standards.

General range

C. 'Autumn' Simple leaf, scalloped edge, soft rusty autumn colourings. ★

C. 'Black Prince' (St) Simple leaves, almost black, self-coloured. Vigorous, makes a good standard. Lovely contrasted with 'Lemon Dash'. ★

C. 'Bronze Gloriosa' Large rippled leaf, green with purple and bronze markings towards tip. Vigorous. ★

C. 'Buttermilk' Bright green leaves with cream mottling and spotting. Upright. ★

C. 'Carnival' Green and red with white and brown splashes, very attractive. Soft-leaved and rather difficult to grow but distinct. ★

C. 'Chamaeleon' Variable pink, green and yellow leaves. No two shoots alike. Curious but difficult to grow. ★

PLATE V *Coleus*

All plants shown at approximately ½ size

C. 'Inky Fingers'

C. 'Black Prince'

C. 'Wisley Flame'

C. 'Winter Sun'

C. 'Coppersmith'

C. 'Pineapple Beauty'

C. 'Firebrand'

C. 'Kiwi Fern'

C. 'Scarlet Ribbons'

C. 'Lemon Dash'

C. 'Walter Turner'

Coleus 'Winsome' is a lovely coleus, whose colouring varies with age and light. Older plants and those grown in full sun have much deeper, richer colourings.

C. **'Crimson Ruffles'** (Ex and St) Frilled edge to leaf, rich beetroot, plus purple veins, faint green edge. Striking and vigorous. ★

C. **'Dairy Maid'** Delicate cream leaves mottled green. ★

C. **'Dazzler'** (Ex) Large leaves with irregular markings of maroon, green and white. Medium habit. ★

C. **'Display'** (Ex) Large, velvety, burnt orange leaves with black veins and green margin. An old Victorian cultivar of medium habit. ★

C. **'Firebrand'** (Ex) Large flat scarlet leaves with broadly scalloped edge in green and yellow. Very compact. ★

C. **'Firedance'** Green mottled red, arrow-shaped leaf, resembling 'Speckles'. ★

C. **'Freckles'** Simple leaf, apricot orange with red blotches. ★

C. **'Funfair'** Large leaf, yellow dappled pink and white, irregular margins. Impressive when mature. Similar to 'Carnival' and also difficult to grow. ★

C. **'Gloriosa'** (Ex) Waved and crimped arrow-shaped leaves, terracotta with green central mottling and edge. A good cultivar. ★

C. **'Glory of Luxembourg'** (Ex and St) Reliable old variety with soft velvety red leaves with yellow edges. Trains well. ★

C. **'Joseph's Coat'** Simple leaf with irregular bands of green, red, purple and pink. ★

C. **'Juliet Quartermain'** (Ex and St) Splendid cultivar with large tapering leaves with some crimping, dappled crimson. Good windowsill plant. ★

C. **'Kentish Fire'** Small leaves, salmon pink with brown halo and green scalloped edge. Compact old Victorian cultivar. ★

C. **'Klondike'** Simple leaf, bright orange with yellow tip and faint scalloped edges. Lovely. ★

C. **'Lemon Dash'** Pale lemon leaves, slight red veining, medium habit. Challenging to grow but worth the effort. ★

C. **'Mission Gem'** Large leaf, pink stippled purple, fine yellowy green marbled edge. ★

C. **'Mrs Pilkington'** Teardrop leaves, red with darker centre, cream edge and tip. Compact. ★

C. **'Nettie'** Short arrowhead leaves with scalloped edges, coloured a mixture of green, purple and pink. An unusual cultivar. ★

C. **'Paisley Shawl'** Rich multi-coloured mottling. Often sports and reverts. ★

C. **'Percy Roots'** Sport from 'Juliet Quartermain', shapely dark purple leaves, fine green margin, well-proportioned plant. ★

C. **'Pineapple Beauty'** (Ex and St) Old variety with large leaves, lime green to gold with dark maroon centre. Sturdy, trainable and reliable. Good for bedding. ★

C. **'Pineapplette'** (St) Yellow leaf with frilled edge and red speckles, colouring well in summer. Vigorous but sturdy. One of the best, and a good windowsill plant. ★

C. **'Primrose Spire'** Small dappled green and lemon foliage. Irregular scalloped leaf edge. ★

C. **'Red Mars'** Small feathery leaves, mainly dull red, some green in winter. Very dwarf. A good cultivar useful for bedding. Inclined to revert, so propagate carefully. ★

C. **'Red Nettie'** Large arrow-shaped leaf, medley of red and green with yellow ageing to maroon. ★

C. **'Red Paisley Shawl'** Elongated leaf with crimped edge in green and maroon with pink and ivory edge. Upright. ★

C. **'Rose Blush'** Large nicely shaped leaves, white dappled with green, crenulated edge. Good vigorous habit. ★

C. **'Rosie'** Simple leaves in bright luminous cerise with green marbling. Medium vigour. ★

C. **'Royal Scot'** Small pointed leaf, orange and red with bright golden edge. Upright and sturdy. ★

C. **'Scarlet Ribbons'** Narrow leaf, dark red ground, central cherry red splash, green margin. ★

C. **'Speckles'** Yellow with red blotches and spots. ★

C. **'Sunbeam'** Large pale yellow leaf with delicate greenish-cream markings. ★

C. **'Treales'** Mixture of greens, pinks and purples. Beautiful, very vigorous and should be more widely grown. ★

C. **'Walter Turner'** (Ex) Large leaves, dark cherry red to maroon with pronounced gold edge. Sturdy, compact and one of the best. ★

C. **'White Gem'** Large smooth leaf, green with pure white blotch. Vigorous. ★

C. **'White Pheasant'** Large leaves, central splash of white with wide green margin and deeply snipped edge. ★

Coleus 'Inky Fingers' is an example of the group of croton-leaved and fantasia coleus.

C. **'Winsome'** Lovely combination of orange, red and pink edged with green and yellow, darkening to rich brown with age. ★

C. **'Winter Sun'** (Ex) Soft cinnamon orange with very finely lined lemon border. Challenging. Always looks at its best at the end of the season. ★

Croton and fantasia types

All have curious leaves, the crotons narrow and straplike, the fantasia type twisted and frilled like parsley, ferns or curly kale. Many were raised in Lancashire by Roy and Kenneth Pedley in the 1950s-1970s.

C. **'Beauty of Lyons'** Deeply cut leaf, much frilled and twisted. ★

C. **'Bizarre Croton'** Cream with pink veins, petioles and stems. Graceful. ★

C. **'Coppersmith'** Fantasia type, intricate cut leaves, in bronze-red edged green. ★

C. **'Fire Fingers'** Deeply cut and twisted leaves, red and maroon with green edge. ★

C. **'Inky Fingers'** Small finely fingered leaves, dark purple and green with some white. Very compact. ★

C. **'Jupiter'** Copper darkening to rich red, leaves frilled and crested. ★

C. **'Kiwi Fern'** (Ex) Finely cut leaves, dark maroon with green and ivory edge. Very compact. Strikingly attractive and easy. ★

C. **'Laings Croton'** Delicate feathery leaves, smoky pink centres with green and white markings and purple edge. Nice habit. ★

C. **'Leopard'** Sport from yellow croton, fingerered leaves, yellow with red spots. Good habit. ★

C. **'Pink Shawl'** Fantasia, pink, green, brown, crinkly, pointed leaf. ★

C. **'Primrose Cloud'** Much divided and contorted leaf, pale primrose yellow, very sturdy. Much curiosity value. Two forms of this cultivar are available, one with chunkier habit and greener foliage. ★

C. **'Red Croton'** Narrow wavy croton leaves, bright cerise with black ribbon edge. ★

C. **'Salmon Plumes'** Cut and twisted leaves, cherry red centres and yellowish-green edge. Compact. ★

C. **'Wisley Flame'** Coppery-bronze, long, tapering leaf. ★

C. **'Wisley Tapestry'** Prostrate, tiny fingered leaves in red, green and yellow, quite distinct, good for patio pots and bedding. Should be suitable for carpet bedding. ★

C. **'Yellow Croton'** (syn. 'Green Ball') Narrow ribbon leaves, irregular dull yellow/green plus red veins. Very compact. Good as an edging plant for bedding. ★

Basket Types

All make low spreading plants with heart-shaped leaves, good in planters, windowboxes and hanging baskets. The names of these may not be accurate, although they are all distinct.

C. **'Blackheart'** (name doubtful, possibly *C. rehneltianus*) Almost black with green margin, vigorous and spreading. ★

C. **'Lord Falmouth'** Crimson red and brown with green margin. ★

C. **'Rob Roy'** (syn. *C.* 'Picturatum') Bright cerise centre, surrounded with black halo and green scalloped edge. ★

CONVOLVULUS
Convolvulaceae

This genus of over 250 species of annuals and perennials, scramblers, climbers, shrubs and sub-shrubs is found in subtropical and temperate areas. Although the genus is probably best known for antisocial monsters such as bindweed there are some very fine garden plants, of which a few tender perennial types are listed.

C. **althaeoides** Needs a dry sunny situation and is almost hardy. It will trail or climb, producing fine silver filigree leaves and large pale pink trumpets. 20 cm (8 in) ★★★★

C. **sabatius** (syn. *C. mauritanicus*) Also hardy in most seasons, given a dry sunny location. It can also be grown in baskets or planters where it trails, producing an endless supply of pale blue silky 'bindweed' flowers. Totally prostrate. 10 cm (4 in) ★★★ ♛

C. s. **dark form** This is a lovely selection with splendid, rich royal blue flowers. It deserves a better name! 10 cm (4 in) ★★★

COPROSMA
Rubiaceae

A genus of 90 or so evergreen shrubs and small trees which originate from Indonesia to Australia, New Zealand and the Pacific Islands. They are mainly grown for their handsome foliage and brightly coloured small fruits, for which separate male and female plants are needed. Many are almost hardy in sheltered locations. Below is a small selection from the many species and cultivars available.

C. **'Beatson's Gold'** Tiny gold leaves with bronze margins covering shapely spreading plants. In many areas it is said to be hardy and it should be more widely grown. In a sheltered spot it may achieve 90 cm (3 ft). ★★★★

C. **'Coppershine'** Popular for its glossy green leaves, tinted coppery purple. 1 m (3¼ ft) ★★★

C. **kirkii** **'Kirkii Variegata'** Makes a spreading but not unruly small shrub. It has small waxy pale grey-green leaves with white edges. It can easily be trained into a rather small weeping standard. 30 cm (12 in) ★★★

C. **repens** **'Marble Queen'** Peppery cream mottling but very tender. ★★

C. r. **'Pink Splendour'** Fat, glossy leaves multi-coloured in pink, bronze, cream and green, darkening in cold weather. ★★★

CORDYLINE
Agavaceae

These tender shrubs from South-East Asia and the Pacific, including Australasia, are grown for their spiky rosetted foliage. Attractive when young as small stocky tufted plants, they become even more dramatic with age as the stem grows and they start to resemble palm trees, giving them the common name of cabbage palm. If they

The spiky leaves of *Cordyline australis* 'Sundance' are valuable in adding an exclamation to a planting scheme.

become damaged by frost or lose their leaders in some way they will often grow a number of side-shoots from near the base, developing into curious and dramatic shapes. Named cultivars are difficult to propagate unless they produce suckers. In recent years a whole host of new cultivars have been introduced and these are commercially micropropagated.

C. australis The simple green species, toughest of all and will in mild locations eventually flower with huge panicles of creamy-white, sickly sweet-smelling flowers. Toughest of all and worth gambling outside in many areas. Easily grown from seed. 1.8 m (6 ft)+ ★★★ ♉

C. a. 'Albertii' Choice variegated type with red midribs and cream and pink stripes. Somewhat tender so always return under glass for winter or grow as a conservatory plant. 1.8 m (6 ft) ★★ ♉

C. a. 'Pink Stripe' New cultivar with dark dull brown leaves with smoky pink veins. 1.8 m (6 ft) ★★

C. a. 'Purple Tower' A good form with wide, richly purple leaves. 1.8 m (6 ft) ★★★

C. a. 'Purpurea' Deep rich purple leaves. Fairly tough but not as hardy as the species. Comes fairly true from seed. 1.8 m (6 ft) ★★★

C. a. 'Sundance' Mid-green leaves with red central vein and red leaf bases which give the 'crown' a concentration of colour. 1.8 m (6 ft) ★★★

C. a. 'Torbay Dazzler' A white-variegated form tougher and easier to grow than 'Albertii'. 1.8 m (6 ft) ★★★

C. a. 'Torbay Red' Richer, deeper purple than the older 'Purpurea', although possibly less hardy. 1.8 m (6 ft) ★★★

CORREA

Rutaceae

These small evergreen shrubs from Australia are frost tender and require a lime-free soil. Grow as conservatory plants, in tubs for patio display or in very sheltered outdoor locations.

C. backhouseana Graceful but dense spreading shrub with small green leaves and rusty red stems. Variable creamy green tubular flowers are produced during the winter months. Almost hardy and withstands salt spray in maritime locations. 1–2 m (3¼–6½ ft) ★★★ ♉

C. 'Dusky Bells' Carmine red flowers borne on a wide-spreading bush. 30–90 cm (1–3 ft) ★★★

C. 'Mannii' (syn. 'Harrisii') Possibly two separate cultivars. Both are red. 1–2.4 m (3¼–8 ft) ★★★ ♉

C. pulchella A charming low spreading plant. Small clear pink bells. 0.3–1.5 m (1–5 ft) ★★★

C. reflexa This is a very variable species with many recognized varieties. The most familiar colour is red, although green, white and pink variations are possible. 0.3–3 m (1–10 ft) ★★★ ♉

COSMOS

Asteraceae/Compositae

From this genus of mainly annual flowers, just one species is of interest here: ***C. atrosanguineus*** (syn. *Bidens atrosanguinea*). The flowers are a dark maroon, almost black, produced on long wiry stems. It needs paler colours to set it off well. The scent is delicate and evocative of a hot chocolate drink, hence the common name hot chocolate plant. Sadly, it is now thought to be extinct in its native Mexico. This is in part due to the fact that all known forms of this plant are now sterile, so no seed is produced. Work is underway at Kew Gardens on this plant with the hope of reintroducing it to the wild again. Fortunately, it has been rescued as a garden plant and is now widely available.

Cosmos is propagated from cuttings produced from its small dahlia-like tubers which should be started into growth in a warm greenhouse in early spring. Cuttings should be taken when quite small and the use of a hor-

Cuphea cyanea is an easy plant for a long-lasting colourful display.

mone rooting powder is advisable as they do not always root reliably. Late-rooted cuttings may make adequate garden plants but will not form large tubers and can therefore be difficult to overwinter. If the tubers are planted deep in the garden, about 15 cm (6 in) below the soil surface, there is a reasonable chance that the plants will survive outside from year to year. 60 cm (2 ft) ★★★★

CUPHEA
Lythraceae

A sub-shrubby genus from warmer parts of the USA, Mexico and South America, widely used as bedding plants in the 19th century but many are almost unknown today. They are floriferous, easily grown plants that are valuable for container growing or conservatory display. All prefer a sunny well-drained site. Propagation is generally by tip cuttings, which need overwintering in a frost-protected greenhouse. Most grow to around 30 cm (12 in).

C. caeciliae Green leaves, dark stems and small bright orange trumpets with feathery tips, borne on spreading plants. It looks splendid with *Helichrysum petiolare* 'Limelight'. ★★

C. cyanea (formerly *C. strigilosis*) This sturdy little plant produces masses of tubular red flowers with yellow tips, the colour intensifying as the season progresses. The stamens protrude and there are two black dots towards the flower tip, giving the plant its common name of 'goldfish plant'. It will flower up to Christmas in a good year and is just about hardy. ★★★

C. c. hirtella A recent variation with bluish-green foliage. The rich pink flowers blend into yellow with dark maroon anthers and markings. It is a striking colour combination and more tasteful than it sounds. Plants are weak in winter. ★★

C. hyssopifolia Tiny green leaves cover a diminutive but stocky plant, sometimes called 'false heather'. Masses of vivid cerise flowers are produced throughout the summer and it seeds prolifically, though seedlings do not always come true. It makes a good windowsill plant and can be trained into a small standard. ★★ ♀

C. h. 'Alba' A snowy white form of this pretty little plant. ★★

C. h. 'Riverdene Gold' Similar to the species but with rich gold foliage. It makes a rather brash mix of colours. ★★

C. ignea Often called the cigar plant because of its tiny red tubular flowers with white 'ash' tips. It flowers on and on. Propagation is from cuttings or seed; under good

conditions it seeds itself. It is amazingly hardy and seedlings can appear in unexpected places. ★★ ♀

C. i. 'Variegata' Rather vivid form of the above with bold yellow blotches on leaves. The effect is not always seen as attractive, appearing to some people to be disease. ★★

C. macrophylla A larger plant in both leaves and flowers. Spikes of bright 'whiskery' flowers open yellow and mature to soft orange. It is quite upright and aristocratic. ★★

DAHLIA
Compostae

A genus of only 30 species but with an incredible 20,000 recorded cultivars. These tender tuberous perennials are widely grown for their flamboyant flowers and are available in an immense range of cultivars. Gardeners tend to love or loathe them; Gertrude Jekyll loved them. The name commemorates Dr Anders Dahl (1751–89), who was a Swedish botanist and a pupil of Linnaeus. They are natives of Mexico and were discovered by Dr Francisco Hernandez, who found two species growing in a mountainous area and used as food by local people. They were introduced to England by the Marchioness of Bute in 1798 but it was not until 1804 when *D. coccinea*, *D. pinnata* and *D. rosea* were sent from Spain to Holland House in Kensington that interest was really kindled. Most modern cultivars derived from these original species. By the 1850s a wide range of cultivars had been produced.

The compact habit of *Dahlia* 'Bednall Beauty' makes it admirably suitable for bedding.

Dahlias are greedy plants and need a well-cultivated soil, thoroughly enriched with organic matter, in a sunny position. Generous feeding and watering during the season is desirable. Propagation is by short cuttings taken from the tubers, which should be started into growth in early to mid-spring as established clumps. Dry tubers can be planted directly into the garden in late spring but growth can be slow in a cold season. If planted deep and mulched in the autumn, established clumps will survive winter temperatures of −15°C (5°F) indicated below by first star rating. Green plants will tolerate only 5–10°C (41–50°F) indicated below by second star rating.

Here are some less common species and cultivars that may be of interest to the grower of tender perennials.

D. 'Bednall Beauty' Similar to 'Bishop of Llandaff', (see below) but shorter and darker blood red. Foliage more finely cut but slightly lighter in colour. 45 cm (18 in) ★★★★/★★

D. 'Bishop of Llandaff' A lovely old cultivar, recently rediscovered. Flowers are single and bright scarlet with a central boss that starts maroon and turns yellow. These are contrasted by rich dark bronze foliage and stems. Raised by Fred Treseder in the 1920s and named after his friend the Right Reverend Joshua Hughes, who was bishop of Llandaff, an ancient cathedral city now part of Cardiff, Wales. Comes true from seed. 60 cm (2 ft) ★★★★/★★

D. coccinea One of the primary parents of modern dahlias. Pinnate green leaves, single flowers brownish-scarlet with centres varying between yellow, orange and maroon. 1.8 m (6 ft) ★★★★/★★

D. imperialis A dramatic monster producing huge green, purple-hued pinnate leaves on plants up to 3 m (10 ft) tall. Sometimes called the tree dahlia. Apparently the Aztecs used the long hollow stems as water pipes. It rarely flowers so should be considered as a garden foliage plant. Lovely for a subtropical bed. If grown in a conservatory it may flower by mid to late winter with small, pendant, whitish flowers tinged with lilac and streaked with blood-red at the base. ★★★★/★★

D. merckii A wiry plant topped with a scattering of small, delicate, single, shell-pink flowers. It is somewhat more refined than the average dahlia. A white cultivar, often called alba or just white form, is also available. 90 cm (3 ft) ★★★★/★★

D. 'Moonfire' Stocky plants, purple foliage, single apricot/yellow flowers with red tints. 45 cm (18 in) ★★★★/★★

D. sherffii Similar to D. merckii, but producing pale

lavender-pink flowers with wavy petals. 90 cm (3 ft) ★★★★/★★

DENDRANTHEMA PACIFICUM See Ajania pacifica

DIASCIA
Scrophulariaceae

The name of this genus, which is correctly pronounced with a hard 'c', is of Greek derivation. It is sometimes thought to refer to the two spurs behind most flowers but in fact indicates the two small translucent 'windows' in the corolla found on the species D. bergiana. It was first recorded in 1820. The genus includes 60 or so annual and perennial species and originates from South Africa.

These are generally low-growing, mat-forming perennials, all rather delicate in appearance in various shades of pink and lavender. Diascias associate well with many plants, especially penstemons, which share a similar part of the spectrum. At Powis Castle in Wales some are successfully used as groundcover under the partial shade of roses and are reputed to last for up to five years. They can also be used in hanging baskets, containers and rock gardens.

In their native home, most diascias would flower in the spring and then go dormant during the hot dry South African summer. However, in more temperate climates many of them respond to constant spring-like conditions by flowering continuously until the colder autumn weather.

BOTANY

Diascias are semi-evergreen, sometimes suckering perennials. They are generally prostrate or semi-erect. The leaves are opposite, ovate or heart-shaped to elliptic or linear. They produce terminal racemes of tubular five-lobed flowers. The lower lobes are broad and create a prominent lip. The upper lobes have two backward-pointing spurs and a translucent 'window' at each base.

HISTORY

Nicholson's Dictionary of Gardening, published in 1885, gives scant reference to diascia, although it reports that there are probably a score of species, all natives of South Africa, and describes them as 'pretty greenhouse annuals'. D. barbarae is the only species mentioned by name, although D. bergeriana had been recorded earlier. At some stage in the first half of the 20th century a salmon-coloured version called D. salmonae was introduced.

PLATE VI *Diascia*

All plants shown at approximately life size

D. 'Lilac Mist'

D. vigilis

D. 'Joyce's Choice'

D. 'Coral Belle'

D. 'Jacqueline Joy'

D. 'Twinkle'

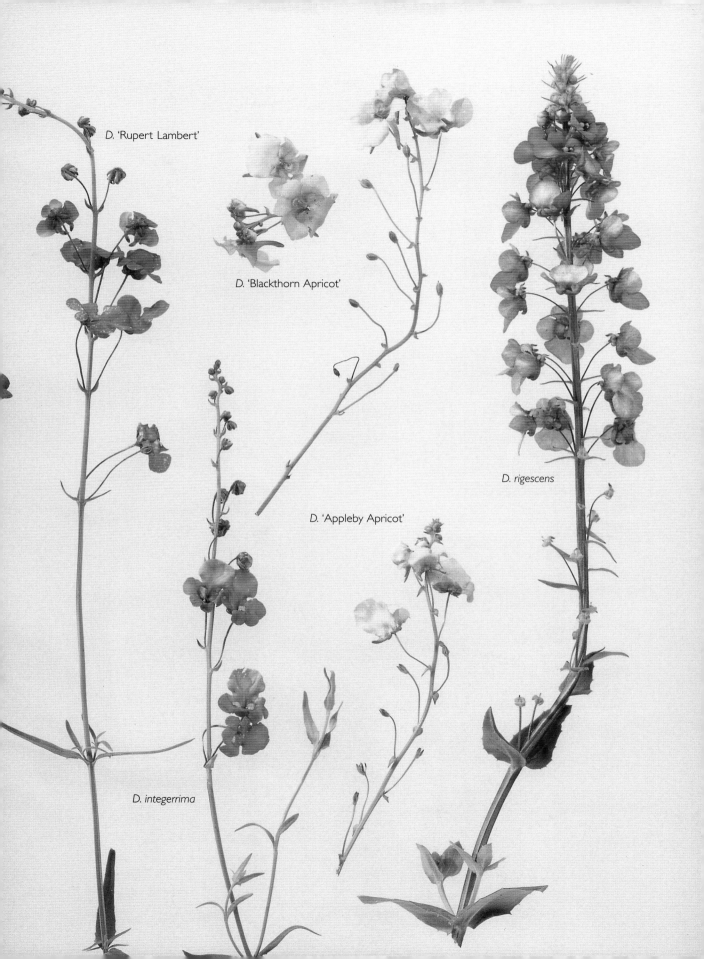

D. 'Rupert Lambert'

D. 'Blackthorn Apricot'

D. rigescens

D. 'Appleby Apricot'

D. integerrima

Little interest seems to have been shown in this genus until the 1970s, when a richly coloured hybrid appeared from *D. barbarae*, named 'Ruby Field'. In recent years a large number of new cultivars have appeared, many of which are the result of a patient hybridization programme by Hector Harrison, a retired market gardener from Yorkshire. Starting with just a few available species, he has produced a whole host of lovely hybrids with a long flowering season and a wider colour range. In 1994 the RHS commenced a two-year trial of diascias in their garden at Wisley, and 12 cultivars and one species received Awards of Garden Merit, *D. rigescens* and *D. vigilis* having already gained the award. In 20 years, diascias have risen from near obscurity to be one of the most popular ranges of patio and basket plants available today.

PROPAGATION AND CULTIVATION

Many diascias are hardy given a suitable situation but can be slow to regrow and flower in subsequent seasons. It is therefore common practice to take a few cuttings each autumn and overwinter under frost-free glass. As well as autumn cuttings, they can be propagated in early to mid-spring and produce good plants for planting out when the danger of frosts has passed. Although the technique for preparing cuttings is quite routine, it can sometimes be difficult to find suitable propagation material as the growths are often thin and fragile and have very soft tips. This is one genus where it can be better to take a longer shoot and remove the soft flimsy tip back to the point where the nodes are closer together. When inserting the delicate cuttings it may also be necessary to use a dibber. Diascias are self-incompatible and are pollinated by a particular bee with specially long forelegs that are adapted to reach into the spurs of the flower. Under controlled conditions the same results can be achieved with a small paintbrush.

Diascias are amazingly tolerant and will thrive in most soils, and in sunny or partially shaded situations, though they do not like to be too dry. After the first flush of flowers, they can look untidy but respond well to a trim with shears and recover to flower again within a few weeks. Apart from slugs outside and red spider mite when grown under glass, they suffer from virtually no pests or diseases.

PLANT LIST

The original parents of many early hybrids were *D. cordifolia* and *D. barberae*, both of which have really been superseded by the hybrids for garden performance. They mostly survive winter temperatures of −1°C (30°F) when established.

As well as the perennial diascias there are numerous annual species, few of which are available in the regular seed lists.

Species
D. fetcaniensis A floriferous species with rich pink flowers in short spikes. It has a bushy habit and is actually stoloniferous. 30 cm (12 in) ★★★

D. integerrima Also stoloniferous but has thin wiry stems with tiny leaves. Flowers are a deep rose pink. It winters well and can be quite long-lived. 45 cm (18 in) ★★★

D. lilacina Of limited value as a garden plant. Its flowers are small and almost insignificant but it is of note as a parent of most of the new lilac cultivars. 20 cm (8 in) ★★★

D. patens Produces thin wiry stems with tiny leaves, topped with dark crushed strawberry-pink flowers. Very lax open habit. 60 cm (2 ft) ★★★

D. rigescens Huge floppy cushion of wiry stems tightly packed with whorls of leaves and topped with immense spires of bright sugar-pink flowers. Closer inspection shows a darker eye. It should be planted in a warm site

Diascia 'Blackthorn Apricot' used in a planter with *Abutilon* 'Savitzii', *Sutera cordata* 'Snowflake' and *Pelargonium* 'The Boar'.

and left to overwinter for an even better display in the second year. 45 cm (18 in) ★★★ ♈

D. stachyoides (syn. *D. flanaganni*) Elegant spreading habit and light pink flowers. 45 cm (18 in) ★★★

D. vigilis Soft, slightly hairy leaves. Quite free-flowering with pale pink flowers. 30 cm (12 in) ★★★ ♈ There is a cultivar available called **'Jack Elliott'** which is hardly distinguishable from the species.

Cultivars

D. 'Appleby Apricot' Wiry, bushy habit, salmon-apricot flowers slightly smaller than those of 'Blackthorn Apricot'. The older 'Hopleys' Apricot' is also similar but is probably superseded by these new apricots. 30 cm (12 in) ★★★

D. 'Belmore Beauty' A recent cultivar with gold-edged leaves and ruby pink flowers. Compact habit. 20 cm (8 in) ★★★

D. 'Blackthorn Apricot' Large flat flowers in a lovely rich apricot, with hints of yellow, pink and orange, produced continuously. Good planted in a border and lovely in baskets. 30 cm (12 in) ★★★ ♈

D. 'Blush' This, the palest of all diascias, opens white and fades to a pale blush pink. Elegant spreading habit. Discovered in the wild in South Africa as a chance mutation. 30 cm (12 in) ★★★

D. 'Coral Belle' Introduced in 1996, this plant has bright apple-green foliage that sets off the myriad warm coral pink-apricot flowers that appear continuously all summer. 30 cm (12 in) ★★★

D. 'Dark Eyes' A strong pink with a deeply recessed flower, flushed deep pink. 20 cm (8 in) ★★★ ♈

D. 'Frilly' Strong purplish-pink flowers with a distinct frilly outline. 30 cm (12 in) ★★★ ♈

D. 'Jacqueline Joy' Pinky purple, prominent purple eye, prostrate and vigorous. 20 cm (8 in) ★★★

D. 'Joyce's Choice' Large apricot flowers over compact mound-shaped plant. 20 cm (8 in) ★★★ ♈

D. 'Lady Valerie' Very pale apricot-pink flowers. Bushy habit. 30 cm (12 in) ★★★ ♈

D. 'Lilac Belle' One of Hector Harrison's early hybrids; forms a very free-flowering, pale lavender carpet. 30 cm (12 in) ★★★

D. 'Lilac Mist' Lovely new cultivar, with a vigorous floppy, spreading habit, a little like *D. rigescens*, which is one of its parents. The colour of the many flowers is a soft silvery lilac. 30 cm (12 in) spreading to 60 cm (2ft) ★★★ ♈

D. 'Louise' Large upturned flowers in soft salmon. 30 cm (12 in) ★★★

D. 'Pale Face' Very pale pink flowers with deep apricot reverse. 30 cm (12 in) ★★★

D. 'Ruby Field' Probably the first modern hybrid, bred by John Kelly and still justly very popular, having a perfect cushion habit. Flowers are a rosy salmon, borne on slender stalks from early summer to the frosts. Almost hardy. 20 cm (8 in) ★★★★ ♈

D. 'Salmon Supreme' Another salmon form bred from 'Ruby Field' and with the same compact habit and therefore distinct from the more lax apricots described above. 20 cm (8 in) ★★★

D. 'Sydney Olympics' Pinky apricot, floriferous. 20 cm (8 in) ★★★

D. 'Twinkle' One of the darkest, with strong purplish-pink flowers borne on a compact plant. 20 cm (8 in) ★★★

At the 1994/95 diascia trial, 'Fischer's Flora', 'Elizabeth', 'Hector's Hardy' and 'Rupert Lambert' were all also given Awards of Garden Merit and are well worth consideration. However, with such a large number of cultivars available, there is inevitably similarity between them.

The furry silver leaves of *Dicliptera suberecta* act as a perfect foil for its orange tubular flowers.

DICLIPTERA
Acanthaceae

A genus of 150 species of annuals, sub-shrubs, perennials and climbers found in many tropical and warm temperate regions.

D. suberecta Upright habit, small furry silver leaves and deep orange tubular flowers produced up the stems in the leaf axils. Tender. Originates from Uruguay. Propagate from cuttings. Lovely when well grown but can be very disappointing. 45 cm (18 in) ★

ENSETE
Muscaceae

There are some seven species of these banana-like perennials originating from tropical Africa and Asia. They all have enormous paddle-like leaves which emerge from a pseudostem, formed from the bases of the old leaves. Although the fruits resemble bananas, they are dry and unpalatable.

E. ventricosum The commonest species, easily grown from seed. It has an amazing speed of growth and can reach enormous proportions, although 3 m (10 ft) would be a likely size for specimens grown outside in the UK. During the winter it should be lifted and kept in a frost-free greenhouse. Large old plants may be difficult to accommodate but can be cut down hard to a mere 15 cm (6 in) and will regenerate from the growing point, which is hidden almost at ground level. Alternatively some gardeners have success with removing the green leaves in the autumn and wrapping the 'stem' with insulating material such as straw or bubble wrap, taking care to waterproof the whole structure. Given a mild winter they will sometimes survive. There is a lovely much sought-after bronze-leaved version that is slowly becoming available under various names. ★★

EURYOPS
Asteraceae/Compositae

This genus of around 100 species, mainly from South Africa, encompasses shrubs, sub-shrubs, herbaceous perennials and annuals. All the half-hardy species are small shrubs. Listed here are two popular tender perennials and a couple of less common species, all of which are almost hardy and require only minimal winter protection.

E. abrotanifolius Available from a few specialist nurseries. It makes a small fresh green shrub with finely divided delicate foliage. Yellow daisies are occasionally produced. 75 cm (2½ ft) ★★★

E. chrysanthemoides Small green oak-like leaves, with dark stems and masses of buttercup-yellow daisies. It branches naturally and has a good stocky habit, although this makes it impossible to produce standards as a single stem cannot be achieved. It is often erroneously sold as an argyranthemum as it is very similar. It is an excellent species, readily available from garden centres and nurseries. 75 cm (2½ ft) ★★★

E. pectinatus Quite similar to the above, although taller and more upright and does not branch so freely. It is grown for its delicate dissected grey foliage, rather like the feathers on an arrow, and its yellow flowers which, although attractive, are not so freely produced as with the previous species. 90 cm (3 ft) ★★★

E. tenuissimus A curiosity that is occasionally available and may also be grown from seed. Its main value is its long, whip-like foliage that gives the plant the overall appearance of a small grey pine. 90 cm (3 ft) ★★★

EVOLVULUS
Convolvulaceae

Only one species from this large genus is commonly grown, and that is usually available in the cultivar form.

***E. pilosus* 'Blue Daze'** A slender trailing evergreen sub-shrub with hairy silvery-grey leaves and powder-blue bell-shaped flowers. I have rarely found it growing well in the UK but have seen it in Florida as an excellent groundcover. Its native habitat stretches from Montana and South Dakota through to Texas and Arizona. Spread 45 cm (18 in) ★

FELICIA
Asteraceae/Compositae

This genus of mainly blue-flowered daisies originates from tropical and southern Africa and the Arabian peninsula. They are almost without exception very floriferous. A few people are allergic to the foliage and should avoid handling them.

F. amelloides This species has provided most of the cultivars regularly grown in Western gardens but is now less commonly grown than the various selections. It is a small, bushy sub-shrub with mid-blue daisies. 30 cm (12 in) ★★

***F. a.* 'Astrid Thomas'** Large vivid blue flowers with closely overlapping petals on a compact plant with small pointed leaves. It is rarely out of flower. 30 cm (12 in) ★★

***F. a.* 'Read's Blue'** Very similar to 'Astrid Thomas', a compact plant bearing flowers with tightly packed

petals. 30 cm (12 in) ★★

F. a. **'Read's White'** Clear white flowers with yellow centres, freely produced on a compact plant. 30 cm (12 in) ★★

F. a. **'Santa Anita'** Large sky-blue open daisies with yellow centres and more widely spaced petals. A compact and well-proportioned plant with rounded leaves. 45 cm (18 in) ★★ ♈

F. a. **'Santa Anita Variegated'** As above but with white-variegated foliage. A sport that occurred at Kew Gardens. ★★ ♈

F. a. **'Variegata'** Greyish-green foliage with delicate creamy white margins, small blue flowers but looks good with or without flowers. 30 cm (12 in) ★★

F. amoena (syn. *F. pappei* or *Aster pappei*) Compact plant with tiny leaves and small clear blue daisies with yellow centres. Widely available. 20 cm (8 in) ★★

F. petiolata A pink-flowered species, shy-flowering in first season but almost hardy and produces splendid crop of pale pink daisies early in second season. Prostrate and spreading; don't prune or the flowers are lost. Plant in warm dry spot. Well worth the wait. 30 cm (12 in) ★★★

FUCHSIA

Onagraceae

This well-known and highly cultivated genus is really a specialist group on its own and many monographs have been published on these justly popular plants. There are some 100 species and over 8000 cultivars. They are widely grown for garden purposes and for exhibition, and although some species and cultivars are hardy most can be regarded as tender perennials, needing frost protection overwinter. In a book such as this it is appropriate to mention only a few distinct types, which inevitably reflect the author's personal preferences.

Fuchsias respond well to simple propagation by autumn or spring cuttings and overwintering in frost-free conditions. Plants are worth saving from year to year and with careful pruning will make substantial specimens excellent on a patio or in a cool conservatory. Fuchsias can be trained as standards or pyramids and such specimens are particularly valuable to keep over winter. They make good container plants and there are many trailing cultivars that grow well in hanging baskets and windowboxes.

F. arborescens The common name 'lilac fuchsia' helps to describe the tiny rose-magenta flowers that are produced in large panicles in midsummer. It makes a large shrub or small tree and is therefore good as a conservatory plant

Fuchsia splendens is not a well-known plant, but is well worth growing for its delicate green-tipped flowers.

or specimen for a planter. 2 m (6½ ft) ★★

F. boliviana A tree fuchsia originating from southern Peru to northern Argentina. Huge trusses of fluorescent red tapering trumpets are produced from long branches with peeling bark rather like a birch. Makes an excellent conservatory plant or specimen for a patio planter. 1.5 m (5 ft)+ ★★

F. b. **'Alba'** White, tinted pink, otherwise as the species. ★★ ♈

F. fulgens Terminal trusses of long tubular salmon-orange flowers with small red petals and greenish tips to sepals. 75 cm (2½ ft)+ ★★ ♈ Very similar to *F. cordifolia*, which produces its flowers individually.

F. **'Lottie Hobby'** Tiny magenta flowers, freely produced on a compact plant. Good with *Verbena* 'Sissinghurst' and the vivid leaves of *Iresine herbstii* 'Brilliantissima'. ★★

F. paniculata Large leathery green leaves, huge panicles of tiny pink flowers with prominent stamens. Useful container or conservatory plant. Similar to *F. arborescens*. 2 m (6½ ft) ★★

F. splendens An old species, long red flowers tinged green, good in conservatories, showy. 2 m (6 ft) ★★ ♈

F. **'Thalia'** One of the Tripylla group of fuchsias, characterized by leaves being borne in threes and flowers in large terminal bunches. 'Thalia' is vigorous and upright with leaves tinged purple on the undersides and rich orange tubular flowers. 45 cm (18 in) ★★ ♛ **'Koralle'** and **'Gartenmeister Bonstedt'** are similar, in a soft orange and in brick red respectively.

GAZANIA
Compositae/Asteraceae

These bright, theatrical daisies originate from tropical Africa and revel in hot dry conditions; many of those with single flowers close up on dull days. Although there are many seed-raised strains available, some of the best are the named cultivars that are grown from cuttings. All are low bushy plants growing to no more than 30 cm (12 in). They are easy to grow but prefer a sandy loam-based compost in the production stage rather than a peat-based loamless one. No particular pests or diseases. All are very drought-tolerant.

G. **'Aztec'** Very silvery-white fingered foliage. Flowers with cream petals graduating to wine red plus a yellow daisy centre. Quite brash. 30 cm (12 in) ★★ ♛

G. **'Bicton Orange'** Produces masses of single orange flowers over silvery linear foliage. Simple but prodigious and reliable. 30 cm (12 in) ★★

G. **'Christopher Lloyd'** Rich pink with sage-green zone and yellow centre, fresh green leaves. 30 cm (12 in) ★★

G. **'Cookei'** Rich terracotta daisies with olive green disc and yellow centre and pewter grey, finely fingered foliage, a good-looker. 30 cm (12 in) ★★ ♛

G. **'Cream Dream'** Grey foliage, cream-coloured flow-

The simple orange flowers and reliable performance make *Gazania* 'Bicton Orange' a good choice for bedding.

ers with dark green blotches at the base of the petals. 30 cm (12 in) ★★

G. 'Dorothy' Yellow flowers with green ring, white dots and yellow centre, green leaves. Striking, almost reptilian colourings. 30 cm (12 in) ★★ ♔

G. rigens var. uniflora Felted silvery-white fingered foliage, large yellow flowers. 30 cm (12 in) ★★ ♔

G. r. 'Variegata' Bright orange flowers, cream and green foliage. 30 cm (12 in) ★★

G. 'Yellow Buttons' Fully double yellow flowers, green foliage. Does not close up on dull days. 30 cm (12 in) ★★

GREVILLEA
Proteaceae

In this genus there are over 250 species of evergreen shrubs and trees, most native to Australia with a few from Indonesia, New Guinea and New Caledonia.

G. robusta Commonly known as the silk oak, it is sometimes grown as a pot plant in the UK for its finely divided bronzy pinnate leaves. It is fast-growing and can be treated as an annual, making a valuable plant within one season from seed. It is also of great value planted out in subtropical foliage displays or used as a dot plant in formal bedding displays. Under conservatory conditions it will make a small graceful tree over several seasons, although far less than the 35 m (120 ft) that it can achieve in its native Queensland. Around 1.2 m (4 ft) in a season from seed. ★★ ♔

Other, hardier members of this genus are listed on page 158.

HEDYCHIUM
Zingiberaceae

The ginger lilies are a genus of exotic perennials from Asia that flower in late summer. The colour range is basically shades of white, yellow and orange, and many have the bonus of a rich, heady scent. Although very popular in the 19th century, they are only rarely seen nowadays in the UK, partly because of the misapprehension that they are all very tender and require continual greenhouse space. They have been popular in Asia and the Far East for centuries and have recently become fashionable in the USA. In New Zealand they are banned due to their prodigious spread and the threat they pose to native flora.

BOTANY

All hedychiums have large, glossy, lanceolate, elliptical or oblong leaves. The flowers are large and showy, although short-lived. They are borne in a terminal spike. The calyx is tubular and split into three for the top third of its length. Many species have a long prominent anther and stigma which is combined and showy 'petals' which are actually staminodes. Overall, the flowers generally have a very spidery effect. The plant grows from a tough, fleshy rhizome.

HISTORY

The first species of this genus to be introduced was *H. coronarium*, in 1791, and the genus was named for its sweet-smelling snowy-white flowers, *hedys* meaning sweet and *chion* meaning snow. Although these plants are commonly called ginger lilies the genus does not contain the true ginger, which is *Zingiber officinale*, a member of the same family. A number of those regularly grown today were first introduced in the 19th century and were regarded at the time as stove house plants. However, their value for subtropical bedding was soon realized and they were grown outside in summer in the same way as cannas.

While in 1856 there were 22 recorded types in cultivation, by 1871, when William Robinson wrote *The Subtropical Garden*, all but four seem to have been lost to cultivation. The 20th century has seen the introduction of lovely cultivars such as *H. coccineum* 'Tara', *H. densiflorum* 'Assam Orange' and *H. d.* 'Stephen', but it is only quite recently that they have really started to regain their popularity. Interest in the USA has resulted in the introduction of new and interesting hybrids, particularly from a botanist called Tom Wood, who aims to create new cultivars which are shorter-growing, larger-flowered and in bloom earlier in the year.

PROPAGATION

Hedychiums are propagated by division of the fleshy rhizomes in spring. These are tough and woody and may require a stout knife or small saw. The divisions should be at least 15 cm (6 in) in size and have a growing shoot or distinct bud. Such divisions are best established in pots of potting compost in a warm greenhouse before planting out in their final positions. Hedychiums resent disturbance, so should only be divided when new stock is required or when clumps are very overcrowded.

CULTIVATION

Hedychiums are rarely seen grown as permanent plantings in the UK. Those adventurous gardeners that do grow them usually opt for caution and use them as conservatory plants or at the most bed them out for the summer in subtropical displays. Several species are however quite hardy in the UK and given careful siting are well worth trying.

Choose a sheltered, sunny or lightly shaded site, ideally with the protection of a brick wall. Gingers respond well to a rich, moisture-retentive but well-drained soil, which should be prepared with ample dressings of organic matter and grit. Liberal watering in dry seasons will ensure that growth continues. The foliage will be blackened by the first frost and they can then be cut back to ground level. A good deep mulch of rough open compost, straw or chopped bracken will help to insulate the roots from winter frost; as the rhizomes tend to come towards the surface however deeply planted, this is essential. In very wet areas a cloche or pane of glass can be used to direct excess water away from the crowns. In the open, gingers can be very slow to come into growth and may well not show above ground until late spring or even early summer. Outside they suffer from few problems except slugs. Under glass they may be

Hedychium densiflorum 'Stephen' was collected by Tony Schilling in 1966 in East Nepal and named after his son, who was born in Kathmandu in the same year.

attacked by whitefly, mealy bug and, especially, red spider mite.

PLANT LIST

H. coccineum This one comes from the Central and Eastern Himalayas, India and Bangladesh. It has many forms which are variable, although orange is the basic colour. It was first introduced from the Himalayas in 1920 by Reginald Farrer and the original stocks are still thriving in both Kew and Edinburgh Botanic Gardens. 1.8 m (6 ft) ★★★ ♛

H. c. 'Tara' Slightly glaucous leaves and flowers of a deep orange. Perfume is slight but it has proved to be a very hardy cultivar of this species. 2 m (6½ ft) ★★★★ ♛

H. coronarium The most commonly grown white ginger lily, with very fragrant flowers. It is tender and will therefore need to be grown as a tender perennial or conservatory plant. It originates from the tropical and subtropical Himalayas and is widely cultivated in Sri Lanka

Hedychium densiflorum is worth growing for its exotic foliage alone, the orange flowers being a valuable bonus.

and the Malay Archipelago, where its name *gandasuli* means 'queen's perfume'. The flowers are used as garlands or headdresses. 1.5 m (5 ft) ★★

H. densiflorum Less dramatic but easier to grow and still produces small but fragrant orange-yellow flowers. As the name would suggest, the flowers are more densely packed on the spike and open from the apex down, unlike other gingers. The species originates from the temperate Himalayas, from Nepal through to Bhutan and Assam. It is generally fairly hardy. 2 m (6½ ft) ★★★★

H. d. 'Assam Orange' Particularly tough and frost-hardy and of a good dark orange. ★★★★ ♔

H. d. 'Stephen' A cultivar with apricot flowers. 1.5 m (5 ft) ★★★★

H. gardnerianum Probably the most popular species in cultivation and has huge stems crowned with enormous cream flowers with prominent red anthers. It is a dramatic plant with a rich scent. 2 m (6½ ft) ★★★ ♔

H. greenei Of particular interest for its leaves, which are dark glossy green on the upper surface and deep maroon beneath. Flowers are large and deep orange. It is somewhat less hardy and should be grown under glass or bedded out for summer display and lifted before the winter. It needs a copious water supply and will grow happily at the waterside. 1.5 m (5 ft) ★★★

H. spicatum acuminatum Quite commonly available and generally hardy in most temperate areas. It grows outside at Kew Gardens, the RHS gardens at Wisley and at Sissinghurst in Kent. Flowers are white with an orange or yellow basal blotch and are lightly perfumed. 1.5 m (5 ft) ★★★★

HELICHRYSUM
Compositae

From this large and varied genus a few popular foliage plants are listed below. They are almost too widely planted, but are nevertheless valid inclusions in many planting schemes.

H. argyrophyllum (syn. *H.* 'Mo's Gold') Prostrate silver foliage plant with tiny shiny leaves and white stems. Flowers sparse and lemon-yellow to brown like tiny everlastings. Tricky to propagate and grow. Needs frost protection. 10 cm (4 in) ★★

H. microphyllum See *Plecostachys serpyllifolia*.

H. petiolare A vigorous silver foliage plant. If left to grow naturally it will make a soft cushion 1 m (3¼ ft) or more across in a single season. Because of its vigour it should only be planted in large containers; in a small hanging

The compact habit of *Helichrysum petiolare* 'Roundabout' makes it suitable for smaller baskets and planters.

basket it can smother all its neighbours. Under cannas and other larger exotics, it makes a splendid silver carpet. It can be trained as a pillar on a cane, up a wire frame as a spiral or over wire netting shapes to make small animals. (See pages 173–4 for details of training.) Late in the season it may produce mustardy flowers which do not enhance the plant and should ideally be removed. A truly versatile plant. 60 cm (2 ft) ★★ ♔

H. p. 'Goring Silver' This smaller version of the typical species is a much better-behaved plant with a compact habit and slightly smaller leaves. It makes an excellent basket plant. It is now becoming available through nurseries but under a range of different names. It originated as a sport from 'Roundabout'. 45 cm (18 in) ★★

H. p. 'Limelight' A lovely soft sulphur-yellow counterpart of the species, but not quite so invasive. It is still best in a sizeable planter. 60 cm (2 ft) ★★

H. p. 'Roundabout' As 'Goring Silver' but foliage is variegated silver and gold. It probably originated as a compact sport from 'Variegatum'. 45 cm (18 in) ★★

H. p. 'Variegatum' The variegation is a coarse yellowy cream around the silver centre and the plant is of dubious ornamental value. 60 cm (2 ft) ★★ ♔

HELIOTROPIUM
Boraginaceae

I have vivid childhood memories of the gaudy bedding plants adorning a so-called knot garden in a historic town that had better be nameless. It was not the colour that particularly caught my attention, but the honeyed, cherry pie scent of a patch of deep blue heliotropes. I soon acquired a plant and added it to the ever-expanding collection of plants that marked my adolescent love affair with plants and gardens. Since then I have always had a soft spot for heliotrope and its scent always reminds me of that first sighting. Like many favourite 19th-century plants, it is now becoming popular again after a period of almost total neglect. The name *Heliotropium* is derived from *helios*, meaning sun, and *trope*, meaning to turn, from an original erroneous belief that the flowers followed the sun.

BOTANY

The garden heliotrope is characterized by a small range of cultivars of similar appearance, but the genus actually contains over 250 species widely dispersed throughout tropical and subtropical regions. Most are unknown in cultivation and of little garden value. The leaves of this genus are generally simple, usually oblong to lanceolate, entire but roughly hairy and usually alternate. The small tubular blue or white flowers are produced in cymes. They are attractive to butterflies and generally sweetly scented.

HISTORY

Most of the hybrids grown today are derived from crosses between *H. arborescens* (formerly *H. peruvianum*) and *H. corymbosum*, both from Peru. Although the former had been in cultivation since 1757 it was not until 1808 that the latter was introduced, whence came popularity with the Victorians and the flood of cultivars listed in old books. In 1860 the RHS ran a trial of heliotropes at Chiswick. The detailed classification and long list of cultivars illustrates the importance of the plant at that time. Sadly few of these old cultivars are available today.

No Victorian head gardener would have been caught without a few pots of heliotrope in flower at almost any time of the year. Being an accommodating plant it will, with very little trouble, flower throughout the winter months as well as the summer. In the 'big houses' it was frequently used alongside the more flamboyant plants purely for its sweet perfume. Old references also suggest that it was cut for small arrangements and used in bouquets and corsages for personal adornment. In posies which were designed to have a meaning, heliotrope conveyed the idea of devotion or fidelity.

Large plants would also be trained up conservatory pillars to provide a permanent background fragrance. In addition many hundreds would often have been propagated for use outside in bedding displays. As such, heliotrope would often be used in beds near the house or in urns adjacent to paths and steps where the fragrance could be appreciated at close quarters. It is truly a versatile plant.

Like so many plants, heliotrope has over the years been endowed with various non-horticultural properties. In *Flowers and their History*, Alice Coats reports that it is 'supposed to cure warts'. She also comments that as well as being a constituent of perfumes it was used to manufacture an astringent lotion of great service in 'clergymen's sore throat'!

PROPAGATION

Heliotropes root easily from softwood cuttings taken at almost any time, although spring and late summer are probably the most practical. For standards and large specimens autumn cuttings will provide the longer growing season, but for bedding purposes cuttings rooted in spring will provide quite adequate plants. They require a very well drained rooting medium such as equal parts of peat, bark and perlite.

The greatest problem with propagation is finding adequate non-flowered shoots. If none are available flowering shoots must be used, removing the buds or flowers to allow a sideshoot to develop. Old, woody plants will not yield quantities of good cuttings.

Like so many Victorian tender perennials, heliotropes have in recent years been more regularly raised from seed. The commonest seed strain is 'Marine', which should not be confused with the old cultivar 'Princess Marina'. This is a vigorous plant producing enormous trusses of deep purple flowers. The results are quite spectacular in visual terms but disappointing for perfume. There is a

Heliotropium 'Princess Marina', the darkest of all the heliotropes, with bronze-tinted foliage and rich purple flowers.

variation called 'Dwarf Marina' which is more compact. All seed strains are without scent. The RHS seed list sometimes offers seed of *H. arborescens*, which produces vigorous plants with lavender-blue flowers. Seed needs to be sown in warmth in late winter to obtain sizeable flowering plants for the summer.

CULTIVATION

Most of the normal potting composts, either soil-based or loamless, will provide an adequate growing medium, provided they are open and well-drained. Small plants for bedding can be produced in 9 cm (3½ in) pots. Potting on into larger pots will give more substantial plants. Three plants in a 30 cm (12 in) pot or small tub will produce a splendid display. They should be pinched regularly until flowering is required.

Standards can be grown in much the same way as fuchsias, argyranthemums or coleus would be trained. The best cultivar for growing as a standard is 'Chatsworth'.

Heliotropes are not unduly tender, although they will not tolerate frost. Overwintering at a temperature of 8–10°C (46–50°F) will keep them ticking over but with little growth; for winter flowering or active winter growth, a temperature of 10–12°C (50–54°F) is needed.

Where standards or large specimen plants are kept from one season to the next they can be pruned in early spring to a short framework. At such time they should be repotted, using larger pots or knocking off some of the old rooting medium and replacing with new.

Apart from the inevitable whitefly and occasional aphid, heliotropes are free from pests, diseases and general disorders. Occasionally they show signs of chlorosis, which can be corrected with a feed of chelated iron or a liquid feed containing trace elements.

GARDEN DISPLAY

When used in garden displays, heliotropes need to be added surreptitiously purely for their scent or combined carefully with other colours if they are not to be lost. For example, *H.* 'Princess Marina' with its deep purple hues contrasts well with the sea-green leaves and primrose-yellow flowers of *Argyranthemum maderense*.

Most of the silvers blend well with heliotropes. At Knighthayes in Devon, there is a splendid old lead cistern in a secluded corner which is filled each year with a pale lilac heliotrope festooned with the filigree trails of *Lotus berthelotii*.

Heliotrope also looks good with purple foliage such as that of *Tradescantia pallida* 'Purpurea' (syn. *Setcreasea purpurea*) or 'McGregor's Ornamental' beet and could be backed with *Salvia guaranitica* for an autumn finale. Remember though that dark colours need to be placed in a sunny position or contrasted with paler surroundings if they are not to remain sombre.

PLANT LIST

Heliotrope is distinct within the Boraginaceae in having a scent and only a few species within the genus are scented. Most of the old named types of heliotrope have some scent, which has been likened to vanilla, almonds, marzipan, marshmallows, honey, cinnamon and even a well-known brand of baby powder. All grow to around 45 cm (18 in).

H. arborescens Tall and gracefully lanky, with sweetly scented pale lavender flowers. 60 cm (2 ft) ★★
H. 'Chatsworth' Crisp, slightly hairy leaves and large, globular, bluish-purple, scented flowers. Its vigorous,

PLATE VII
Heliotropium
All plants shown at approximately ¾ size

H. 'Princess Marina'

H. 'Gatton Park'

H. 'Mrs Lowther'

H. 'The Speaker'

H. 'White Lady'

H. 'Chatsworth'

H. 'President Garfield'

H. 'Dame Alicia de Hales'

H. 'Lord Roberts'

H. arborescens

upright habit makes it suitable for training as a standard or pyramid. ★★ **'Gatton Park'** is similar but slightly paler and less vigorous.

H. 'Dame Alicia de Hales' A recent introduction described as pink. Although there is a hint of warmth in the colour, it is nearer pale lavender. Nevertheless it is a welcome renaissance of a colour that was available in the 19th century. Seedling from 'White Lady' × 'Chatsworth'. Slightly taller than the others. ★★

H. 'Lord Roberts' Soft violet flowers on compact plants. ★★

H. 'Mrs Lowther' Has a good scent and lavender-blue flowers. Also offered as 'P. K. Lowther' and 'W. H. Lowther'. I am told that 'The Speaker' was raised at Campsea Ashe in Suffolk by the head gardener to Lord Ullswater who became Speaker to the House of Commons. However at the time when he was Speaker, he was plain Mr Lowther. Possibly the Lowther variations come from the same origin. ★★

H. 'Netherhall White' A very compact form with dark green foliage. Pale pink buds open to white. ★★

H. 'President Garfield' An old cultivar that has been in use at Hampton Court regularly since the 1920s. It produces masses of tiny mauve heads with a good scent. ★★

H. 'Princess Marina' The darkest of all with huge, flat, almost square heads of rich regal purple flowers with a white eye and dark, almost purple leaves. It makes a short plant suitable for edging. Although not actually a trailer, it sprawls enough for use in hanging baskets. It is lightly scented and probably the most familiar of all, having found its way back into popularity as a 'patio plant' in garden centres. ★★

H. 'The Speaker' A very wide-spreading multi-branched habit and open heads composed of many tiny flowers. The colour is mid-purple. ★★

H. 'White Lady' A free-flowering cultivar with flowers in a steely white, pale enough to be called white but not pure enough to include in a white border. This is one of the few old 19th-century cultivars remaining and has the strongest scent. **'White Queen'** is another similar pale cultivar. ★★

HERMANIA
Sterculiaceae

A large genus from South Africa, of which few are regularly cultivated. Pershore College in Worcestershire are trialling some new species from Kirstenbosch in South Africa which may be worth growing more widely.

H. incana (syn. *H. candicans*) A small shrub with tiny yellow pendant bell-like flowers. Plant in a tall container to appreciate it fully. Very fragrant and unusual, worth searching out. 45 cm (18 in) ★★

IMPATIENS
Balsaminaceae

Busy lizzies have been well known as windowsill plants for years and more recently the new F_1 hybrid strains have proved to be excellent bedding plants. All are tender perennials and can be easily rooted from cuttings, although most are raised annually from seed. They are generally quite tender and will not tolerate any frost. Over winter they need to be kept at a minimum of 10°C (50°F). Listed below are a few less common types that are generally cutting-raised as true tender perennials. All make good subjects for patio planters or in the conservatory.

I. New Guinea Group These are large-flowered types generally grown and sold as pot plants. Names are numerous. The colour range is wide, with the exception of blue and pure yellow, and some have bronze or variegated leaves. 23 cm (9 in) ★

I. niamniamensis 'Congo Cockatoo' Erect stocky habit, extraordinary beaked flowers of green, yellow and crimson. Flowers all the year. 60 cm (2 ft) ★

I. pseudoviola 'Alba' Tiny miniature white busy lizzie flowers borne on compact plants. Also a pink cultivar called **'Woodcote'**. 15 cm (6 in) ★

I. walleriana The species in which most seed-raised bedding types should be botanically grouped. There are also the various double-flowered cultivars with flowers like tiny rosebuds which are propagated from cuttings. They are available in white, pink, red and lilac. There are many varied names. 20 cm (8 in) ★

IOCHROMA
Solanaceae

A genus of 20 species of shrubs and small trees originating in tropical and South America. All have trumpet-shaped hanging flowers.

I. cyaneum Erect spreading shrub with grey-green leaves and large trusses of deep Oxford blue tubular flowers. Tender, propagate from tip cuttings. Good conservatory

The glowing colours of Impatiens *'Calipso' from the New Guinea Group with the newly introduced* Verbena *'Boon' make a suitable colour mix for a planter in a sunny position.*

The golden foliage of *Iresine herbstii* 'Aureoreticulata' contrasted with the dark leaves of aeonium.

plant but prone to red spider mite. All parts of the plant are poisonous. 1.5 m (5 ft)+ ★★

IRESINE
Amaranthaceae
These brilliantly coloured plants originate from South America and Australia. The flowers, if produced at all, are insignificant. They need higher temperatures than most tender perennials and require at least 12–16°C (54–61°F) to overwinter successfully. They are easily propagated from tip cuttings and are excellent in subtropical bedding or as dot plants in formal bedding schemes.

I. herbstii Erect and bushy, with small round purple leaves. 45 cm (18 in) ★

***I. h.* 'Aureoreticulata'** Almost succulent foliage plant, coccineal red stems, green leaves suffused gold. Very striking. 45 cm (18 in) ★

***I. h.* 'Brilliantissima'** Vivid magenta leaves and stems, very startling. Sometimes called the 'beefsteak plant'. Goes well with *Verbena* 'Sissinghurst'. Good in a warm conservatory. 45 cm (18 in) ★

I. lindenii Narrow, dark beetroot-purple leaves, upright habit. 60 cm (2 ft) ★ ♛

ISOPLEXIS
Scrophulariaceae
A genus of three species of evergreen sub-shrubs or shrubs closely related to *Digitalis* and found in Madeira and the Canary Isles.

I. canariensis Erect bushy shrub, wonderful burnt orange hooded flowers. Comes from the Canary Islands and needs overwinter frost protection. Propagate from softwood cuttings. 75 cm (2½ ft) ★★

LAMPRANTHUS
Aizoaceae
A large genus with over 200 species, of which relatively few are commonly grown. All are succulents from semi-desert areas of South Africa and have daisy-like flowers. They are all frost tender. In milder areas grow outdoors in a hot sunny site and leave undisturbed, as the best

displays are on older, well-established plants. Alternatively grow in pots in a gritty compost and overwinter under frost-free glass. Propagate from seed or stem cuttings.

L. aurantiacus Spreading succulent with cylindrical grey-green leaves and brilliant orange flowers. 45 cm (18 in) ★★

L. haworthii Semi-erect habit, grey-frosted green leaves and huge pale lavender daisies with narrow petals. 45 cm (18 in) ★★

L. spectabilis Variable succulent with mid-green leaves and reddish-purple or white flowers. Grows wild on suitable cliffs in sheltered coastal areas. 30 cm (12 in) ★★★ Several selections such as **'Tresco Apricot'**, **'Tresco Brilliant'**, **'Tresco Fire'** and **'Tresco Red'**.

LANTANA
Verbenaceae

These tropical shrubs originate from North, Central and South America and South Africa. All are very floriferous, producing many tiny flowers like verbenas. Under glass they suffer badly from whitefly and so are best bedded or stood out in the summer to reduce the problem. They are highly attractive to butterflies. The foliage has a strong, almost pungent citrus scent, redolent of hot dusty days and cool evenings in exotic locations. All parts of the plant are highly poisonous and in some countries it is considered to be a serious weed.

L. camara Reddish-orange flowers change colour at maturity, giving a variable effect. Cultivars are very variable and the naming is highly muddled. They are often

Lantana 'Radiation', another good plant for either patio display or bedding.

offered merely as colours. 45 cm (18 in) ★★

L. c. **'Feston Rose'** Lovely rich bicoloured flowers, opening yellow from the centre of the truss and deepening to rose as they age. 45 cm (18 in) ★★

L. c. **'Mine d'Or'** Rich golden-yellow flowers. 45 cm (18 in) ★★

L. c. **'Snow White'** Soft creamy-white flowers contrasting well with rich green leaves. 45 cm (18 in) ★★

L. **'Gold Mound'** Dwarf yellow form with small green leaves and yellow flowers. 30 cm (12 in) ★★

L. montevidensis (syn. *L. sellowiana*) Lovely spreading plant with masses of sugary pink to lilac flowers. If planted in a basket will trail gracefully. Foliage matures to bronze, especially outside in a cold season. 30 cm (12 in) ★★

L. m. **'Boston Gold'** Golden-yellow flowers on compact plant with verbena-scented golden-variegated leaves. Makes a splendid standard with patience. Originally introduced to the UK from Boston, USA, by Brockings Exotics but recently more available under other names such as 'Aloha'. 45 cm (18 in) ★★

L. m. **'White Lightning'** Lovely delicate white form, spreading habit. ★★

L. **'Radiation'** Another bicolour with orange and red flowers. 45 cm (18 in) ★★

LEONOTIS
Labiatae/Lamiaceae

A genus with 20 species, including annuals, perennials, sub-shrubs and shrubs, mostly aromatic. The majority originate from South Africa.

L. ocymifolia (syn. *L. leonurus*) Upright semi-evergreen with lance-shaped green leaves. From late summer through to autumn whorls of light orange flowers are produced in the upper leaf axils. 1.8 m (6 ft) ★★

L. o. **'Harrismith White'** Rare white-flowered form. 1.8 m (6 ft) ★★

LEUCOPHYTA
Compositae

Originating from Australia, these wiry-leaved plants thrive in hot dry sites. They can be tricky to propagate – use short stocky sideshoots and root in a very well-drained open compost.

L. brownii (syn. *Calocephalus brownii*) The wire wool plant, with scrunched up silvery foliage, useful contrast with gaudy plants. Looks splendid with deep blue or purple flowers such as *Verbena* 'Homestead Purple' or *Heliotropium* 'Princess Marina'. 30 cm (12 in) ★★★

Lobelia laxiflora var. *angustifolia* is a lesser-known member of this familiar genus but worth growing for its curiosity value.

The stately spikes and vibrant colours of *Lobelia tupa* make it worth gambling on this plant overwintering in a sheltered spot.

LOBELIA
Campanulaceae

This genus is well known for the familiar blue edging plant that is so widely planted with the ubiquitous white alyssum. Most lobelias are perennial, although the ease of growing from seed means that many of the bedding types are not kept from year to year. The genus comes from tropical and temperate areas ranging through North, Central and South America and a variety of habitats.

L. erinus **'Kathleen Mallard'** This is an old Victorian cultivar of the common bedding lobelia but with double blue flowers. It looks pretty in pictures and when well grown but can be tricky in propagation and in the garden, easily succumbing to fungal diseases. Worth growing as a curiosity but not to be relied upon for a big display! Propagate by small tip cuttings or dividing up the small clumps into rooted offsets. 15 cm (6 in) ★★

L. × *gerardii* **'Vedrariensis'** Clump-forming perennial, almost totally hardy. Graceful spikes of soft violet flowers with dark green foliage. Propagate from seed or division of crowns. Likes a moist site. 75 cm (2½ ft) ★★★★★

L. laxiflora **var.** *angustifolia* A shrubby type with narrow linear leaves and tubular red and yellow flowers.

Propagate by tip cuttings and overwinter under frost-free glass. 60 cm (2 ft) ★★★★

L. **'Queen Victoria'** Rich bronze foliage and tall regal spikes of brilliant scarlet flowers. Grows best as a waterside plant and must never go short of water or the spikes wilt and then recover with kinks. Makes a useful addition to any summer display as a dot plant or interplant. Propagate from seed or by division of crowns. Herbaceous perennial and almost hardy but best lifted and overwintered under cold glass. 90 cm (3 ft) ★★★ ♆

L. × *speciosa* **cultivars** Several strains of clump-forming lobelia have been introduced in recent years, such as the Fan Series and Compliment Series. Colour range is through reds, purples and pinks. 75 cm (2½ ft) ★★★

L. richardsonii The best of the trailing lobelias, it flowers profusely with masses of powder-blue flowers with a white eye, very reliable. Far better than any of the seed-raised trailing lobelias for baskets and planters. Because of its vigour, use fewer plants in a container. Propagate by small cuttings in early to mid-spring. Pinch soon after rooting to get a bushy plant. Spreads to 30 cm (12 in) ★★

L. tupa Robust perennial with large greyish leaves. Chunky spikes of curious brick-red flowers, two-lipped and with prominent globular calyx. Originating from Chile but hardy in well-sheltered sites. 1.2 m (4 ft) ★★★★

LOTUS
Leguminosae/Papilionaceae

Although this is a diverse genus those listed here all make good basket plants. They have long, slender, trailing stems and delicate feathery silver foliage. They rarely flower in the first year but are well worth growing on their own in a basket as a conservatory display and will make trails up to 1.2 m (4 ft) in a single season. Kept overwinter they will then flower freely early the next season, giving a waterfall of colour over the silver background. The flowers are curiously shaped, rather like a lobster claw.

L. berthelotii Splendid scarlet flowers and silvery-white foliage in long, many-branched trails. Commonly available in garden centres and rightly so. Originates from the Canaries and Cape Verde Islands. ★★ ♔

L. b. × *maculatus* Hybrid with good grey foliage and red and yellow flowers, freely produced. ★★

Lotus berthelotii used as a silvery foil for the spiky accents of agave and astelia.

L. maculatus Similar to the above but with pale silvery sea-green leaves and orange and yellow flowers, native to Tenerife. ★★ ♔

L. sessilifolius (syn. *L. mascaensis*) More compact and bushy with very silvery-white foliage and pure yellow flowers. Slow-growing but rather special. More compact than the others. 90 cm (3 ft) ★★

LYSIMACHIA
Primulaceae

A large genus from which is selected just one species which has recently become popular. There are several variations of it available.

L. congestiflora (syn. *L. lysii*) Very low-growing trailing plant, free-flowering, yellow, lovely. Spread 30 cm (12 in) ★

L. c. 'Outback Sunset' Golden-leaved form of the above. Some leaves pure yellow, others with irregular green blotch. Spread 30 cm (12 in) ★

MALVASTRUM
Malvaceae

A genus of 30 species of hardy or tender spreading and erect perennials and shrubs, found in both North and South America.

M. lateritum Shiny green mallow leaves, pale apricot flowers with chocolate centres, spreading prostrate habit. Can be grown up wire netting as a climber, when the flowers are better displayed. Originates from Argentina and Uruguay. Almost hardy. Spread 1 m (3¼ ft) ★★★★

MALVAVISCUS
Malvaceae

A genus of three species of evergreen shrubs originating in tropical North and South America.

M. arboreus Tall, airy conservatory shrub with bright green heart-shaped leaves and sealing wax red flowers, mainly in summer. 1.5 m (5 ft) + ★

MELIANTHUS
Melianthaceae

This small genus has just six species, all native to southern Africa. They can be raised from seed or propagated from short basal cuttings, produced from the new growth in mid-spring.

M. major Grown for its sharply toothed grey-green pinnate foliage. It makes a large rounded bush which gives a striking aristocratic effect. Maroon flowers are

Although shy to flower in all but the warmest climates, *Melianthus major* is well worth growing for its foliage alone.

occasionally produced very late. They give off an unfortunate smell when touched, so grow out of reach. Good in a conservatory or sheltered spot outside. Frost will kill most of the top growth but if mulched well in winter to cover the crown it will usually regrow from the base each year. Well worth growing. 1.2 m (4 ft) ★★★ ♛

MIMULUS
Scrophulariaceae
A large genus, found in Africa, Asia, Australia and North, Central and South America. They are grown for their trumpet flowers, rather like antirrhinums. Those of interest here are all slender-stemmed shrubs. Propagate by short stem cuttings taken in spring or autumn. All are sticky-leaved, making propagation tedious; dampening foliage before taking cuttings helps. Young plants need to be kept warm at around 12°C (54°F) during the winter, although older stock plants will tolerate lower temperatures provided they are kept frost-free.

M. aurantiacus (syn. *Diplacus glutinosus*) This small shrub produces erect branches, which may with time become procumbent. Foliage is a rich glossy green. Flowers are a soft apricot orange with pale velvety throats. 75 cm (2½ ft) ★ ♛

M. a.* var. *puniceus Blood-red flowers with yellow throat. Free-flowering plant with clear dark green foliage and upright wiry habit. 60 cm (2 ft) ★

M. longiflorus Dusky orange, quite compact and stocky. 30 cm (12 in) ★

***M.* 'Popacatepetl'** Pure white, well-formed flowers on glossy green foliage. A lovely form of this plant. 60 cm (2 ft) ★

***M.* 'Quetzalcoatl'** A hybrid curiously and subtly coloured in a dusky maroon blended to orange. 60 cm (2 ft) ★

***M.* 'Verity Buff'** Soft butterscotch-coloured trumpets over a well-clothed stocky plant. 45 cm (18 in) ★

***M.* 'Verity Magenta'** Vivid purple form of the above. A little difficult to grow especially in the winter, when it suffers from botrytis which causes the stems to die back. 45 cm (18 in) ★

M. 'Verity Rose Blush' Large rose-pink flowers with dark throat. 45 cm (18 in) ★

MONOPSIS
Campanulaceae

This genus comprises 18 species, most of which are annuals originating in South Africa.

M. lutea Fast growing, sprawling plant, bearing bright yellow flowers. Useful for baskets. 20 cm (8 in) ★★

NEMESIA
Scrophulariaceae

This genus is well known for the multi-coloured, seed-raised, annual bedding plants. It also includes over 50 species of annuals, perennials and sub-shrubs from South Africa. The flowers are generally small, open and trumpet-shaped. The tender perennial types are regarded by many as superior to the annual strains commonly grown. They root easily from short tip cuttings, although it may sometimes be difficult to find material without flowers.

The diminutive flowers of *Nemesia* 'Joan Wilder' contrasted with a New Guinea *Impatiens*.

However, this does not seem to matter as almost any stem section will root and grow.

N. denticulata (also sold as *N. d.* 'Confetti') Delicate smoky pink, frilled petals, yellow eye, faint scent, very floriferous and seems to be fully hardy. 40 cm (16 in) ★★★★

N. caerulea (syn. *N. fruticans*, *N. umbonata*) Nomenclature is muddled and botanists would probably distinguish three botanically different plants. Horticulturally they are similar short-lived perennials with masses of pinkish-blue flowers. Petals are strongly reflexed, displaying a prominent yellow eye. Flowers are produced continuously from late spring to autumn. 30 cm (12 in) ★★

N. 'Fragrant Cloud' New cultivar with pale pink scented flowers. 30 cm (12 in) ★★

N. 'Innocence' Pure white with yellow eye, large open trumpet flowers, free-flowering. Very stocky, nicely shaped clump. 30 cm (12 in) ★★

N. 'Joan Wilder' Dense spikes of pale violet-blue, white-eyed flowers. Fresh clear colours. Scented. 30 cm (12 in) ★★

N. 'Melanie' Also new, with deep pink flowers. 30 cm (12 in) ★★

N. 'Woodcote' Recent hybrid with dark lavender-blue flowers, robust and floriferous. Lightly scented. 30 cm (12 in) ★★

NERIUM
Apocynaceae

There is only one species in this genus – **N. oleander.** These distinctly Mediterranean-looking shrubs make excellent conservatory plants or specimens in large tubs to move outside in summer. They need to be well established to flower well. The leaves are narrow and leathery and the trusses of flowers which appear throughout the summer come in white, yellow, pink, red, purple and lilac. Many are fragrant. Propagation is by semi-ripe tip cuttings in the autumn. Young plants should be pinched to encourage bushy growth and older plants may be pruned in late winter to maintain shape and reduce the size. Overwinter they should be grown at a minimum of 5–8°C (40–46°F). The species is variable, growing 2–6 m (6½–20 ft) high and producing flowers in pink, red or white, and although it is widely naturalized in Mediterranean areas it is generally superseded for garden purposes by the many cultivars, which include one with variegated foliage, 'Variegatum', which has creamy leaf margins and double pink flowers. Some are more frost-tolerant than others and some will withstand temperatures

down to as low as −12°C (10°F) for short spells. 2 m (6½ ft) +

N. o. 'Alsace' Single white with a pink hue, free-flowering. ★★

N. o. 'Angiola Pucci' Single, light yellow with orange throat, free-flowering. ★★

N. o. 'Géant des Batailles' Double red, fragrant and cold-tolerant. ★★★

N. o. 'Luteum Plenum' Double yellow and scented.★★

N. o. 'Madame Allen' Double pink and cold-tolerant. ★★★

N. o. 'Margaritha' Single pink, free-flowering and cold-tolerant. ★★★

N. o. 'Papa Gambetta' Single fiery red with orange throat, free-flowering. ★★

N. o. 'Souer Agnes' Double white and fragrant. ★★

NICOTIANA
Solanaceae

A familiar genus, best-known for the seed-raised tobacco plants grown for bedding. There are some 67 species native to Australia, North America and tropical South America. Included here are three species which, although short-lived perennials, are generally seed-raised. In mild areas, plants left over winter will often regrow a second year. Seed is very fine and should be surface sown at 18°C (64°F). They will breed true from self-saved seed.

N. glauca Fast-growing lanky shrub with bluish-grey leaves. Bright yellow tubular flowers are produced late in the season. 1.8 m (6 ft) ★★★

N. langsdorffii True apple-green tobacco plant, with waxy lime green skirted bells with reddish stamens on wiry stems. Very sophisticated and much more attractive than modern so-called green bedding strains. Originates from Brazil. 90 cm (3 ft) ★★ ♔

N. sylvestris Splendid tall tobacco plant with graceful spikes of long trumpet-like white flowers with a sweet scent. Native to Argentina. 1.5 m (5 ft) ★★ ♔

OLEA
Oleaceae

This genus encompasses about 20 species of evergreen trees and shrubs from the Mediterranean and Africa to Central Asia and Australasia.

O. europaea Although the well-known olive originates from the Mediterranean, it is surprisingly tough and virtually hardy. In sheltered areas it can be grown outside against a warm wall and when established will produce creamy white flowers and, in a good season, fruit. Specimens grow well in large tubs and look very effective for their grey-green foliage alone. When too large or leggy, they can be pruned quite hard. Propagation is by cuttings in summer or seed sown in spring. Eventually 10 m (30 ft) ★★★★ ♔

OSTEOSPERMUM
Compositae/Asteraceae

The South African bush daisies are semi-woody evergreens with large glistening daisy flowers in various colours. Most are prostrate, although a few are more upright in habit. The more vigorous cultivars such as 'Nairobi Purple' will scramble up through other plants in climbing fashion. Most of the species come from South Africa, so it is not surprising that they revel in warmth.

BOTANY

The genus contains some 70 species of evergreen sub-shrubs, perennials and annuals. The leaves are linear to obovate, with entire, toothed or lobed margins, and are alternate. The flowerhead is a capitulum, usually in white, pink or yellow, often with a contrasting central disc. The flowers are large and borne singly or in open panicles. The ray florets sometimes have a contrasting colour to the underside of the petals, especially slatey blues or bronzes. This is best appreciated as the sun goes in and the flowers close. Some, such as 'Whirligig', have crimped, spoon-shaped petals.

HISTORY

Osteospermums were originally included within the genus *Dimorphotheca*. *D. barberiae* was introduced from South Africa in 1862 and is still widely grown, but now under the name of *Osteospermum jucundum*. It appears that the genus was not important in the 19th century but late in the 20th hybridization carried out at Cannington College in Somerset has resulted in a wider range of gardenworthy cultivars.

PROPAGATION AND CULTIVATION

Propagation is by semi-ripe cuttings in early autumn or from overwintered stock in early to mid-spring. Autumn is a good season to find a choice of suitable shoots, as is early spring before flower buds form. Over winter most

Osteospermum 'Cannington John' toning perfectly with the seed-raised petunia 'Pink Wave'.

PLATE VIII
Osteospermum

All plants shown at approximately ¾ size

O. 'Buttermilk'

O. 'La Mortola'

O. 'Cannington Roy'

O. 'Nairobi Purple'

O. 'James Elliman'

O. 'Blue Streak'

O. 'Silver Sparkler'

O. 'Pink Whirls'

O. 'Zulu'

O. 'Weetwood'

O. 'Chris Brickell'

O. jucundum

O. 'Whirligig'

O. 'Golden Sparkler'

need minimal heat just to keep them frost-free. They prefer a gritty open potting compost rather than an all-peat mix. The yellow-flowered cultivars and some of the variegated types are more difficult and prefer to be kept somewhat warmer at around 10°C (50°F). Some more vigorous types can be trained into short standards.

Plant out in late spring to early summer in a warm, dry, sunny site. Drainage must be good if you intend to overwinter them in situ. Soil fertility should not be too high or growth will be lush and flowers sparse. The best displays are often seen on stony, sunny banks. In a sheltered site many species and cultivars may overwinter most years but for security a few cuttings should be taken each autumn. Generally the prostrate types are hardier than the upright ones. Osteospermums are generally free of pests and diseases, although plants in poorly drained soils may be affected by a verticillium wilt.

PLANT LIST

Prior to the 1970s there were no more than three or four species and cultivars available. As interest in these plants grew new hybrids were selected and introduced from abroad. There are now over 60 cultivars available and they are freely available in garden centres and nurseries. The National Collection is held at Cannington College, which has been instrumental in breeding and introducing a number of cultivars. In 1994–5, the RHS conducted a trial of osteospermums at Wisley, at which eight cultivars were awarded the AGM. Six others already had the award. The following is a brief selection of some of the more readily available types.

O. 'Blue Streak' Snowy-white daisies with blue centres and reverse to petals. Erect habit. 60 cm (2ft) ★★

O. 'Bodegas Pink' Cream-edged leaves and soft pink flowers with mulberry centres. It has a loose habit and is inclined to be difficult. One of the slowest and most difficult to grow; it should always be overwintered in a warm greenhouse. 30 cm (12 in) ★

O. 'Buttermilk' Green serrated leaves, dark stems, luminous pale yellow flowers with chocolate centres and bronzed reverse. Upright habit. Needs a frost-free greenhouse for overwintering. 45 cm (18 in) ★★ ♔

O 'Cannington John' Spoon-shaped petals in purple and white, compact habit. 20 cm (8 in) ★★★

O. 'Cannington Roy' Prostrate habit. Purple-tipped white flowers aging to mauve, with purple disc. 15 cm (6 in) ★★★

O. 'Chris Brickell' Good single pink, profuse flower-

ing and fairly tough. 60 cm (2 ft) ★★★

O. 'Giles Gilbey' Dark gold variegation on leaf with pink flowers. 30 cm (12 in) ★★

O. 'Gweek Variegated' A very compact cultivar with delicate silver-variegated foliage. Its pink flowers are regularly produced. The habit is prostrate or even trailing, making it suitable for hanging baskets. It is the toughest of the variegated cultivars. 15 cm (6 in) ★★

O. 'James Elliman' A good mid-purple, free-flowering cultivar. Although lighter than 'Nairobi Purple' it is probably more regular in flowering, especially in its first season. 30 cm (12 in) ★★

O. 'Jewel' A new cultivar with strong golden variegation. Mid-pink flowers with dark centres. 30 cm (12 in) ★★

O. jucundum This species is found in Natal, East Transvaal and the Orange Free State. It produces masses of smoky pink flowers and is very prostrate. Totally hardy. 20 cm (8 in) ★★★★★ ♔ There is a good compact form occasionally available under various names including O. j. var. compactum.

O. 'La Mortola' Large rich pink daisy flowers on long stems. 30 cm (12 in) ★★★

O. 'Nairobi Purple' (syn. 'Tresco Purple') A lovely plant when well grown – in fact the best displays seem to be on older, well-established but neglected plantings, where it presents a carpet of deep purple daisies with black centres. Although fairly hardy it needs a warm dry spot and to be left alone. It tends to flower early and late in the season. Habit is compact. 15 cm (6 in) ★★★

O. 'Silver Sparkler' The white-variegated leaves are topped by steely white daisies with a blue reverse and dark centre. The habit is sturdy and upright. A choice cultivar. 45 cm (18 in) ★ ♔ There is a golden-leaved counterpart called **'Golden Sparkler'**.

O. 'Weetwood' Pure white very compact cultivar, sometimes sold as a rock garden plant. Tough and hardy. 15 cm (6 in) ★★★★ ♔

O. 'Whirligig' Erect plant producing unique silvery-white spoon-shaped flowers with a blue centre. Early-season flowers sometimes lack the crimped petal form which can lead to confusion in identification. 60 cm (2 ft) ★★ ♔ There is a pink counterpart called **'Pink Whirls'**. ♔

O. 'White Pim' (previously O. eklonis 'Prostrata') Pure white flowers with dark centres over a spreading, almost flat plant. It is tough, quite hardy and very free-flowering. 20 cm (8 in) ★★★★ ♔

O. 'Zulu' (syn. 'Anglian Yellow') A recent introduction

O. 'Zulu' is one of the best yellow-flowered osteospermums available today and is suitable for bedding or containers.

with rich buttercup-yellow flowers. It produces upright growths and the foliage is delicately cut like a small oak leaf. This is a super plant and much easier to grow than the older and better-known 'Buttercup'. 45 cm (18 in) ★★

PANDOREA
Bignoniaceae
This is a genus of six woody-stemmed evergreen climbers. Although almost hardy, they are most commonly grown as conservatory plants.

P. jasminoides Vigorous twining climber with wiry stems and glossy green pinnate leaves. Trumpet-shaped flowers are produced throughout spring and summer. The species is white flushed with a deep pink, almost crimson in the throat. 5 m (15 ft) ★★ There is also a white form, *P. j.* **'Alba'**, and other named cultivars such as **'Rosea Superba'** ♛, with large pink flowers with purple spotting.

PAROCHETUS
Leguminosae
A genus of just two species, both of them trailing evergreen perennials, found in East Africa, from the Himalayas to Sri Lanka, southwest China and South-East Asia.

P. africana Prostrate perennial with long stems that root freely. The clover-like foliage is attractive in summer and occasional bright blue pea-like flowers are produced throughout autumn and winter. Makes a useful contribution to a mixed basket. Trails to 60 cm (2 ft) ★★★ ♛

PELARGONIUM
Geraniaceae
This genus encompasses around 230 species, mainly from South Africa. The thousands of cultivars are divided into various groupings for ease of classification. All are tender perennials and a book such as this can only touch on these fine plants. The flowering period is long and many have interesting velvety-textured, coloured foliage, sometimes scented. Many modern bedding geraniums, as they are commonly called, are grown from seed but the unusual types such as the old-fashioned coloured foliage and scented types can only be vegetatively propagated.

BOTANY
Most pelargoniums are shrubs or sub-shrubs, although a few are succulents. The leaves are usually alternate, palmately lobed or pinnate and often with long petioles. Many have aromatic foliage, which is a particular feature in those selected as scented-leaved. The flowers are basically five-petalled in terminal umbel-like clusters (pseudoumbels), although there are double forms such as 'Apple Blossom Rosebud' and others where the petals are modified to give a star or butterfly appearance.

HISTORY
Pelargoniums, like most other tender perennials, were first grown as greenhouse plants. One of the first experiments with bedding these plants took place in 1829. Mr Robson, gardener at Linton Park, Kent, took a barrowload of prunings from a greenhouse plant of the variety 'Old Horseshoe' and dibbled them into a bed of rather second-rate annuals. By September there was fine display of rather tall and straggly but splendid red pelargoniums. The next year he repeated the experiment, enclosing the bed with wire basketwork to help support straggly plants. Other colours, dwarfer plants and coloured leaves soon followed, making pelargoniums among the most effective and popular bedding plants of all time.

PROPAGATION AND CULTIVATION
Pelargoniums are propagated by tip cuttings in the early autumn or early spring. Cuttings do not need high humidity for rooting and in fact are more inclined to rot in a mist unit or closed frame. One successful way of propagating is to fill 9 cm (3½ in) pots with potting compost and make a deep hole in the centre, using a dibber. Fill with sharp sand or grit and insert the prepared cutting into this central core. The extra drainage helps to keep

PLATE IX
Pelargonium
All plants shown at approximately ½ size

P. 'Vancouver Centennial'

P. 'Lass O'Gowrie'

P. 'Frank Headley'

P. 'Mr Henry Cox'

P. 'Fragrans Variegatum'

P. tomentosum

P. 'Czar'

P. 'Mrs Pollock'

P. 'Madame
   Salleron'

P. 'White Boar'

P. 'Lady Plymouth'

P. crispum 'Variegatum'

P. 'L'Elegante'

P. 'Variegated Clorinda'

the base of the cutting a little drier, thus avoiding rotting, and after the cutting has rooted it grows straight out into the potting medium without check. While rooting the pots of cuttings can be lightly covered with horticultural fleece, which reduces the excess light and gives a slightly humid atmosphere which is not too wet. Over winter pelargoniums must be kept frost-free, preferably at around 7–10°C (45–50°F).

Despite their popularity, pelargoniums are not trouble-free plants and they can be attacked by aphids and whitefly. Botrytis can be a difficult problem to control over winter and rust disease may also appear.

GARDEN DISPLAY

The possibilities with pelargoniums are endless. Their use as formal bedding plants is well established and I well remember as a young gardener the many beds of the old coloured-leaved varieties that used to be planted out in the seaside parks department where I worked. Nowadays most formal bedding is done with seed-raised types and the older ones are mainly used for smaller displays in containers, where they perform to perfection. It is good to see new ranges of cutting-raised pelargoniums appearing again, such as the Fischer types which have a vigour and size of flower that cannot be matched by the seed-raised types.

Most make superb container plants either for a single season or, when grown as conservatory plants, for several years. Large specimen plants built up over several seasons for conservatory use or patio display should be pruned each year in early to mid-spring just before vigorous growth recommences. At this stage they can be potted on into larger pots or shaken out and repotted into the same size, removing a certain amount of the old soil carefully and repotting in new compost. Pelargoniums will grow in most potting composts but the ideal is a well-drained, slightly gritty soil-based mix.

PLANT LIST

The selection of species and cultivars is inevitably personal, comprising a few favourites and oldies that fit well with other tender perennials. Dates of introduction are included where known.

P. **'Caroline Schmidt'** Probably the most familiar variegated geranium with small double cherry red flowers and white-variegated leaves. 45 cm (18 in) ★★ ♛

P. **'Clorinda'** This vigorous scented-leaved cultivar makes an excellent plant for the conservatory, where it

A rich mixture of tender perennials, including the lovely old coloured-leaved *Pelargonium* 'Happy Thought'.

can achieve 3 m (10 ft) given a large container. Flowers are bright pink feathered purple, like a small regal pelargonium. It will flower as a young plant and can be kept small by restricting the pot size. Outside it will reach 45 cm (18 in) in a season. ★★

P. crispum **'Variegatum'** Old variety introduced in 1817. Has tiny crinkly leaves with a saw-toothed white edge which smell strongly of lemons. It grows with an upright habit and easily trains into pyramids or standards. The tiny individual pinkish flowers are insignificant. 75 cm (2½ ft) ★★ ♛

P. **'Czar'** Lovely old cultivar, yellow leaf with bronze zone, single red flowers. 45 cm (18 in) ★★

P. **'Distinction'** Leaves like crinkly green coins, thin dark zone. Occasional small red flowers. Introduced in 1880 and rarely grown nowadays. 30 cm (12 in) ★★

P. **'Fragrans Variegatum'** Tiny grey-green leaves with white variegation, small white flowers and nutmeg scent. Very compact. 15 cm (6 in) ★★

P. **'Frank Headley'** Green and white leaves, single salmon flowers very freely produced. Looks very traditional but introduced in 1960. Makes a great conservatory plant. 75 cm (2½ ft) ★★

P. **'Golden Harry Hieover'** Lovely old Victorian edging plant, introduced in 1875. Shiny small round golden leaves, single red flowers. Nice edging for formal bedding. 20 cm (8 in) ★★

P. **'Happy Thought'** Green leaves with a white butterfly centre and single cerise flowers. Victorian fancy-leaved type introduced in 1877. 45 cm (18 in) ★★ ♈

P. **Ivy-leaved Types** Very wide range of trailing cultivars derived from *P. peltatum*, with glossy leaves and single or double flowers in small clusters. Excellent basket or windowbox plants. **'Mme Crousse'** ♈ is an example of an old cultivar with long internodes and pale pink flowers. Very floriferous but inclined to be brittle. **'L'Elégante'** ♈ is a lovely old Victorian ivy-leaved pelargonium, introduced from France in 1868, with white-variegated leaves that turn pink when dry or starved. Small pinkish-white flowers are freely produced. Grows only 7.5 cm (3 in) high but spreads to 30 cm (12 in). Recent breeding has produced cultivars such as **'Amethyst'** ♈ with a short jointed habit and mid-purple, semi-double flowers. There are also very lax cultivars, sometimes called 'balcony' or 'continental' geraniums, which make long trailing sheets of flowers. The **'Decora'** range comes in white, lilac, red and pink. ★★

P. **'Lady Plymouth'** Cream-variegated leaves, small pink flowers and a eucalyptus scent. Dates from 1800. 45 cm (18 in) ★★ ♈

P. **'Lass O'Gowrie'** Green and cream foliage marked with red and brown. Single red flowers. 45 cm (18 in) ★★

P. **'Madame Salleron'** Small grey-green leaves, cream margins. No flowers. Good edging plant. 20 cm (8 in) ★★

P. **'Mr Henry Cox'** Very choice tricolour foliage in cream/pink/purple and green. Salmon flowers. Slow-growing. Introduced in 1858. 30 cm (12 in) ★★ ♈

P. **'Mrs Pollock'** Fancy-leaved zonal geranium with green leaves with bronze centres, edged cream. Single soft red flowers. Introduced 1858. 30 cm (12 in) ★★

P. **'Paul Crampel'** Famous old Victorian geranium with scarlet flowers and nicely zoned leaves. Many are affected by virus but clean virus-free stocks are available. If healthy, still one of the best. 45 cm (18 in) ★★

P. **'Preston Park'** Green scalloped leaf with thin black zone, pale salmon flowers. 45 cm (18 in) ★★

P. **'Splendide'** Collectors' item, slow-growing but beautiful. Small silver leaves. Single flowers, upper petals deep cerise with black spot and lower ones white. 30 cm (12 in) ★★

P. **'The Boar'** Slender-stemmed lax habit, small green leaves with black centres and masses of single pink flowers. 45 cm (18 in) ★★ ♈

P. tomentosum Peppermint-scented, soft furry green heart-shaped leaves, tiny pink flowers, very prostrate. Can be grown in a basket but give it plenty of space as it is quite invasive. Introduced in 1710. 75 cm (2½ ft) ★★ ♈

P. **'White Boar'** White version of 'The Boar', not quite as striking. 45 cm (18 in) ★★

P. **'Vancouver Centennial'** Compact stellar type with small bronze and brown leaves. Single orange-red flowers. 30 cm (12 in) ★★ ♈

P. **'Variegated Clorinda'** Just what it says. Variegation stronger in summer and almost disappears in poor light in winter. 2 m (6½ ft) ★★

PENSTEMON
Scrophulariaceae

This is an enormous genus with around 270 species, all but one from North and Central America. There are a number of alpine species suitable for the rock garden as well as border perennials and sub-shrubs. Those that generally concern us here are short-lived, sub-shrubby tender perennials and most are cultivars. There is a wide range of colours, although pastel shades predominate. Most produce stately upright spikes of serried bells rather like a small foxglove.

Penstemons associate well with many other garden plants and are often used in mixed borders with herbaceous perennials and roses. The pastel-coloured cultivars mix well with diascias, adding height and colour contrast. They can be used in containers but tend to be more at home in beds and borders, where their classical spikes are shown to perfection.

BOTANY

Penstemons are generally evergreen or semi-evergreen perennials or sub-shrubs. The leaves are linear to lance-shaped and often sessile (stalkless). The flowers are tubular or bell-shaped, produced in racemes or panicles. The individual flowers are composed of two lips, the upper having two lobes and the lower three. The outer part of the tube is called the mouth and the inner the throat.

HISTORY

The genus was first identified by Dr John Mitchell, a physician living in Virginia, but a number of the big-name Victorian plant hunters such as William Lobb, Carl Hartweg, David Douglas and Archibald Menzies collected penstemon seed. Very soon the garden value of these plants was recognized and new hybrids and strains were developed. The first RHS trial of penstemons took place in 1861.

PLATE X Penstemon

All plants shown at approximately ½ size

P. 'Stapleford Gem'

P. 'Midnight'

P. 'Rich Ruby'

P. 'Pershore Pink Necklace'

P. 'Sour Grapes'

P. 'Garnet'

P. 'Chester Scarlet'

P. 'White Bedder'

P. 'Countess of Dalkeith'

P. 'Catherine de la Mare'

P. 'Evelyn'

CULTIVATION AND PROPAGATION

All penstemons like full sun and a sheltered spot with good drainage. A rich soil will encourage leaves rather than flowers, so don't overfeed. If plants overwinter successfully, prune as soon as there are signs of new growth, cutting back above the point at which it occurs. Propagate by semi-ripe cuttings taken in early autumn or in spring. Pinch young plants to give a well-branched stocky plant. Over winter, keep them cool but free from frost. Planting out can take place from late spring onwards.

PLANT LIST

The naming of penstemons attracts considerable controversy, only partly solved by the most recent trial held by the RHS at Wisley, between 1991 and 1993. As is the case with many popular plants, the names used by nurserymen are not always accurate. Reliably named collections are grown at the RHS gardens at Wisley in Surrey and Kingston Maurward Gardens in Devon.

P. **'Alice Hindley'** Huge dignified spikes of white-throated lilac flowers, almost purple in bud. Easy to grow but distinctly tender. 90 cm (3 ft) ★★ ♛

P. **'Apple Blossom'** Blush pink but with a white throat. 75 cm (2½ ft) ★★★ ♛ **'Beech Park'** and **'Thorn'** have similar colouring.

P. **'Blackbird'** Deep rich purple flowers on dark stems, really funereal. Contrasts well with light blue and pale pink. 75 cm (2½ ft) ★★

P. **'Catherine de la Mare'** Low-growing, small-flowered cultivar with many variably bluish-purple flowers densely packed on wiry stems. 45 cm (18 in) ★★★ ♛

P. **'Chester Scarlet'** Sparse foliage, intense bright red flowers on dark stems. Purplish sheen to flowers and faint markings at throat. 90 cm (3 ft) ★★ ♛

P. **'Countess of Dalkeith'** ('Newby Gem') Tall, erect plant with deep purple flowers and open white throat. 1 m (3¼ ft) ★★★

P. digitalis **'Husker Red'** One of a new range of penstemons bred by Dr Dale Lindgren from the University of Nebraska. Its deep beetroot-red foliage is unique and provides a perfect foil for the pinkish-white flowers. 45 cm (18 in) ★★★★

P. **'Evelyn'** Another compact cultivar. Flowers are small and a delicate light pink, mounted in graceful spikes. Like most of the small-leaved types, it is quite hardy. 60 cm (2 ft) ★★★★

P. **'Garnet'** (syn. 'Andenken an Friedrich Hahn') Although correctly known by its synonym, it is more

P. 'Alice Hindley' is one of the loveliest of the penstemons but its use in the border is limited by its distinctly tender nature.

usually offered under the name 'Garnet', given by Graham Stuart Thomas. Small cerise-wine flowers on wiry stems. It is tough and fairly hardy. 75 cm (2½ ft) ★★★★

P. **'Hidcote Pink'** Flowers are pale shell pink, small and freely produced. It is fairly hardy. 1 m (3¼ ft) ★★★ **'Pennington Gem'** is similar.

P. isophyllus Very tall slender nodding spikes. The small delicate flowers have long pedicels and are of a rich deep salmon pink. Useful at the back of a border or among low-growing plants. 1 m (3¼ ft) ★★★ ♛

P. **'King George V'** Introduced in 1911 and still one of the best reds. Vigorous. The bright clear red flowers have a white throat with red flecking. 75–90 cm (2½–3 ft) ★★★ **'Firebird'** and **'Chester Scarlet'** are other good reds.

P. **'Midnight'** One of a number of deep rich purple cultivars. This one also has dark stems. 75 cm (2½ ft) ★★★ **'Port Wine'**, **'Raven'** and **'Blackbird'** are similar.

Penstemon 'White Bedder' in a mixed planting with Verbena bonariensis and Datura inoxia.

P. 'Pershore Pink Necklace' Lovely recent cultivar in rich pink with a deep ruby ribbon around an almost white throat. 60 cm (2 ft) ★★

P. 'Rich Ruby' Very erect cultivar with rich purple stems and deep purple-red flowers with dark patches at mouth. White throat with red streaks. 1 m (3¼ ft) ★★

P. 'Rubicundus' A massive red with a white throat. 75 cm (2½ ft) ★★★

P. 'Sour Grapes' An elusive cultivar that has caused much controversy. The similar **'Stapleford Gem'** has often been offered erroneously in the past. The true 'Sour Grapes' has deep purple flowers overlaid with blue, the throat is white and there is a distinct green marking on the upper tube. A collector's cultivar. 60 cm (2 ft) ★★★★

P. 'White Bedder' (syn. 'Snowstorm') Pure white flowers. 60 cm (2 ft) ★★★★ ♔ **P. hartwegii 'Albus'** is another good white. ♔

PERICALLIS
Asteraceae/Compositae

A genus of 15 species of perennials and sub-shrubs occurring naturally in the Canary Islands, Madeira and the Azores. The best-known plant in the genus is the annual pot plant known as cineraria.

P. lantana (formerly *Senecio heritieri*) Silvery maple-shaped leaves, flowers white with cerise pink-tipped petals and strawberry boss. Wiry habit. 45 cm (18 in) ★★ Dwarf form available under various names including **'Kew form'** with more finely formed leaves and richer pink colouring to flowers.

PETUNIA
Solanaceae

Originating from South America, petunias have been hybridized for so many years that the species are rarely seen outside botanic gardens. Most of our modern petunias have been derived from two species, *P. axillaris* and *P. integrifolia* (syn. *P. violacea*). For many years seed strains, grown as annuals, have dominated the bedding plant market, although petunias are actually tender perennials.

More recently superior strains of vegetatively propagated types such as the 'Surfinia' petunias have been produced. They are available in whites, pinks, magentas, lavenders and blues, many with delicate veining. All make huge spreading plants and are excellent for hanging baskets. **'Priscilla'** is double with prettily veined lilac flowers. **'Million Bells'** is more compact with smaller flowers and botanists question whether the 'Million Bells' strains are actually petunias or belong in their own genus, *Calibrachoa*.

These are propagated from cuttings taken in autumn or winter. Most types are covered by the Plant Propagators Rights, which means that although the private gardener may take cuttings for his own use, he may not sell them, neither may any nursery without paying the correct fees. Most are produced by the huge commercial propagators and sold as plugs to nurseries to grow on. They suffer badly from viruses which can easily be transmitted when taking cuttings, so it is often better to buy fresh healthy 'plugs' each spring. ★★

PHYGELIUS
Scrophulariaceae

This genus contains only two species from South Africa and a few cultivars. They are almost hardy. In sheltered areas and in mild winters they remain shrubby but after severe frost die down to ground level and regrow as a herbaceous perennial. They root easily from tip cuttings.

P. aequalis 'Yellow Trumpet' Stocky spires of creamy-yellow trumpets freely produced. 90 cm (3 ft) ★★★★

P. capensis The cape figwort is a tall suckering shrub with orange flowers with yellow throats. Against a warm wall will grow to 1.5 m (5 ft) ★★★★ ♔

P. × rectus 'African Queen' Pendant pale red flowers with orange-red lobes and yellow throats. Upright habit. 30 cm (12 in) ★★★★

P. × r. 'Pink Elf' Pale pink flowers with dark crimson lobes. 75 cm (2½ ft) ★★★★

P. × r. 'Winchester Fanfare' Arching stems bearing red tubular flowers with lemon centres. 1.2 m (4 ft) ★★★★

PLECOSTACHYS
Asteraceae/Compositae

P. serpyllifolia (formerly *Helichrysum microphyllum*) Delicate small silver leaves, spreading habit, well behaved in small hanging baskets and planters. 20 cm (8 in) ★★

PLECTRANTHUS
Labiatae

Although there are over 350 species in this genus, relatively few are regularly grown. They are all tender, originating from areas such as Africa, Madagascar, Asia, Australasia and the Pacific Islands. They are often aromatic and are generally grown for their foliage. They root from tip cuttings very easily.

P. amboin Sometimes sold as *Coleus aromaticus*, this small plant has succulent green leaves with a lovely spicy citrus smell. Small insignificant blue flowers. Makes a nice windowsill plant. 20 cm (8 in) ★

P. argentatus Grey-green leaves with silvery hairs. Tiny bluish-white flowers. Spreading habit, useful in baskets and planters. 10 cm (4 in) ★

P. forsteri **'Marginatus'** Long trails of lemon-scented, white-variegated foliage. Familiar basket plant. Trails to 75 cm (2½ ft). ★

P. madagascariensis **'Variegated Mintleaf'** Small, chunky shrub bearing large almost succulent leaves with white variegations and minty smell. 30 cm (12 in) ★

P. oertendahlii Beautifully marbled pewtery leaves with mauve undersides. Delicate racemes of white or pale blue flowers. Should be more widely grown. Lovely mix with violet, lavender or pink flowers. 20 cm (8 in) ★ ♔

PLUMBAGO
Plumbaginaceae

These tropical climbers and shrubs make excellent conservatory plants. They can be grown in containers and used outside as patio features. They need tying to a support to remain tidy and can be pruned quite hard in early spring. They are rather inclined to be brittle.

P. auriculata (syn. *P. capensis*) Cape leadwort. Soft powder-blue flowers are freely borne in dense racemes. In frost-free locations, it can be allowed to sprawl and make a low groundcover. 1.8 m (6 ft) + ★★★ ♔

P. a. **'Alba'** As above but snowy white. Just as easy to grow. ★★★

Plectranthus are generally grown for their attractive leaves but the delicate flowers can be a valuable bonus.

POLYGALA
Polygalaceae

This huge genus of annuals and evergreen perennials and shrubs is found almost worldwide. Its members are grown for their pea-like flowers.

P. × dalmaisiana Erect, rounded evergreen conservatory shrub. Purple pea-like flowers with white fringe-like style. 1.5 m (5 ft) ★★ ♔

P. myrtifolia Shrubby species from South Africa but almost hardy. Small purple pea-like flowers all summer. Grow in a conservatory. 1.2 m (4 ft) + ★★

PORTULACA
Portulacaceae

A genus of 100 succulent species, most of which are annuals. They are natives of dry, sandy soils in warm temperate and tropical regions.

P. grandiflora Spreading succulent with chunky moss-like leaves. Native of Brazil, Argentina and Uruguay, though most of those grown are of garden origin, with single or double satiny flowers like small roses in many colours. Can be grown from seed or named cultivars such as the 'Sundial' series from cuttings. 15 cm (6 in) ★★

PROSTANTHERA
Labiatae/Lamiaceae

This is a genus of 50 species of small evergreen shrubs and trees from Australia. Most have aromatic foliage and small cup- or bell-shaped flowers in various colours.

P. cuneata The alpine mint bush is almost hardy and can be grown outside in a sheltered position. It makes a small spreading evergreen shrub with tiny aromatic leaves. In summer, masses of pretty little white flowers with purple and yellow markings in the throat are produced. Fully hardy in many areas. 60 cm (2 ft) ★★★★ ♔

P. rotundifolia Not so hardy, therefore grow in a tub and take under cover for the winter in most areas. Clouds of lavender flowers in the spring. 90 cm (3 ft) ★★★ ♔ There is a pink form called **'Rosea'**.

PSEUDOPANAX
Araliaceae

A genus of 12–20 evergreen trees and shrubs from Tasmania, New Zealand and Chile, most of which have striking foliage and strong architectural shapes.

P. lessonii **'Goldsplash'** Handsome erect shrub or small tree with evergreen three- or five-lobed, palmate leaves, suffused with golden yellow. Needs to be kept just frost-protected. Good cool conservatory plant. 1.5 m (5 ft) + ★★ ♔

P. l. 'Purpureus' Similar to above with bronze-purple foliage. 1.5 m (5 ft) + ★★ ♔

RHODANTHEMUM
Compositae
A genus of 10 species of prostrate perennials and sub-shrubs originating mainly from North Africa.

R. gayanum This plant has undergone many name changes and is often sold as a marguerite, which it once was. The botanists then changed its name to *Chrysanthemum*, then *Chrysanthemopsis* and *Pyrethropsis* before its present identity. Naming aside it is a lovely little sub-shrub with soft sea-green leaves rather like tiny carrot foliage. Flowers are borne freely throughout the summer, single daisy heads in a pinkish-maroon with yellow centres. Under cool glass it will flower on into the winter and then start again early the next spring. It originates from Morocco and Algeria. 30 cm (12 in) ★★★

RUSSELIA
Scrophulariaceae
This is an almost unknown genus of about 50 species of shrubs and sub-shrubs. The stems are rush-like and the leaves are often reduced to mere scales.

R. equisetiformis Most curious plant that looks like a rush or mare's tail with thin, wiry, scale-like leaves. Lax habit with masses of pendant tubular gaudy scarlet flowers. Originates from Mexico and needs an overwinter temperature of 10°C (50°F) Propagated by division or softwood cuttings. 75 cm (2½ ft) ★★ ♔

SALVIA
Labiatae
This is a large genus with over 900 species. Many are found in the Americas and the rest are spread all over the temperate and sub-tropical areas of the world except Australasia. Most of the tender salvias come from South America, Mexico, and Texas, Arizona and New Mexico in the USA.

The flowering sages are a group of plants that gardeners either love or hate. Many gardeners still equate the name with the garish red bedding type, though this is a vast genus of plants with flowers in a spectrum of colour from soft powder blue through to the hottest of reds, many also having aromatic foliage. Their late flowering is often seen as a disadvantage, although there are few other genera which will provide the same interest in the border in autumn. Some of them flower so late that there is real risk that the display will be frosted before its peak. To avoid disappointment some growers use the really late salvias as display plants for the cool conservatory.

BOTANY
All the salvias have the square stems characteristic of members of Labiatae. The leaves are opposite and generally simple, although with such a diverse genus there is some variation in shape and margins, for example *S. greggii* has smooth margins whereas *S. blepharophylla* is fringed with hairs.

The flowers are arranged as spikes, racemes or panicles. The calyx has three upper and two lower segments. In some species, the calyx holds on after flowering and may become part of the seed structure. The corolla is formed from petals joined together to form a tube with two lips. The upper lip may be hooded and hairy, giving a velvety appearance.

Many species have ordinary fibrous roots but some, such as *S. uliginosa*, have underground runners and others, for example *S. patens*, tuberous roots.

HISTORY
Many of the well-known half-hardy salvias were introduced in the 19th century, and when the bedding salvia *S. splendens* was introduced in 1822 from Brazil its startling scarlet flowers must have caused quite a sensation. At that time it was regarded as a 'pretty greenhouse shrub', though nowadays it is always grown from seed as a summer bedding plant. Gertrude Jekyll used a 'good form' of it in her September flower borders at Munstead Wood.

There was a steady stream of introductions following *S. splendens, S. involucrata* arriving from Mexico in 1824, *S. confertiflora* from Brazil in 1838, *S. leucantha* from Mexico in 1847, *S. discolor* from Peru in 1883 and *S. greggii* from Mexico in 1885. The pale blue form of *S. patens* known as 'Cambridge Blue' was well known by 1887 and is still a good cultivar today, though the variegated form of *S. fulgens* that was grown in the 19th century is now lost.

Interest in salvias has continued in the 20th century, although they have never been particularly popular plants. *S. blepharophylla* was collected in Mexico in 1930 and *S.* 'Indigo Spires' was raised in 1979 at the Huntingdon Botanic Garden in California. On a recent expedition to Mexico, Compton, Darby and Rix discovered a range of natural hybrids between *S. greggii* and *S. microphylla* which were named *S. jamensis* after the local village of Jame. There are now several named cultivars in this group.

CULTIVATION AND PROPAGATION

In general all salvias like full sun and a well-drained site. Avoid excess nitrogen as this results in sparse flowering. Most have to be treated as tender perennials and replaced each year, although it is worth mulching plants in a sheltered position; even if the top parts die they may sprout again from the base of the plant. Virtually all the tender salvias are shrubby and so can be propagated easily from cuttings. Generally salvias need no more than frost protection overwinter. Young plants of *S. greggii* easily succumb to botrytis at low temperatures, which can be avoided by growing warmer at about 10°C (50°F). This in turn can result in very soft over-large plants by spring. Being fairly tough, they can be planted a little earlier than many tender perennials in late spring.

PLANT LIST

The trial of tender salvias by the RHS at Wisley in 1995 and 1996 has evaluated a number of traditional types and highlighted some lesser known but gardenworthy types, many of which are listed here.

S. africana-lutea (syn. *S. aurea*) Crinkly, aromatic, grey-green leaves, cinnamon-brown flowers. As the name suggests, a native of South Africa. Quite unusual and striking. 30 cm (12 in) ★★★

S. coccinea pseudococcinea Long racemes of well-spaced small strong red flowers over a bushy plant flowering well in late summer. 75 cm (2½ ft) ★★ ♔

S. confertiflora Woody perennial with towering wiry spikes of orange-red flowers produced late summer. Unpleasant scent. 1.2 m (4 ft) ★★★

S. discolor Produces steely wands of greyish, white-backed leaves topped with almost black nodding flowers. Lax habit. By growing it in a basket or high planter the contrasting foliage can be best appreciated. Foliage can be sticky, which makes the taking of cuttings a bit messy. 75 cm (2½ ft) ★★★ ♔

S. elegans 'Scarlet Pineapple' (syn *S. rutilans*) Pineapple sage, sweetly aromatic foliage and bright scarlet flowers, produced in early autumn. Too late flowering for any real value so just an odd plant somewhere convenient for pinching the foliage to release the aroma. 90 cm (3 ft) ★★

S. greggii Makes a small wiry shrub with tiny red sage flowers. There are many cultivars. Gardeners should be warned that the plant is very brittle and should be han-

Salvia involucrata 'Bethellii' growing among the seed-raised *Salvia farinacea* 'Victoria'.

dled with care. For this reason it is not often available by mail order. 75 cm (2½ ft) ★★

S. g. 'Alba' Produces pure white flowers, but is rather temperamental and easily dies off during the winter both outside and under glass. 45 cm (18 in) ★

S. g. 'Peach' Flowers of a soft peach colour. 60 cm (2 ft) ★★ ♔

S. g. 'Raspberry Royal' A deep rich red. 60 cm (2 ft) ★★

S. guaranitica Deep purple, almost black, very late flowering. 1.5 m (5 ft) ★★★ ♔ Several improved cultivars available such as **'Blue Enigma'** ♔, which starts to flower in midsummer. Contrasts well with the orange *Dahlia* 'Moonfire'.

S. 'Indigo Spires' This is a hybrid between *S. farinacea* and *S. longispicata*, raised in California. It produces long spikes of deep indigo-blue flowers from midsummer to late autumn on a tall and somewhat lax plant. Useful for the back of the border. 1.5 m (5 ft) ★★★ ♔

S. involucrata 'Boutin' Stately plant bearing large spikes of chunky rosy magenta flowers in midsummer. 1.5 m (5 ft) ★★★★ ♔ The cultivar **'Bethellii'** is similar and very showy.

S. × jamensis 'La Luna' Like *S. greggii* in form and habit

PLATE XI
Salvia

All plants shown at approximately ¾ size

S. coccinea pseudococcinea

S. africana-lutea

S. × jamensis 'La Luna'

S. greggii

S. leucantha

S. × jamensis 'Los Lirios'

S. patens 'Cambridge Blue'

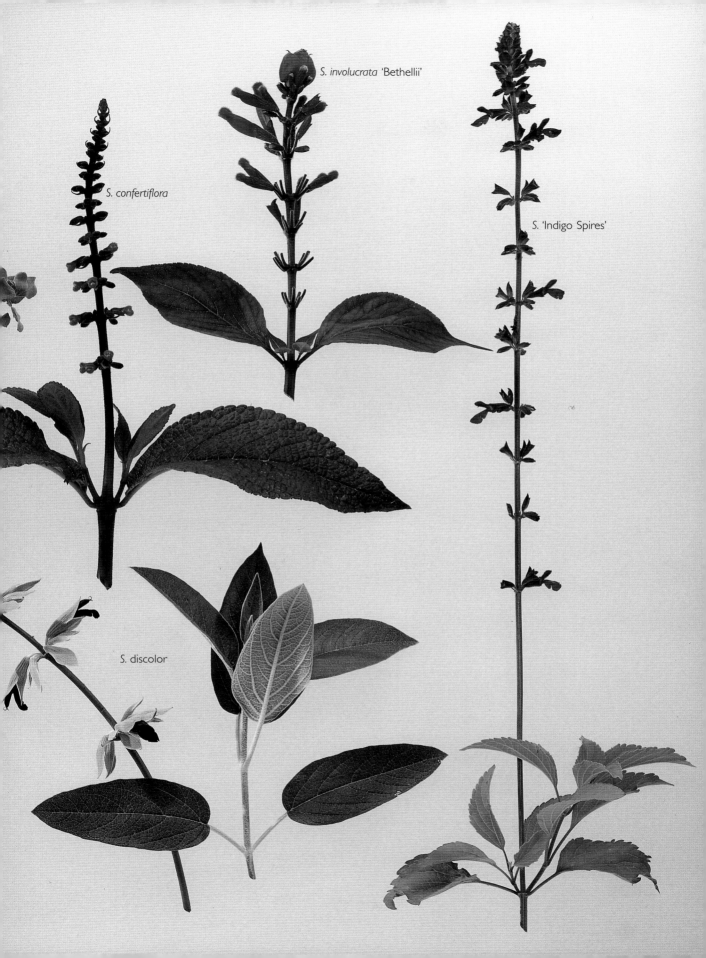

S. confertiflora

S. involucrata 'Bethellii'

S. 'Indigo Spires'

S. discolor

Salvia patens provides one of the richest blues in the late summer border.

but flowers greeny cream with a hint of raspberry pink. One of a series of hybrids from *S. greggii* × *S. microphylla*. 45 cm (18 in) ★★

S. × ***j.*** **'La Tarde'** Pale shell pink with cream throat. 45 cm (18 in) ★★

S. × ***j.*** **'Los Lirios'** Dusky pink and showy. 45 cm (18 in) ★★ ♔

S. leucantha Chenille sage, narrow felted leaves, thin spikes of violet and white flowers. 75 cm (2½ ft) ★★ ♔

S. microphylla (syn *S. grahamii*) Bushy evergreen with variable red, pink or mauve flowers from late summer to the frosts, almost hardy in a sheltered spot. 90 cm (3ft) ★★★★ Various named selections such as **'Newby Hall'** ♔ and **'Kew Red'** ♔, both with rich scarlet flowers. There are also pink selections such as **'Pink Blush'** ♔ and **'Pleasant View'** ♔, both of which flower freely and seem to be fairly hardy.

S. patens A tender species from Central Mexico. Flowers are large, royal blue, hooded and produced on slender stems. It can be grown from seed or by cuttings, but as it is tuberous propagation must take place in late summer to allow for the establishment of small tubers before the winter. 45 cm (18 in) ★★★ ♔ **'Cambridge**

Blue' is a paler blue form and **'White Trophy'** is a dirty white.

S. uliginosa Known as the bog sage because of its moisture-loving character. From late summer onwards, elegant spires of softest sky-blue flowers are produced. Very graceful, good for the back of a border. Contrast with darker flowers and silver foliage. 2 m (6½ ft) ★★★★ ♔

SCAEVOLA
Goodeniaceae

From this genus of around 96 species including trees and shrubs only two plants are well known and these have rightly become popular patio plants. Although they are easily propagated from tip cuttings, it is sometimes difficult to find suitable non-flowered material. All are low-growing and suitable as basket plants or trailers in a planter.

S. aemula Tiny delicate pale blue fan-shaped flowers. Sometimes sold under the cultivar name 'Petite'. 15 cm (6 in) ★★

S. a. **'Blue Fan'** Vivid light violet-blue flowers copi-

Scaevola aemula 'Blue fan' with *Verbena* 'Aphrodite', making a good long-lasting mix for a planter or basket.

ously produced, spreading. Good in baskets. Also sold as 'Blue Wonder'. 15 cm (6 in) ★★

SEDUM
Crassulaceae

This vast genus of over 400 species, most of them fleshy-leaved or succulent, contains only a few tender perennials.

S. lineare 'Variegatum' Low-growing mat-forming plant with tiny variegated leaves. Useful in planters or baskets. Almost hardy. 15 cm (6 in) ★★★

S. spathulifolium 'Cape Blanco' Tiny rosettes of succulent foliage with powdery white bloom. Yellow flowers. Used for carpet bedding. Hardy but often produced under glass for ease. 10 cm (4 in) ★★★★★ ⑨

S. s. 'Purpureum' Similar to above but suffused with purple. Also hardy but used for carpet bedding. 10 cm (4 in) ★★★★★ ⑨

SENECIO
Compositae

A large genus of over 1000 species including many different types of plants from various habitats worldwide. The two species listed here both make good conservatory subjects and are also worth trying in patio planters.

S. confusus Bushy twining climber with vivid orange daisies. 3 m (10 ft) ★★

S. macroglossus 'Variegatus' This plant looks very much like a variegated ivy and is sometimes known as the Cape or Natal ivy. The slightly succulent leaves are arrow-shaped and variegated with creamy white. It climbs by twining and produces yellow daisy flowers. 2 m (6½ ft) + ★★ ⑨

SENNA
Leguminosae

This is a large genus of 260 species better known under the generic name of *Cassia*, in which these plants are often included. It encompasses trees, shrubs and perennials from dry tropical and warm temperate regions, generally grown for their yellow pea-like flowers.

S. corymbosa (syn. *Cassia corymbosa*) A large evergreen shrub or small tree with pinnate leaves and clusters of bright yellow pea-like flowers. Grow in a large tub for summer patio display or as a conservatory plant under frost-free conditions. Light pruning may be necessary to keep under control. Propagate from seed or cuttings in spring or autumn. 1.8 m (6 ft) + ★★

SOLANUM
Solanaceae

This enormous genus of over 1400 species includes such important plants as potato and tomato and undesirables such as the poisonous nightshades. There are a few worthwhile tender perennials.

S. laciniatum Commonly known as kangaroo apple, this plant has deeply cut leaves and shoots tinged with purple. Deep blue flowers. Grows easily and quickly from seed, making a worthwhile plant within the first season. Often treated as an annual and grown afresh each year. 2 m (6½ ft) ★★★

S. quitoense Enormous furry purple leaves and stems with spines. Looks sinister. Grow from seed. 2 m (6½ ft) ★★

S. rantonnetii (syn. *Lycianthes rantonnetii*) Papery lavender potato flowers with darker markings and golden stamens. This vigorous lanky shrub makes a lovely conservatory plant and can also be trained as a small standard for a summer planter. Propagate from cuttings in autumn to achieve a sizeable plant. 2 m (6½ ft) + ★★

SOLENOPSIS
Campanulaceae

There are about 25 species in this genus, originating from dry areas of Australia and Central and South America. Most have linear foliage and small star-like flowers.

S. axillaris (syn. *Isotoma axillaris* or *Laurentia axillaris*) Small starry five-petalled blue flowers are produced over delicate finely cut foliage on compact bushy plants. Prodigious flowering, a lovely basket plant from Australia. Can be propagated from seed or cuttings. Some new strains of this are now available with pink and white flowers. Frost tender. 20 cm (8 in) ★★

SOLLYA
Pittosporaceae

This small genus has three species of twining evergreen climbers, originating from Australia. They need frost protection, but only just. They can be grown from seed or cuttings rooted in spring or early summer.

S. heterophylla Bushy, twining climber of most use as a conservatory plant. Blue bell-shaped flowers are followed by blue berries. 2 m (6½ ft) + ★★ ⑨

SPARRMANNIA
Tiliaceae

A small genus of evergreen shrubs and compact trees, found in tropical Africa and Madagascar.

Solenopsis axillaris, sutera and lobelia in a stone planter set against a background of fig foliage.

S. africana Large shrub with huge, hairy, light green vine-like leaves. Makes a good conservatory plant but does need plenty of space, or can be grown in a large tub for summer outdoor display. Flowers on young wood so can be quite hard pruned. 1.8 m (6 ft) + ★★ ♈ There is a double form called **'Flore Plena'** and also a variegated form, **'Variegata'**.

SPHAERALCEA
Malvaceae
A genus of about 60 species including annuals, perennials, shrubs and sub-shrubs. They are natives of dry areas of North and South America.

S. miniata Small shapely upright shrub, tiny leaves, beautifully marked coral pink flowers. Should be more widely grown. 45 cm (18 in) ★★

S. munroana Wide spreading habit, greyish, hairy, finely cut leaves, small strawberry pink mallow flowers. Virtually hardy in most locations. Good in large basket or planter. Pale pink form available, not yet named. 45 cm (18 in) ★★★★

STREPTOCARPUS
Gesneriaceae
This genus is mainly known for the exotic large-flowered hybrids known as Cape primroses. They originate from tropical areas such as South Africa, Madagascar and parts of China, often being found in rainforest conditions. Most are fleshy-leaved rosette-forming herbaceous plants. All are tender and prefer light shade. Over winter they should not go below 10°C (50°F).

S. saxorum This species is a small sub-shrub with succulent stems and small velvety leaves. It has a prostrate habit and produces copious quantities of small, pale lavender-blue flowers. Good in baskets. 20 cm (8 in) ★ ♈ The many large-flowered hybrids make excellent cool conservatory and windowsill plants and might well be of use in the garden in sheltered shady locations.

STREPTOSOLEN
Solanaceae
There is only one species in this genus and it is from open woodland habitats in Columbia, Peru and Equador. It is easy to propagate by tip cuttings in either autumn or spring.

S. jamesonii A loose spreading shrubby plant, commonly known as marmalade bush, with small green leaves. Vivid orange flowers are produced freely from late spring to autumn. Makes a valuable conservatory plant or specimen for a patio planter. Worth keeping for several seasons to build up a strong well-branched specimen. Can be trained into a standard as a dot plant for summer bedding. Prune lightly each spring for shape and size restriction. 90 cm (3 ft) + ★★ ♈

S. j. 'Yellow Form' Lovely golden-yellow form of the above. Can be shy-flowering as a young plant but settles down to regular flowering when well established. 90 cm (3 ft) ★★

SUTERA
Scrophulariaceae
This genus of 130 species of annuals and perennials mainly from South Africa was almost unheard of until the recent introduction of *S. cordata* 'Snowflake', better known as *Bacopa*.

S. cordata 'Knysna Hills' Delicate spreading habit, open and airy plant covered with masses of delicate lilac pink flowers. 45 cm (18 in) ★★

S. c. 'Pink Domino' Lilac pink, compact habit similar to 'Snowflake' ★★

S. c. 'Snowflake' (syn. *Bacopa* 'Snowflake') Very prostrate, mat-forming plant with tiny leaves, covered with masses of small white flowers like broderie anglaise. Long flowering season. Excellent basket plant, but requires

plenty of water in summer. Spreads/trails to 45 cm (18 in) ★★

The petit-point flowers of *Sutera cordata* 'Snowflake' are produced in copious quantities throughout the season.

TIBOUCHINA

Melastomataceae

A genus of 350 species of evergreen shrubs, sub-shrubs and perennials found in Mexico, the West Indies and tropical South America to Brazil. It is mainly known in cultivation for one species.

T. urvilleana (syn. *T. semidecandra*) Erect shrub with velvety dark green leaves with a hint of purple. Big open flat flowers in rich purple with prominent curly stamens. Makes a good conservatory shrub or specimen for patio planter and therefore worth keeping from year to year. Propagate from tip cuttings in spring. 1.5 m (5 ft) + ★★ ♛

TRADESCANTIA

Commelinaceae

Most people know this genus as dusty house plants tolerant of almost total neglect! They originate from North, Central and South America and include both tender and hardy species. Some tender perennial types are selected here. In fact almost all the types grown as houseplants can be used in baskets or planters. All root very easily as tip cuttings at almost any time of the year.

T. 'Bridesmaid' Small green pointed leaves, branching habit. In summer totally hidden under a cloud of tiny white flowers like a bride's veil. Good addition to a hanging basket. 30 cm (12 in) ★

***T.* 'Maiden's Blush'** Green leaves. Tips of shoots have white blotches tinged pink. Best colourings in shade. 30 cm (12 in) ★

***T. pallida* 'Purpurea'** (syn. *Setcreasea purpurea*) Curious habit with floppy stems bearing long strap-like leaves in deep funereal purple. Contrasts well with pink and lavender verbenas and also silver foliage such as *Leucophytta brownii*, the wire wool plant. 30 cm (12 in) ★ ⚱

TROPAEOLUM
Tropaeolaceae

Many members of this genus of 80–90 species of annual and herbaceous perennials have tuberous roots. They originate from Central and South America and many are climbers or scramblers. Most of them are more commonly known as nasturtiums. The foliage has a pungent aroma.

***T. majus* 'Hermine Grashoff'** Perennial nasturtium with lovely frilly double flowers in rich orange. Good in baskets. Must be propagated by tip cuttings. Keep frost-free over winter. Spread 60 cm (2 ft) ★★

Tulbaghia violacea 'Silver Lace' is attractive as a foliage plant alone but the delicate scented flowers are a useful bonus.

***T. m.* 'Margaret Long'** A pale apricot-yellow version of the above. Spread 60 cm (2 ft) ★★

***T. m.* 'Red Wonder'** (syn. 'Empress of India' or 'Crimson Wonder') Dark crimson flowers, deep blue-green leaves with reddish petioles. Compact bushy habit. Best propagated from cuttings but will set seed and often breeds true. 30 cm (12 in) ★★

***T. tuberosum* 'Ken Aslet'** This tuberous cultivar produces thick purplish stems and orange flowers wth red calyces in midsummer. Tubers must be planted just below the surface in late spring and lifted again in the autumn for storage in peat in a frost-free shed, though in many areas they may be left outdoors with a good protective mulch. 2 m (6½ ft) + ★★★ ⚱

TULBAGHIA
Alliaceae/Liliaceae

A genus of 24 species of clump-forming perennials, most of which have strap-like foliage and smell strongly of garlic, although the flowers may be sweet-scented.

T. simmleri (syn. *T. fragrans*) Bulbous perennial with clusters of narrow leaves. Sweet-smelling, pale lavender flowers, produced in midsummer. 60 cm (2 ft) ★★★

***T. violacea* 'Silver Lace'** Very delicate striped grey-green strap leaves, palest lavender umbels like miniature agapanthus. Grow as a potted specimen for conservatory display or move outside for the summer. A large specimen several years old can be an impressive sight when in full foliage and flower. 45 cm (18 in) ★★

VERBENA
Verbenaceae

Verbena is a genus of around 250 species of annuals, perennials and sub-shrubs. They occur naturally in open ground in tropical and temperate regions of North, Central and South America as well as southern Europe. Just a few species are hardy. They were much loved by the Victorians, and are rightly the stars of the show in many planters and baskets. All produce flattened trusses of small flowers in a wide colour range.

BOTANY

Verbenas have erect or procumbent square stems (not to be confused with Labiatae). The leaves are opposite, simple and usually deeply toothed. The small salverform (tubular) flowers are occasionally solitary but more commonly made up into spikes, panicles, cymes or corymbs. They are usually brightly coloured and some are scented.

HISTORY

Verbenas were popular in Victorian bedding displays, being available in a wide range of colours and having a naturally compact habit, and until the development of the dwarf pelargoniums in the mid-19th century they were one of the main ingredients of a summer display.

Most verbenas are hybrids resulting from crosses originally made between *V. peruviana*, *V. incisa* and *V. tweedii*, all introduced from South America between 1826 and 1837. One of the best reds, still grown today, is *V. phlogiflora*, introduced from Brazil in 1834 by Henry Fox. However, by the 1860s there are references to verbenas becoming unpopular due to disease problems and subsequently seed strains replaced many of the old cultivars. Nevertheless, some of the old perennial types have persisted due to their vigour and *V.* 'Lawrence Johnston', originally named and distributed in the 1940s, is still one of the finest reds available today. Recent hybridization has produced some of the excellent modern strains such as the Tapien and Temari hybrids.

PROPAGATION AND CULTIVATION

Verbenas propagate easily from tip cuttings in autumn or spring. If the shoots are leggy, short sections without a terminal growing point will root easily. They grow very fast and produce a sizeable plant very quickly, so spring propagation is the norm for most uses. They should be pinched frequently to create a bushy plant.

Verbenas are very prone to attack by whitefly and may also suffer from powdery mildew. Their main use is in hanging baskets and planters but they also make excellent bedding plants and fillers for the mixed border.

PLANT LIST

Most of those listed here are hybrids. Because of their popularity, verbenas are produced in the million each year by numerous growers using a multiplicity of confusing names. Many modern cultivars are protected by propagation rights which require commercial nurserymen to pay a royalty to grow and sell them.

V. **'Aphrodite'** (syn. 'Carousel') Purple and white-striped flowers, curious but not very effective in a planting. 20 cm (8 in) ★★

V. bonariensis Stiff and upright, rose pink flowers. Hardy but associates well with tender perennials. 1.2m (4ft) ★★★★

V. **'Boon'** New trailing cultivar, lavender-rose flowers and finely cut foliage. Trails to 45 cm (18 in) ★★

V. corymbosa **'Gravetye'** A tough, wiry plant with a stoloniferous habit; it spreads and weaves its way through other plants. Soft lavender-blue flowers. Virtually hardy so worth leaving in place from year to year. Flowers in flushes through the summer and autumn. 45 cm (18 in) ★★★

V. **'Foxhunter'** Intense bright scarlet. 30 cm (12 in) ★★

V. **'Hidcote'** Large flowers, deep blue. Old, well-established variety. 20 cm (8 in). ★★

V. **'Homestead Purple'** Good solid deep lavender, virtually hardy. 30 cm (12 in) ★★★

V. **'Kemerton'** Large flowerheads in rich clear mid-lavender. 45 cm (18 in) ★★

V. **'La France'** Recent cultivar with enormous well-rounded flowerheads in a soft lavender blue. Vigorous plants with strong green foliage and a bushy habit. 30 cm (12 in) ★★

V. **'Lawrence Johnston'** Large cardinal red flowers. 30 cm (12 in) ★★ ♛

V. peruviana (syn. *V. chamaedrifolia*) Very compact carpet-

With its bright raspberry-ripple coloured flowers and its sturdy constitution, *Verbena* 'Pink Parfait' is a welcome addition to any border or larger planter. It also has a delicate and delicious perfume.

PLATE XII *Verbena*

All plants shown at approximately ½ size

V. 'Homestead Purple'

V. 'Kemerton'

V. tenuisecta

V. phlogiflora

V. 'Sissinghurst'

V. 'Pink Parfait'

V. peruviana

V. Tapien® 'Pearl'

V. 'La France'

V. 'Hidcote'

V. bonariensis

V. peruviana 'Alba'

V. 'Silver Anne'

The prostrate-growing *Verbena tenuisecta* used as an edging to a raised bed of *Argyranthemum* 'Jamaica Primrose'.

ing plant with bright scarlet flowers. Virtually hardy in most situations. Plant in gritty site or on well-drained rockery. 15 cm (6 in) ★★★

V. p. **'Alba'** Pure white form of the above, looser habit. Best white verbena. Not so hardy as the species, so best treated as a tender perennial. 20 cm (8 in) ★★

V. phlogiflora 19th-century cultivar with rich scarlet flowers. Can be difficult to grow. 30 cm (12 in) ★★

V. **'Pink Parfait'** Stunning fragrant, two-tone, pink raspberry ripple-coloured flowers. 30 cm (12 in) ★★

V. rigida (syn. *V. venosa*) Erect species with magenta flowers, primarily used as an interplant among other bedding. Although perennial and virtually hardy, it is usually grown from seed each year. 60 cm (2 ft) ★★★ ♛

V. **'Silver Anne'** Sugar-pink flowers in large trusses, fading gracefully with age to soft pink, compact, some scent. One of the best. 30 cm (12 in) ★★ ♛

V. **'Sissinghurst'** Probably the best known and most widely grown of all verbenas. Vivid cerise flowers through until the frosts, wiry spreading habit, finely cut foliage, tough and almost hardy, one of the best. Very floriferous. 20 cm (8 in) ★★★ ♛

V. **Tapien range** Recent introductions. Very vigorous, prostrate. Floriferous, with fine foliage rather like 'Sissinghurst'. Available as **'Lilac'**, soft pale lavender blue, **'Pearl'**, very light hint-of-blue colour, **'Pink'**, light smoky pink, **'Violet'** deep royal purple. All excellent cultivars. Plant Protected. Trailing to 45 cm (18 in) ★★

V. **'Temari Scarlet'** New trailing cultivar with large, rich scarlet heads. Trails to 30 cm (12 in) ★★ Also 'Temari Violet'.

V. tenuisecta The common name moss verbena describes its prostrate habit and delicate finely-cut green foliage. Sold under a host of other names. Masses of violet-blue flowers. Looks good with bidens. Originates from South America but is very tough and will sometimes overwinter outside. Trails to 30 cm (12 in). ★★★

V. **'White Knight'** White verbena with delicate foliage rather like *V. tenuisecta* but looser habit and more upright, delicate. 30 cm (12 in) ★★

WIGANDIA
Hydrophyllaceae

A genus of five species of shrubs and sub-shrubs occurring in regions of tropical America. Contact may cause skin irritation.

W. caracasana (syn. *W. macrophylla*) Now almost unheard of, this evergreen sub-shrub used to be widely grown by the Victorians for its huge, hairy, remarkably veined leaves and pale blue flowers. William Robinson regarded it as one of the finest of garden plants. Performs best in a warm, sheltered location with well-drained soil. 2 m (6½ ft) + ★★

ZAUSCHNERIA
Onagraceae

The four species of sub-shrubs in this genus are sometimes included within *Epilobium*. They originate from North America and are of borderline hardiness. Propagate from spring cuttings. All are inclined to be brittle, so handle carefully. All flower in late summer.

Z. californica (syn. *Epilobium canum*) Californian fuchsia, with greyish foliage and tubular orange-scarlet flowers. Clump-forming. 30 cm (12 in) ★★★ ♛

Z. c **'Albiflora'** White form. 30 cm (12 in) ★★

Z. c. **'Dublin'** Good selection with bright deep red flowers. 30 cm (12 in) ★★★ ♛

Z. c. **'Solidarity Pink'** Pale pink flowers, but inclined to be a weak grower. 20 cm (8 in) ★★

Z. c. **'Western Hills'** Good wiry form with bright red flowers. 20 cm (8 in) ★★★

Verbena 'Temari Scarlet', one of a new range of vigorous and floriferous verbenas. In this picture it is used on its own to create a ball of colour in a hanging basket.

Part Three Planting Schemes

4 Using & Displaying Tender Perennials

Just as the pigments laid out on an artist's palette can be used in many ways and bear no resemblance to the finished masterpiece, so garden plants can be arranged in many diverse ways and styles. As with paints and the artist, the end product – in this instance a garden – is an expression of the gardener's interests, preferences and horticultural skills.

As garden components, tender perennials are no different from any other groups of garden plants, although their speed of growth means that the end result can be judged within a matter of only weeks rather than years. Also, any mistakes can be rectified the next year. This makes them ideal for experimentation with different colour and foliage themes.

Tender perennials have traditionally been looked upon as simple variations on summer bedding plants,

perhaps with a particular value as container plants, but this is an underestimation of their possibilities. In fact, there are many ways of using them to create different effects and garden styles.

DESIGN

With all of the plant groupings and styles within this chapter, the basic rules of garden design and plant association apply; the planned use of colour, texture, structure, contrast and light and shade are essential to achieving an effective display.

Generally, the most effective planting schemes are planned with some thoughts on colour groupings. Either one or more colours are chosen as a theme; blues, blue and pink, reds or red and yellow. With monochromatic selections it is important to have a contrast between dark

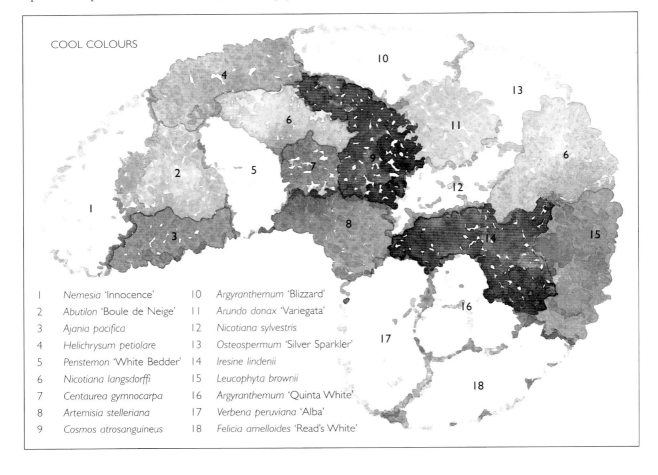

COOL COLOURS

1	Nemesia 'Innocence'	10	Argyranthemum 'Blizzard'
2	Abutilon 'Boule de Neige'	11	Arundo donax 'Variegata'
3	Ajania pacifica	12	Nicotiana sylvestris
4	Helichrysum petiolare	13	Osteospermum 'Silver Sparkler'
5	Penstemon 'White Bedder'	14	Iresine lindenii
6	Nicotiana langsdorffi	15	Leucophyta brownii
7	Centaurea gymnocarpa	16	Argyranthemum 'Quinta White'
8	Artemisia stelleriana	17	Verbena peruviana 'Alba'
9	Cosmos atrosanguineus	18	Felicia amelloides 'Read's White'

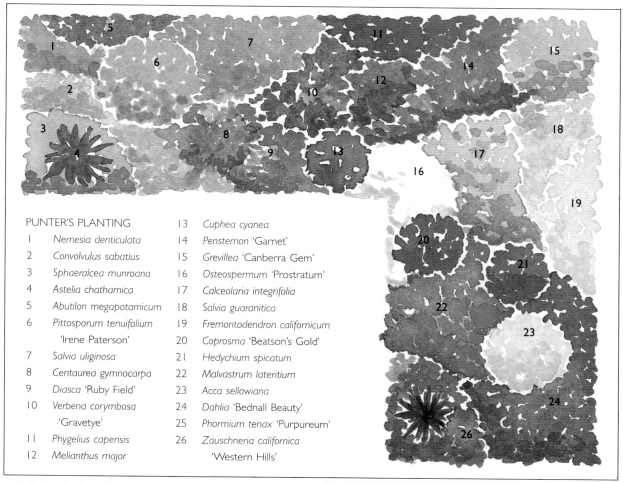

PUNTER'S PLANTING

1	*Nemesia denticulata*	13	*Cuphea cyanea*
2	*Convolvulus sabatius*	14	*Penstemon* 'Garnet'
3	*Sphaeralcea munroana*	15	*Grevillea* 'Canberra Gem'
4	*Astelia chathamica*	16	*Osteospermum* 'Prostratum'
5	*Abutilon megapotamicum*	17	*Calceolaria integrifolia*
6	*Pittosporum tenuifolium*	18	*Salvia guaranitica*
	'Irene Paterson'	19	*Fremontodendron californicum*
7	*Salvia uliginosa*	20	*Coprosma* 'Beatson's Gold'
8	*Centaurea gymnocarpa*	21	*Hedychium spicatum*
9	*Diasca* 'Ruby Field'	22	*Malvastrum lateritium*
10	*Verbena corymbosa*	23	*Acca sellowiana*
	'Gravetye'	24	*Dahlia* 'Bednall Beauty'
11	*Phygelius capensis*	25	*Phormium tenax* 'Purpureum'
12	*Melianthus major*	26	*Zauschneria californica*
			'Western Hills'

and light shades of the same colour. Contrast can be provided by the use of simple white flowers and silver foliage; remember that dark colours especially need the contrast of lighter shades or they are lost. In the same way, deep colours such as the rich crimson of *Cosmos atrosanguineus* are lost in dark shady sites.

The value of contrasting heights seems to have been lost in many modern plantings. Both nurserymen and plant breeders appear to have a fixation with dwarf and compact plants which can often result in tediously flat planting schemes. Among the tender perennials there are many fine tall plants which will add stature to even the smallest of planting schemes. *Nicotiana sylvestris*, *Arundo donax* 'Variegata', *Salvia involucrata* 'Bethellii', some of the penstemons, many abutilons and virtually all the cannas will add a lofty presence, all without the need for staking. *Dahlia imperialis* is the loftiest of all, reaching 3 m (10 ft) in a good season, and is not surprisingly known as the tree dahlia.

FORMAL BEDDING

Traditional formal bedding is now often dismissed in elitist horticultural circles as brash and lacking in taste. Rather than comparing it with other forms of garden design and groups of plants, it should be seen for what it is. David Welch, chief executive of the Royal Parks, describes bedding as horticultural showmanship or floral entertainment. As such, enjoy it!

Within the historic garden, where authenticity is important, it is quite possible to re-create a Victorian-style bedding display with some of the remaining species and older cultivars available. Likewise, where there is a need to devise a distinctive display, tender perennials can provide just what is required. The many flower beds either side of the Broad Walk at Kew Gardens near London are filled each year with an amazing range of unusual bedding plants, many of which are tender perennials.

Formal flower beds are often contrived with a combination of colourful groundwork or carpet plants that

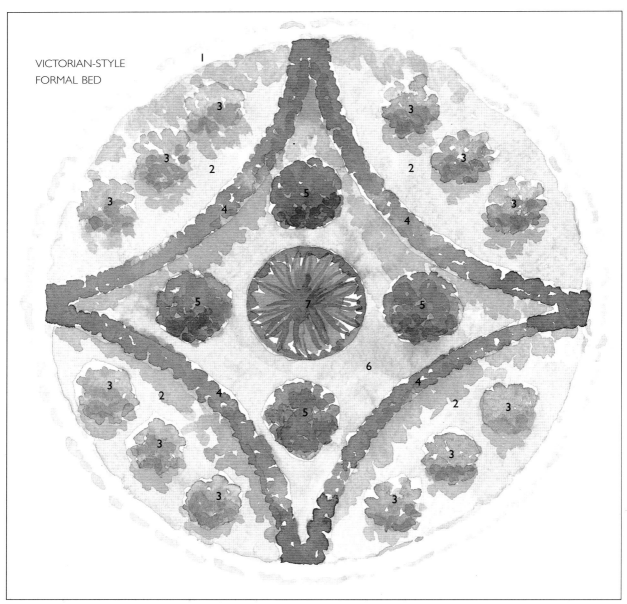

VICTORIAN-STYLE
FORMAL BED

1   *Heliotropium* 'White Lady'
2   *Pelargonium* 'Chelsea Gem' and
      Verbena venosa (interplant)
3   *Centaurea gymnocarpa*
4   *Iresine herbstii* 'Brilliantissima'
5   *Canna* 'Shenandoah'
6   *Coleus* 'Dazzler'
7   Terracotta urn containing
      Cordyline australis 'Atropurpurea' and
      Heliotropium 'White Lady'

cover the majority of the bed, possibly with an edging and a number of 'dot plants' that give height and accent to the display. Such plants as bidens, verbenas, pelargoniums, nemesias, gazanias, diascias and cupheas have a good carpeting habit and would all make a bright display. Interplants are used in smaller numbers, interspersed between the groundwork. They are generally taller and to be effective will often have an upright habit. Penstemons, *Lobelia* 'Queen Victoria', helichrysums, nicotianas and iresines make good contrasting interplants.

Most dot plants are tender perennials and will have been grown on since the previous autumn to achieve a

Formal bedding display using cannas, melianthus, cupheas and dahlias in a scheme linked by the colour orange.

good-sized specimen or possibly saved from year to year, being lifted from the beds in the autumn and overwintered under glass. Such dot plants may be trained into particular formal shapes such as standards; heliotrope, pelargonium, fuchsia and argyranthemum look especially good. Abutilons make a natural pyramidal shape without any particular training and lax plants such as plumbago, helichrysum and *Solanum rantonnetii* are best tied to a cane, being initially treated as a pillar and then allowed to flop as they grow.

Dot Plants

Abutilon – all the large-flowered hybrids, from autumn cuttings

Centaurea gymnocarpa – autumn cuttings

Cordyline australis – keep for several seasons

Arundo donax 'Variegata' – lift and keep from year to year

Argyranthemum – taller and stronger cultivars, such as 'Snowflake', 'Vancouver' and 'Jamaica Primrose'

Euryops chrysanthemoides – autumn cuttings

Helichrysum petiolare- can be trained to almost any shape but a pillar is the easiest

Heliotropium – grow as a standard

Lantana cvs – grow as a standard and keep from year to year, pruning hard each spring

Pelargonium – standards, will last two or three seasons

Plumbago auriculata – lift and keep from year to year

Salvia involucrata 'Bethellii' – autumn cuttings

Solanum rantonnetii – lift and keep from year to year

Streptosolen jamesonii – lift and keep.

CARPET BEDDING

Regarded by some as the very depths of poor taste and now rarely seen other than in seaside and other tourist gardens, the carpet bed is another relic of Victorian gardening. In the 19th century it was a distinct art form that enabled the Victorian gardener to exhibit his skills of design and culture. A well-grown carpet bed still exhibits a high degree of horticultural dexterity and should not be despised.

One of the best displays of this type is regularly seen in the RHS garden at Wisley, where a Victorian carpet bed is re-created each year, often to a traditional design. It is appropriate to include this type of gardening in this book as many of the species used to produce a carpet bed are tender perennials. All are low-growing, generally foliage plants that either stay very compact or can be clipped to shapes that make up the pattern of the carpet.

Carpet-bedding plants

Alternanthera – many variations, naming confused

Aptenia cordifolia 'Variegata'

Coleus – compact cultivars with small leaves such as 'Green Ball', 'Red Mars' and 'Wisley Tapestry'

Crassula cooperi

C. milfordiae

A traditional carpet bedding scheme using many low-growing plants clipped into intricate shapes.

Echeveria secunda var. *glauca*
Sedum spathulifolium 'Cape Blanco'
S. s. 'Purpureum'
Senecio serpens
Soleirolia soleirolii 'Aurea'

The following are also common constituents of a carpet bed, although they are not tender perennials:
Ajuga reptans cvs
Arenaria balearica
Cerastium tomentosum
Helichrysum angustifolium
Herniaria glabra
Mentha requienii
Tanacetum parthenium 'Golden Moss' (better known as *Pyrethrum* 'Golden Moss')
Raoulia australis
Sagina glabra 'Aurea'
Sedum acre 'Aureum'
Sempervivum cultivars.

Planning

The first and most important stage of a carpet bed, however small, is the planning. Draw the design to scale in detail, remembering that complicated patterns may be difficult to replicate in a small area. The use of squared paper may help in this exercise. From the design it should be possible to calculate the quantities of each species required. Approximately 400 plants are required to fill 1 m² (1¼ sq yd) of the bed, which rapidly multiplies up to large quantities.

The plants are produced under glass, generally being grown in small cells or multipacks so that large quantities can be produced in a small space. Small plants planted out at a close density will eventually produce the most even pattern. The tender constituents of the display should be thoroughly hardened off and planting not attempted until early summer when all risk of frost has passed.

A carpet bed looks best if it is placed on a slope or in a position where it can be viewed from above. Alternatively, it may be appropriate to contour the bed in some way to create a more dramatic effect. The soil should be thoroughly cultivated, well firmed and raked down to a very fine tilth. Because of the problems of weeding the eventual display, it is practical to top the bed with a layer of sterilized soil or potting compost to reduce the amount of weed growth.

In order to transfer the design accurately to the bed, it is usual to mark off the plan in squares and then to do the same to the bed, using string. The patterns can then be marked with trickles of sand. To avoid spoiling plants and overcompacting the soil surface, a carpet bed is often planted from a ladder placed across the bed, supported 30 cm (12 in) or so above the surface. The gardener lies across the ladder to plant and tend the bed. Any specimens such as agave or cordyline are planted first, then the patterns, spacing the plants about 5 cm (2 in) apart.

Once the bed is planted it must be carefully watered. As the display grows it will be necessary to trim many

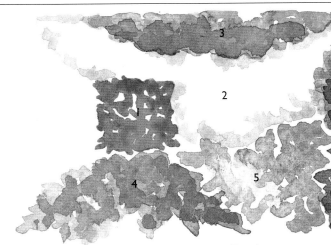

LONG MIXED BORDER	1	clipped yew (*Taxus*)
	2	*Nicotiana sylvestris*
	3	*Clematis* 'Etoile Violette'
	4	*Verbena tenuisecta*
	5	*Heliotropium* 'Princess Marina'
	6	*Rosa* 'Charles de Mills'

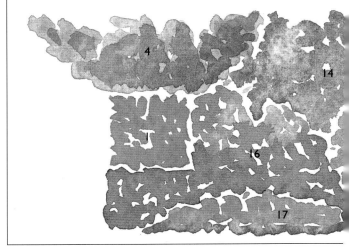

of the plants regularly to keep the design and particularly any lettering neat and clear. Obviously, a carpet bed is very expensive and labour-intensive – the reason why this jewel of the Victorian garden is so rarely seen today.

As far as most amateur gardeners are concerned carpet bedding plants are almost unknown, yet even if a carpet bed is beyond most capabilities, the plants could well provide interesting additions to small planters or baskets.

MIXED BORDER PLANTING

This style of planting, which originates from the traditional cottager's mix of shrubs, roses, and bulbs together with fruit and vegetables in a relaxed profusion, is also often seen on the grand scale in formal gardens such as Sissinghurst and Hidcote. Both of these gardens make full use of this complex style of planting, including tender perennials both as gap fillers and for impact. Many gardeners will know the famous red borders at Hidcote, where shrubs and herbaceous plants are the permanent setting for tender perennials such as *Cordyline australis* 'Purpurea', *Canna* 'King Humbert' and *Verbena* 'Lawrence Johnston', named after the garden's creator. At Sissinghurst, tender perennials feature in many of the pots, urns and troughs throughout the garden and in the

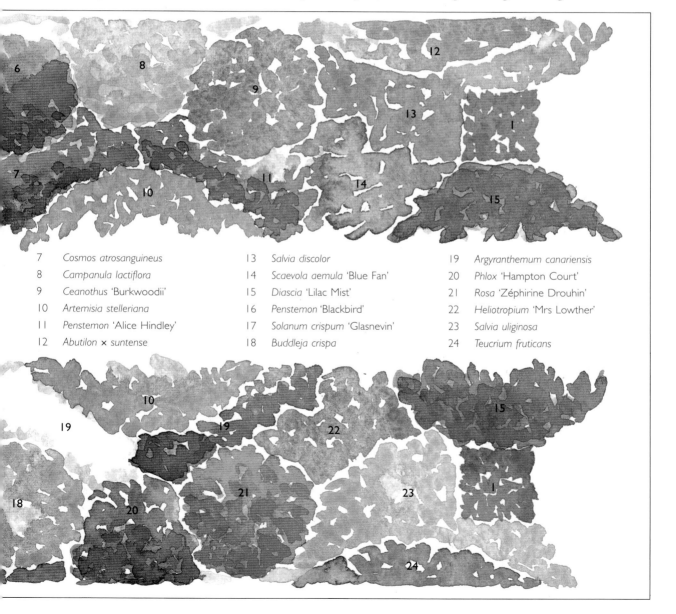

7	*Cosmos atrosanguineus*	13	*Salvia discolor*	19	*Argyranthemum canariensis*
8	*Campanula lactiflora*	14	*Scaevola aemula* 'Blue Fan'	20	*Phlox* 'Hampton Court'
9	*Ceanothus* 'Burkwoodii'	15	*Diascia* 'Lilac Mist'	21	*Rosa* 'Zéphirine Drouhin'
10	*Artemisia stelleriana*	16	*Penstemon* 'Blackbird'	22	*Heliotropium* 'Mrs Lowther'
11	*Penstemon* 'Alice Hindley'	17	*Solanum crispum* 'Glasnevin'	23	*Salvia uliginosa*
12	*Abutilon* × *suntense*	18	*Buddleja crispa*	24	*Teucrium fruticans*

more intimate areas; penstemons intermingle with roses in the rose garden and arctotis add extra colour in the cottage garden.

All too often tender perennials are seen as convenient gap fillers in permanent plantings, and indeed their season of planting enables last-minute losses in a border to be corrected well in time for the main summer display. Nevertheless they can also be used to great effect as planned combinations throughout the garden. This may simply be as blocks showing a particular plant in all its own glory. Alternatively they may be used as contrasting or toning shades, textures, backwashes or highlights for other plantings of shrubs, roses or herbaceous plants.

For example, diascias and penstemons associate very well with roses. Osteospermums and argyranthemums go well with silver-leaved and other dry garden subjects. Nemesias, diascias, zauschnerias and the smaller verbenas are quite at home in the rock garden and the tall lobelias are of course really bog plants for use at the side of a pool or stream. Cannas make excellent highlights among foliage shrub plantings.

In the former site of Reading University in London Road, Reading, there is a fine specimen of the variegated *Cornus alternifolia* 'Argentea' with beautifully tiered layers of variegated leaves. The raised bed beneath was for many years planted with tender perennials. One year it was the deep blue *Verbena tenuisecta* with buttercup-yellow *Bidens ferulifolia*. Another year the same bed held bronze *Calceolaria* 'Kentish Hero', *Artemesia stelleriana* and *Arctotis × hybrida* 'Apricot', a metallic mixture of bronze and silver. Possibly the most effective was a simple planting of shocking pink *Verbena* 'Sissinghurst', which contrasted beautifully with the white foliage until autumn when the cornus also turned bright pink. All of these combinations were ways of enhancing a permanent specimen plant with sensational tender ground cover.

Plant associations

Creating plant associations is merely the grouping together of a few well-chosen plants that complement each other and together make an effective 'garden picture'. Well-designed gardens are full of such plant associations. Many types of plants can be used, including tender perennials in combination with hardy plants such as roses, shrubs and herbaceous plants.

On first sight, it is usually the overall composition of a border that catches the eye. Then, as it is examined in more detail, a series of small cameos can be appreciated,

Spiky foliage and strong outlines from cordylines, yuccas and phormiums give a very architectural feel to this planting which is on a grand scale.

with the various groups of plants within the whole interacting together. Making up such groups and then linking them to each other is one of the ways of designing a large border which might at first seem daunting in its scope.

A permanent planting of the deep bluish-red *Rosa* 'Mme Isaac Pereire' could be combined with the real blue of *Ceanothus arboreus* 'Trewithen Blue', and a campanula such as the violet-blue *C. lactiflora* 'Prichard's Variety'. To this perennial group could be added tender perennials such as the inky blue *Heliotropium* 'Princess Marina', the soft sky blue *Salvia uliginosa* and the rich maroon of *Penstemon* 'Port Wine'.

Plants with strong shapes or bold leaf patterns are often termed 'architectural'. An architectural grouping might be composed of the purple-leaved *Phormium tenax* 'Purpurea', the yellow-flowered *Euphorbia characias* ssp. *wulfenii* 'Lambrook Gold' and low golden-leaved *Euonymus fortunei* 'Sunspot'. All of these permanent plants have strong shapes and dramatic foliage. While it is on its own a quite acceptable planting, it could be enhanced with tender perennials such as *Dahlia* 'Moonfire' with bronze leaves and yellow flowers, a canna such as *C.* 'Richard Wallace' for its primrose-yellow spikes and the yellow daisies of *Euryops chrysanthemoides.*

With all such plantings there is of course the chance that some of the temporary additions may prove to be hardier than expected. With the shelter of their permanent neighbours, a whole host of tender perennials may survive the milder winters and give surprise encores for a second season or more.

In a true cottage-garden mix, vegetables, fruit and flowers intermingle freely. One example would be the red 'Lolla Rossa' lettuce planted with redcurrants and finished off with *Tropaeolum majus* 'Red Wonder' for its deep crimson flowers and *Lobelia* 'Queen Victoria', with more red flowers and bronze foliage. Silvery-foliaged globe artichokes would contrast well with a sea of *Verbena tenuisecta*

and bluish savoy cabbages would look good next to deep red-leaved cannas such as *C.* 'Assaut'.

A brown and white border

Borders don't have to be bright with colour – a restrained approach can be very effective. There are many plants with 'brown' colourings in their flowers and particularly in their foliage. Such pigmentation overlaps with bronzes and purples and in planning a brown planting scheme a little artistic licence is necessary. A colour scheme of this nature does not need to be rigid and touches of another colour such as pale blue or red can give the final touch of genius. An approach that is too purist can spell boredom.

Brown contrasts well with creamy whites, creating a satisfying mix of light and shade. Too many deep colours on their own are dull and lifeless but when contrasted with white or pale shades they can appear very rich and opulent. In practice most of the brown will come from foliage and the majority of the whites from flowers.

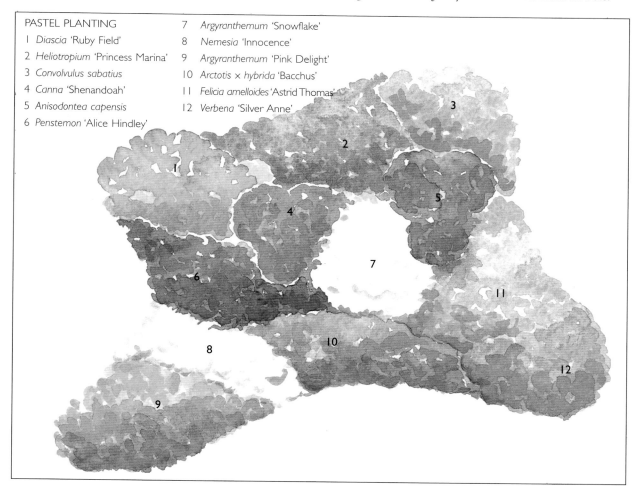

PASTEL PLANTING
1 *Diascia* 'Ruby Field'
2 *Heliotropium* 'Princess Marina'
3 *Convolvulus sabatius*
4 *Canna* 'Shenandoah'
5 *Anisodontea capensis*
6 *Penstemon* 'Alice Hindley'
7 *Argyranthemum* 'Snowflake'
8 *Nemesia* 'Innocence'
9 *Argyranthemum* 'Pink Delight'
10 *Arctotis* × *hybrida* 'Bacchus'
11 *Felicia amelloides* 'Astrid Thomas'
12 *Verbena* 'Silver Anne'

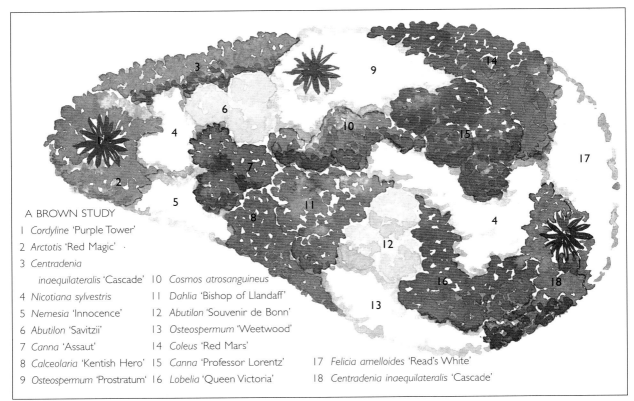

A BROWN STUDY

1 *Cordyline* 'Purple Tower'
2 *Arctotis* 'Red Magic' ·
3 *Centradenia*
    inaequilateralis 'Cascade'
4 *Nicotiana sylvestris*
5 *Nemesia* 'Innocence'
6 *Abutilon* 'Savitzii'
7 *Canna* 'Assaut'
8 *Calceolaria* 'Kentish Hero'
9 *Osteospermum* 'Prostratum'

10 *Cosmos atrosanguineus*
11 *Dahlia* 'Bishop of Llandaff'
12 *Abutilon* 'Souvenir de Bonn'
13 *Osteospermum* 'Weetwood'
14 *Coleus* 'Red Mars'
15 *Canna* 'Professor Lorentz'
16 *Lobelia* 'Queen Victoria'

17 *Felicia amelloides* 'Read's White'
18 *Centradenia inaequilateralis* 'Cascade'

The spiky *Cordyline australis* 'Purpurea' is a good bristly subject for height and impact. Next to it can be planted a chunky white argyranthemum such as *A*. 'Snowflake', which will form a rounded hummock covered with white daisies. Then, coming right down the scale, add a few centradenias for their bronze foliage. Sometimes at the end of the season they will contribute their shocking pink flowers.

Next to this group can be added some medium-height, brown-leaved coleus such as 'Bronze Gloriosa' or 'Winsome', and a splash more low-level white in the form of *Nemesia* 'Innocence'. For striking contrast, one of the darkest-coloured flowers is the hot chocolate plant, *Cosmos atrosanguineus*, with its deep maroon flowers which are just brown enough to justify its inclusion. Its strong chocolatey scent is an added bonus.

To this can be added the weighty foliage of a dark bronze-leaved canna. Most of these will eventually flower and to keep the colour scheme pure it may be necessary to remove the flowers. *Canna* 'Assaut' is relatively easy to obtain and grow and has rich bronze foliage. The flowers, when they come, are rich deep scarlet and can be left to add an extra punch or removed for a purist scheme. If you wish to expand on the 'touch of red' theme, plant the lovely old bronze-leaved *Dahlia* 'Bishop of Llandaff', with its small single red flowers.

Arundo donax 'Variegata', like a giant stripy bamboo with long waterfalls of leaves, will provide another accent, while the tall white *Nicotiana sylvestris*, which is grown

from seed, can be planted freely throughout the scheme. Equally threads of a white *Verbena peruviana* 'Alba' can be allowed to weave throughout the base of the display. Many other plants can be included, such as the rich bronzy *Gazania* 'Cookei', *Penstemon* 'White Bedder', *Pelargonium* 'Chocolate Peppermint' and white felicias, fuschias and osteospermums. Some, such as *Penstemon digitalis* 'Husker Red' with its pink-tinted white flowers, will have to be positioned with care.

A daisy border

Out of the many floral forms within the plant world, one of the commonest is probably the daisy, typical of the members of the family Compositae. Such a large family as this comes from many parts of the world and is in itself quite diverse. Among the tender perennials are many daisies and one way of using them for both botanical and artistic interest is to create a daisy border. Many different colour combinations can be created, choosing either the softer pastel shades which are abundantly represented or the brighter primary colours. Whites such as the many argyranthemums can be added to most schemes. Tedium can be avoided in such a composition by the varying sizes of the flowers, for example the diminutive *Felicia amelloides* with small blue daisies or tiny yellow bidens contrast well with the comparative wagon wheels of *Argyranthemum* 'Jamaica Primrose'.

The overall heights of plants will give further variety in a daisy border. At the bottom of the scale there are 'juniors' such as many of the osteospermums or the various arctotis at a mere 15–20 cm (6–8 in) sitting at the feet of tall plants such as *Dahlia* 'Bishop of Llandaff' or *Argyranthemum canariensis*, reaching a height of around 1 m (3¼ ft).

If seed-raised plants such as *Cosmos* 'Purity', tithonia or some of the new sunflowers are included there is even greater scope possible, all within the general theme of daisies.

Daisies for colour

Arctotis – orange, pink, red and white
Argyranthemum – pastel shades, whites, pinks and pale yellows
Bidens ferulifolia – buttercup yellow
Cosmos atrosanguineus – rich dark maroon
Dahlia – single types such as 'Moonfire' and *D. merckii*
Euryops – yellows
Felicia – blues and whites
Gazania – many bright colours except blue
Osteospermum – glossy flowers, yellows, pinks, whites and purple.

A bright display

Many of the fashionable colour schemes within gardens rely on carefully chosen blends of soft shades of one or two colours, but equally effective displays can be made with the studied use of bright or primary colours. To avoid a rainbow effect, miss out one of the primaries and

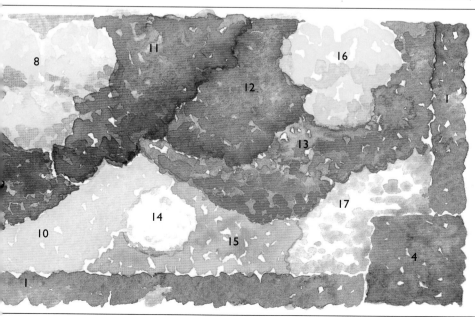

A DAISY BORDER
1 *Santolina* edging
2 *Arctotis × hybrida* 'Apricot'
3 *Felicia amelloides* 'Santa Anita'
4 Box (*Buxus*) block
5 *Dahlia* 'Bishop of Llandaff'
6 *Argyranthemum canariensis*
7 *Argyranthemum* 'Cheek's Peach'
8 *Euryops chrysanthemoides*
9 *Arctotis* 'Red Magic'
10 *Bidens ferulifolia*
11 *Cosmos atrosanguineus*
12 *Dahlia* 'Moonfire'
13 *Arctotis × hybrida* 'Flame'
14 *Argyranthemum* 'Chelsea Girl'
15 *Gazania* 'Dorothy'
16 *Argyranthemum* 'Penny'
17 *Osteospermum* 'Blue Streak'

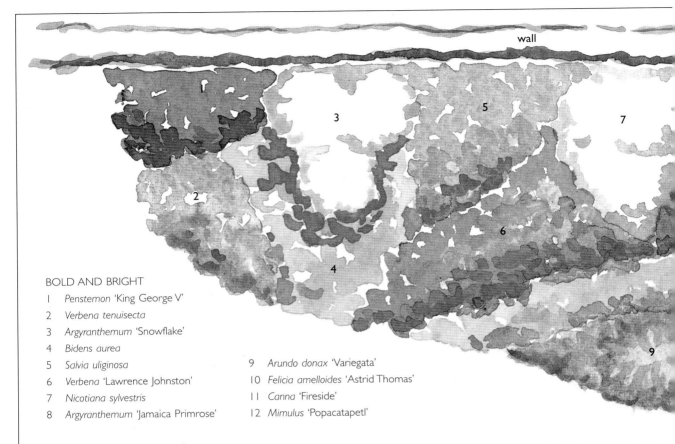

wall

BOLD AND BRIGHT

1 *Penstemon* 'King George V'
2 *Verbena tenuisecta*
3 *Argyranthemum* 'Snowflake'
4 *Bidens aurea*
5 *Salvia uliginosa*
6 *Verbena* 'Lawrence Johnston'
7 *Nicotiana sylvestris*
8 *Argyranthemum* 'Jamaica Primrose'

9 *Arundo donax* 'Variegata'
10 *Felicia amelloides* 'Astrid Thomas'
11 *Canna* 'Fireside'
12 *Mimulus* 'Popacatapetl'

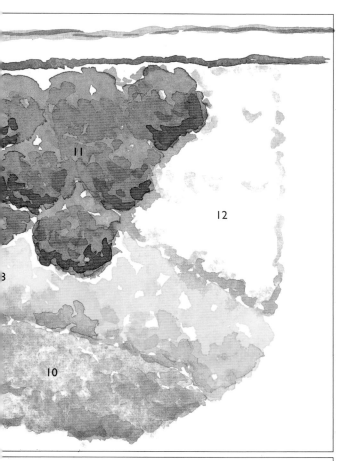

if you feel hesitant about such brash colours add a generous dash of whites. For example red, orange, yellow and white – all the hot colours, but no hints or tints.

Among the rich reds would be *Dahlia* 'Bednall Beauty', *Lobelia* 'Queen Victoria', *Verbena* 'Lawrence Johnston' and *Canna* 'Fireside'. Orange might include *Gazania* 'Bicton Orange', *Streptosolen jamesonii* and *Mimulus longiflorus*. Then yellows could be *Bidens ferulifolia*, *Abutilon* 'Canary Bird', *Argyranthemum callichrysum* 'Etoile d'Or' ('Jamaica Primrose' would be too pale) and *Pelargonium* 'Czar' with yellow leaves and red flowers.

The white element can be added in many ways, for example with argyranthemums, *Sutera cordata* 'Snowflake', *Felicia amelloides* 'Read's White', *Penstemon* 'White Bedder', *Mimulus* 'Popacatapetl', *Nicotina sylvestris* or *Osteospermum* 'Prostratum'.

Canna 'Fireside', a clear bright red useful in a 'hot' colour scheme.

GRAPHIC BORDER

1 *Canna* 'Durban'
2 *Lantana montevidensis*
3 *Gazania* 'Bicton Orange'
4 *Streptosolen jamesonii* (standards)
5 *Nemesia caerulea* 'Woodcote'
6 *Cordyline australis* 'Purpurea'
7 *Arctotis × hybrida* 'African Sunrise'
8 *Verbena* Tapien® Violet
9 *Lantana montevidensis*

5 The Exotic Look

Imagine a lush planting of huge banana leaves, spiky cordylines, strident cannas, waving palms and dripping tree ferns. These and other refugees from faraway lands can be gathered together with reasonable success to give a tropical jungle effect in the unpredictable British climate.

Recently there has been a fresh interest in creating this exotic effect, but it is nothing new; in fact, it is a traditional idea from the late 19th century, when elaborate displays of tender foliage plants were bedded out in private gardens and public parks. Such arrangements were called 'subtropical' or 'picturesque' bedding because of their exotic jungle-like appearance. One of the main

The full exuberance of subtropical gardening at its best in the garden created by Will Giles in Norfolk.

proponents of the style was William Robinson, who published *The Subtropical Garden* in 1871. Exotic schemes relied on foliage plants for their primary interest. One of the big advantages of such foliage beds was their long season of display, and this is just as valid today as it was 100 years ago.

Many British gardeners may immediately picture exotic gardens in places such as Tresco in the Scilly Isles, Abbotsbury in Dorset or other favoured gardens in the southwest of England. However, with ingenuity and a careful choice of plants such an effect can be produced in far less conducive locations. One of the best recent exotic gardens in the UK has been created by Will Giles in the unlikely climate of Norfolk. By planting a sheltering screen of trees, Will has been able to create a microclimate that is distinctly warmer than surrounding areas and expects to have an extra three weeks' freedom from frost at the beginning and end of the summer. Such warm conditions are conducive to the growth of many tender plants, and there are jungle borders with bananas, palms and cannas contrasted with sunny terraces of spiky succulents and vicious-looking cacti.

JUNGLE GIANTS

There are many easily available plants that can be used to create the subtropical look, most of which are half-hardy and so in need of some winter protection. One of the most striking is *Ensete ventricosum*, the Abyssinian banana, perhaps more readily known by its older and now incorrect name, *Musa ensete*. Growth is incredible – during its first season a plant grown from seed can reach nearly 1 m (3¼ ft) and, after overwintering in a frost-free greenhouse, in its second season will produce

A restful corner of Will Giles' garden with potted exotics as well as clipped box.

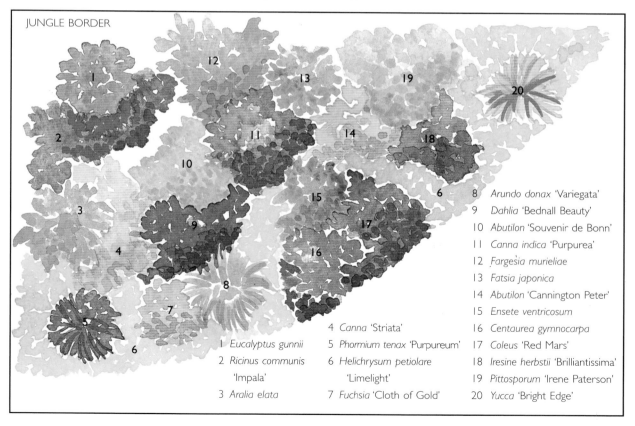

JUNGLE BORDER

1 *Eucalyptus gunnii*
2 *Ricinus communis* 'Impala'
3 *Aralia elata*
4 *Canna* 'Striata'
5 *Phormium tenax* 'Purpureum'
6 *Helichrysum petiolare* 'Limelight'
7 *Fuchsia* 'Cloth of Gold'
8 *Arundo donax* 'Variegata'
9 *Dahlia* 'Bednall Beauty'
10 *Abutilon* 'Souvenir de Bonn'
11 *Canna indica* 'Purpurea'
12 *Fargesia murieliae*
13 *Fatsia japonica*
14 *Abutilon* 'Cannington Peter'
15 *Ensete ventricosum*
16 *Centaurea gymnocarpa*
17 *Coleus* 'Red Mars'
18 *Iresine herbstii* 'Brilliantissima'
19 *Pittosporum* 'Irene Paterson'
20 *Yucca* 'Bright Edge'

As well as being a dramatic and sizeable statement in a border, *Ensete ventricosum* is worthy of close study with its lovely vein patterns and tinted mid-rib.

magnificent paddle leaves up to 3 m (10 ft) high, making splendid centrepieces for any exotic display. There is now a beautiful purple-leaved form of this which is as yet difficult to obtain and has no definitive name. This species should be positioned among low-growing plants such as iresines to show off its impressive stature. The aptly named *Iresine herbstii* 'Brilliantissima' has vivid wine red almost translucent leaves and *I. h.* 'Aureoreticulata' golden leaves with cochineal pink stems and leaf veins. As a contrast to lighter foliage, there is also the dark bronze foliage of *I. lindenii*.

Several of the abutilons also have interesting foliage as well as flowers. Try *Abutilon pictum* 'Thompsonii', with golden spotted leaves, or *A.* 'Souvenir de Bonn', with green and white foliage. Both will grow to 2 m (6½ft) in a warm summer and have the bonus of orange bell-flowers. The smaller *A.* 'Savitzii', with its near-white leaves, is a good contrast to McGregor's Ornamental Beet, which is an annual beetroot, grown from seed but highly appropriate here.

Arundo donax 'Variegata' is a bamboo-like grass with long wands of aristocratic green foliage variegated white. It will stand on its own as a good specimen plant, with a background of something darker like bronze-leaved cannas or surrounded with a tender groundcover of red-leaved coleus.

No traditional subtropical display would be complete without cannas, or Indian shot plants. Once planted out in the garden, growth is rapid and by the end of the season they will have grown into 2 m (6½ ft) sentries with banana-like foliage in green, purple or golden-variegated. The monster-leaved *Canna musifolia* can reach 2.5 m (8¼ ft) in a good season. Most provide a bonus of large flowers in red, yellow, orange or pink. Silver-foliaged plants such as the prostrate *Helichrysum petiolare* contrast well with cannas, providing a swirling silver skirt around their legs. The fine filigree foliage of *Centaurea gymnocarpa* also looks good against the smooth leaves of canna.

Another giant is the rarely grown *Dahlia imperialis*, which will reach 3 m (10 ft) in favourable conditions with huge bipinnate leaves, tinged with purple. Growth is phenomenal and the overall effect is of a small exotic tree. It rarely flowers. Bronze-leaved dahlias such as *D.* 'Bishop of Llandaff' and *D.* 'Moonfire' are also useful.

With the advent of seed-raised geraniums, or more correctly pelargoniums, the older ornamental-leaved cultivars are less commonly seen. It is worth searching out such types as *P.* 'Caroline Schmidt', *P.* 'Mrs Pollock', *P.* 'Czar' and the diminutive flowerless *P.* 'Madame Salleron', which are still available from specialist nurseries. Provided a watch is kept for rust disease, they will add a valuable contribution to a foliage bed. Many date from the late 19th century, so are quite authentic in such a display.

Ricinus communis 'Carmencita' reaches head height in a single season from seed, producing huge purple palmate leaves.

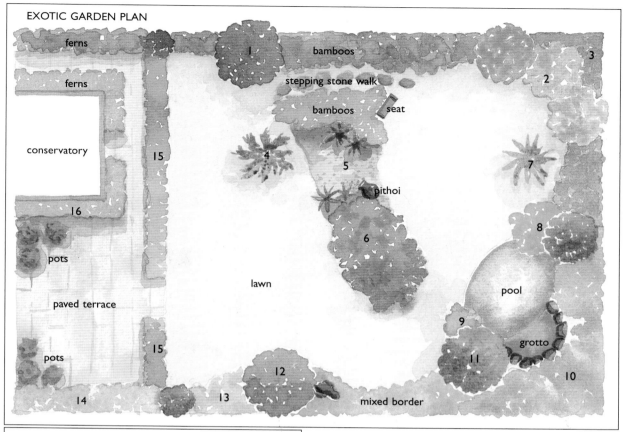

EXOTIC GARDEN PLAN

(Plan labels: ferns, ferns, conservatory, pots, paved terrace, pots, 15, 16, 15, 14, 13, 12, 1, bamboos, stepping stone walk, bamboos, seat, 4, 5, pithoi, 6, lawn, 2, 3, 7, 8, 9, 11, 10, grotto, pool, mixed border)

1	*Paulownia tomentosa*
2	*Eucalyptus gunnii*
3	Mixed planting in pastel shades of roses, penstemons, diascias and argyranthemums
4	*Trachycarpus fortunei* (palm)
5	Gravel and 'spikies', for example *Yucca*
6	Exotic foliage bed of *Canna, Iresine, Dahlia* and *Pelargonium*
7	*Musa basjoo*
8	*Gunnera manicata*
9	*Rheum palmatum* 'Atropurpureum'
10	Background shrubs of *Fatsia, Rhus, Mahonia, Cortaderia* and *Pittosporum*
11	*Catalpa bignonioides*
12	*Robinia pseudoacacia*
13	Hot bank of *Olearia, Pittosporum, Coprosma, Hebe* and *Lavandula*
14	Scented bank of *Jasminium officinale, Hedychium gardnerianum, Cosmos atrosanguineus* and *Eucalyptus citriodora*
15	Hot borders of reds, oranges and yellows bedded out with tender perennials
16	Tender shrubs such as *Polygala, Abutilon* and *Erythrona*

EXOTICS FROM SEED

Seed catalogues list many annuals that will complement tender perennials in an exotic display: for example, the vivid purple *Perilla frutescens* var. *crispa, Coleus* cultivars, *Amaranthus tricolor, Euphorbia marginata* and *Kochia tricophylla*. Then there's ornamental cabbage, kale and Swiss and ruby chard, which bring in the realm of ornamental vegetables.

One of the most dramatic annuals for a subtropical display is *Ricinus communis* (castor oil plant), of which a good bronze-leaved cultivar is 'Carmencita'. Seed sown in mid-spring will provide sturdy plants for planting out in early summer, and by the end of the season they can be 1.5 m (5 ft) high with huge leaves like giant sunburnt hands and prickly red conker-like fruits. However, this is not the plant for a family garden as all parts are highly poisonous.

Zea gracillima (variegated maize) grows to some 2 m (6½ ft) tall, with green and white striped leaves. It became popular in Victorian displays as a substitute for *Arundo donax* 'Variegata', but seed of this plant can be difficult to obtain nowadays.

The rapid speed of growth of many of these plants is just the thing for the impatient gardener as there's no waiting for elusive flowers. A foliage display looks good as soon as it is planted and gets better throughout the season.

SETTING THE SCENE

There are a number of hardy or almost hardy shrubs that have exotic-looking foliage and can be used as a permanent background, providing shelter and also winter colour. *Cordyline australis* (cabbage palm) has lovely spiky leaves and, along with its bronze counterparts in the Purpurea Group, will eventually reach some size and possibly produce white flowers with a sickly sweet perfume. *Trachycarpus fortunei* is a real palm which, although slow-growing, is a splendid addition to a subtropical display, while *Phormium tenax* (New Zealand flax), which is available in a whole series of cultivars, produces long, strap-like leaves in greens, golds, pinks, reds and varied combinations. Beware, though – phormiums don't like wet cold soils and will not survive harsh winters. The yuccas are also spiky-leaved, architectural plants and there are some marvellous new ones such as *Yucca filamentosa* 'Bright Edge' and *Y. flaccida* 'Golden Sword'.

Bamboos such as the tall green-leaved *Fargesia nitida* (syn. *Arundinaria nitida*) and dwarf golden *Pleioblastus auricomus* add a touch of the oriental. The eucalypts will eventually reach tree proportions, given mild winters. *Eucalyptus gunnii* and *E. globulus*, both of which can be raised from seed, are probably the best known. As with all eucalypts, if they grow too big they can be cut back hard and will regenerate from the remaining stump. Then there is *Fatsia japonica*, a good tough evergreen, and the more tender pittosporums, again in a whole host of forms and leaf variations. Even tree ferns such as *Dicksonia antarctica* are possibilities and some gardeners have found ingenious ways of protecting them over winter as they become larger. In a damp situation the giant-leaved *Gunnera manicata* could be grown, although plenty of space would need to be available as it is a giant of monumental proportions.

THE TROPICAL TOUCH

The adventurous gardener might like to add a few house-plants. Some of the palms, such as *Phoenix canariensis*, will

Mixed border incorporating *Brugmansia*, *Helichrysum* and *Fuchsia* with the hardy *Sedum* and houseplants.

The bold green paddle leaves of *Ensete ventricosum* contrast with the silver filigree of *Artemisia* and *Cosmos atrosanguineus*.

perform reliably outside. Other tropicals such as *Dracaena*, × *Fatshedera*, *Ficus*, *Pilea*, *Caladium* and even *Codiaeum* (croton) were used in the 19th century. Why not experiment? Success depends very much on the season and whether they can be provided with a warm spot.

Cacti or succulents can also be included, for example *Agave americana* 'Marginata', which in time will make a splendid specimen. Being armed with vicious spines, it is a bit tricky to handle, so it is best to plunge it into the soil, complete with pot, to allow easy handling in the autumn when it needs to be returned to a frost-free greenhouse. Provided they are kept adequately watered, other specimen plants can be added in the same way. This technique used to be called 'plunge bedding'.

Plants to create the exotic look

Tender perennials
Abutilon pictum 'Thompsonii' (small variegated tree)
A. 'Savitzii' (white-variegated foliage)
Aeonium arboreum 'Arnold Schwarzkopff' (purple-foliaged succulent)

Agave americana 'Variegata' (succulent with spiky variegated leaves)
Arundo donax 'Variegata' (giant variegated bamboo look-alike)
Canna hybrids (many colours and leaf variations)
C. indica 'Purpurea' (purple-leaved canna)
C. musifolia (giant foliage canna)
C. 'Striata' (yellow-variegated canna)
Coleus 'Klondike' (orange foliage)
C. 'Black Prince' (black foliage)
C. 'Red Mars' (tiny red leaves)
C. 'Pineapple Beauty' (yellow and purple leaves)
Centaurea gymnocarpa (silver foliage)
Dahlia 'Bishop of Llandaff' (purple foliage and red flowers)
D. imperialis (tree dahlia with exotic foliage)
Ensete ventricosum (giant banana)
Fuchsia 'Golden Treasure' (yellow foliage)
Helichrysum petiolare (silver carpeting plant)
H. p. 'Limelight' (lemon-yellow carpeter)
Iresine herbstii 'Aureoreticulata' (golden-yellow foliage)
I. h. 'Brilliantissima' (rich ruby foliage)
Lobelia 'Queen Victoria' (bronze leaves and scarlet flowers)
Melianthus major (striking silver foliage)
Musa basjoo (hardy banana)
Pelargonium 'Czar' (golden-leaved 'geranium')
P. 'Happy Thought' (yellow butterfly variegation)
P. 'Madame Salleron' (small white-variegated leaves)
P. tomentosum (furry green leaves and peppermint scent).

Annuals from seed
Amaranthus tricolor (multi-coloured leaves)
Beet 'McGregor's Ornamental' (purple-leaved ornamental beet)
Centaurea cineraria (silver foliage)
Eucalyptus globulus (silver-foliaged small tree)
Hibiscus 'Coppertone' (purple foliage)
Perilla frutescens var. *crispa* (purple foliage)
Ricinus communis 'Carmencita' (huge purple leaves)
Senecio cineraria 'Cirrus' (silver foliage)
Tanacetum 'Golden Feather' (tiny golden-yellow edging plant)
Zea gracillima (variegated maize).

A graceful mix in Will Giles's garden, featuring *Ricinus*, *Cordyline* and *Plectranthus* with the warm terracotta colourings of the clay urn and rhubarb pot.

This well-known *trompe l'oeil* painting is used as a background to the cactus display at Kew Gardens in London.

Houseplants

Agave americana 'Marginata' (succulent)
Caladium bicolor (delicate variegated foliage)
Chlorophytum comosum 'Variegatum' (spider plant)
Codaieum variegatum var. *pictum* (croton, multicoloured leaves)
Dracaena terminalis (purple spiky leaves)
× *Fatshedera lizei* (glossy green leaves)
Ficus elastica (rubber plant)
Grevillea robusta (delicate bronzy leaves)
Pilea cadierei (white-variegated foliage).

Hardy shrubs for exotic effect

Aesculus parviflora (bushy horse chestnut)
Chamaerops humilis (hardy palm)
Cordyline australis (fine spiky leaves)
Eucalyptus gunnii (silver-leaved tree)
Fargesia nitida, syn. *Arundinaria nitida* (bamboo)
Fatsia japonica (glossy-leaved shrub)
Ficus carica (fig, large exotic leaves)
Kalanopanax pictus (fingered foliage)
Mahonia lomariifolia (glossy leaves)
Paulownia tomentosa (large saucer leaves)
Phormium tenax (strap leaves)
Pleioblastus auricomus (small variegated bamboo)
Pseudopanax lessonii 'Gold Splash' (gold-variegated leaves)
Rhus typhina f. *laciniata* (lush-leaved shrub)
Trachycarpus fortunei (hardy palm)
Yucca filamentosa 'Bright Edge' (gold-variegated leaves)
Y. flaccida 'Ivory' (green spiky leaves).

Hardy exotic climbers

Hedera colchica 'Paddy's Pride' (golden-leaved ivy)
Humulus lupulus 'Aureus' (golden hop)

Schizophragma hydrangeoides (hairy-leaved climber)
Vitis coignetiae (huge-leaved vine).

Hardy exotic herbaceous plants
Acanthus mollis (glossy leaves and purplish flower
  spikes)
Cortaderia selloana (pampas grass)
Crambe cordifolia (large leaves and masses of white
  flowers)
Cynara cardunculus Scolymus Group (artichoke)
Macleaya cordata (greyish leaves)
Miscanthus sacchariflorus (tall grass)
Stipa gigantea (oat-like grass).

DRESSING THE SET

Exotic gardeners are often those who are a little more flamboyant; who like exuberant bright colours, bold brash shapes and extrovert expressions of garden style. It is for those gardeners that this piece is written.

Exotic gardening is in many ways make-believe, a touch of theatre – and every show has its setting and props, so why not the garden? Few gardeners are lucky enough to possess grottos, Grecian temples or ruined abbeys, but with ingenuity, imagination and a touch of artistic talent, variations on settings for exotic plants can often be contrived. A trip to a demolition contractor's yard can often yield stone from a demolished church, heavy door-frames, gates, railings, chimneypots and other attractive or curious building materials. Junkyards will reveal farm curios, old cooking pots, pews, Victorian plumbing and endless other talking points.

There are of course many firms that manufacture reproduction urns and other garden stonework. Whether new or old, such items can easily be weathered and encouraged to look established and mossy by the copious application of liquid manure, which tones down colours and promotes the growth of algae and mosses.

If reproduction statues and sculpture are not to your taste or are beyond your budget, various other options are available. Wire netting scrunched and moulded to shape can be used as a base for concrete for simple forms and fibreglass shapes are also possible. Timber carving has been successfully used in many garden settings on its own or coated in some way. In the famous gardens at Tresco Abbey in the Scilly Isles there is a wooden bust of Neptune which each year receives a fresh coat of paint that is dressed with sand before it dries. The end result is a passable stone finish that must have fooled visitors for many years.

Water is always an attractive feature in a garden and it provides another dimension to exotic plantings. Running water gives the added bonus of sound, whereas still water offers reflections. Many hardy waterside plants such as *Gunnera manicata*, *Rheum*, *Podophyllum* and *Rodgersia* all have lush, exotic-looking foliage that would combine well with the overall jungle effect.

Some gardens make use of the technique of *trompe d'oeil*, meaning 'trick of the eye'. At Kew Gardens in London, there is a display of cacti behind which is painted a desert scene. The whimsical gardens at Portmeirion in Wales contain a classical orangery painted on a blank wall as well as various statues throughout the gardens, all painted on flat timber but very plausible at a distance among vigorous planting. The use of mirrors and false perspective can also add to the overall setting of the exotic garden.

6 Pots, Planters & Baskets

'Patio plants' is a horrid, hackneyed phrase with which to describe a marvellous range of versatile plants. Nevertheless, it does emphasize that tender perennials excel when used for display in pots, tubs, windowboxes, baskets and planters of all descriptions. The relatively small numbers used in a planter justifies their higher cost in comparison to seed-raised bedding plants, and their long season of display and prolific flowering make them admirably suited to special locations in key positions.

Planters come in one of two main styles. The 'seasonal planter' stays in position, is planted each season with a mixture of tender perennials for summer display and is then often replanted in the autumn with bulbs and biennials such as wallflower or polyanthus for a spring display. By contrast, there are also those planters or pots containing specimen plants that are brought out into the garden each summer but go back to the greenhouse or conservatory with their permanent occupants each winter.

MIXED SEASONAL PLANTERS

In summer, the seasonal planter will in most cases be an extrovert, exuberant explosion of colour that overflows the container. Planters will need to relate to their setting, but in general the bigger the pot the better the display. Pots should be filled with a good potting compost – the older style loam-based composts such as those based on the John Innes recipes are better than the modern soil-less equivalents. The incorporation of a slow-release fertilizer and a water-retaining gel will help to sustain the display throughout the summer. Planting should always be at a much closer density than would normally be used for similar species in flowerbeds. Good feeding will compensate for the close density and plants will spread out in all directions around a planter.

The actual content of the display will be a matter of personal choice. However, it will often conform to a basic pattern. There will usually be a taller centrepiece such as a spiky cordyline, together with a mass of lower, spreading plants to provide the main colour and trailing species to carry the display over the edge. Basically, plants should be chosen to explode out of the planter in three dimensions! Choosing plants within a particular colour range

This classical terracotta urn is well-filled with an overflowing mixture of tender argyranthemums and fuchsias set against a hardy silver foliage contrast.

will often maximize the impact. Adding scented plants is a logical move, as the additional height of a planter will bring the scent nearer to nose level.

Planter recipe 1
Big and Bold: orange and silver
Canna 'Wyoming'
Dendranthema pacificum
Gazania rigens var. *uniflora*
Melianthus major
Streptosolen jamesonii

Planter recipe 2
Cool and Crisp: white, silver and pale blue
Argyranthemum 'Snowflake' (trained as standard)
Centaurea gymnocarpa

Nemesia 'Innocence'
Scaevola aemula 'Blue Fan'
Verbena tenuisecta

Planter recipe 3
Succulent and Tender: succulents and spikies
Aeonium arboreum 'Atropurpureum'
Aptenia cordifolia 'Variegata'
Astelia chathamica 'Silver Spear'
Cordyline australis 'Torbay Dazzler'
Sedum lineare 'Variegatum'

Planter recipe 4
Floral Sunshine: yellows
Abutilon 'Peaches 'n' Cream'
Argyranthemum 'Jamaica Primrose'
Iresine herbstii 'Aureoreticulata'
Helichrysum petiolare 'Limelight'
Osteospermum 'Buttermilk'

Planter recipe 5
Heaven Scent: aromatic foliage and scent
Cosmos atrosanguineus
Heliotropium 'White Lady'
Nemesia denticulata
Pelargonium crispum 'Variegatum'
Verbena 'Silver Anne'

Planter recipe 6
In the Pink: shades of pink
Argyranthemum 'Petite Pink'
Arctotis × hybrida 'Bacchus'
Canna 'Shenandoah'
Diascia 'Ruby Field'
Leucophyta brownii

PERMANENT PLANTERS

Within this group come a number of tender perennials that remain presentable after the first year. In many cases they do not achieve their full potential or perhaps do not flower until they are several years old. Many are large shrubs, climbers or small trees in their natural habitat and can eventually achieve such status in a permanent planter if judiciously tended.

Most abutilons come into this category. Although they will flower freely as young plants, the blooms are usually hidden at knee height among the foliage. Unless you lie on your back on the ground, their true beauty is lost! As they grow and reach eye level, you can look up into their flowers and only then do you appreciate their full splendour. Brugmansias are similar and also produce more flowers as the older plants become root-restricted. Many growers would suggest that they are grown as standards, leaving the main stem at pruning time, merely shortening back side-shoots.

Anisodontea capensis is a lovely tender shrub, spangled with masses of pink flowers in early summer, but it must have frost protection over winter, hence the need to be pot grown and returned to the greenhouse for the winter. A large, well-grown specimen in full flower is a splendid sight. It doesn't always flower right through the summer, but if it is grown in a tub or large pot it can be moved from centre stage after its main display.

Plumbago auriculata, of which there are blue and white forms, grows well in large planters, as does the blue-flowered *Solanum rantonnetii*. The various cestrums, iochromas, lantanas, melianthus, neriums and streptosolens all make long-lived specimens. In particular *Streptosolen jamesonii* yellow tends to be shy-flowering until more mature, so it is well worth keeping until it comes of age and produces its spectacular show of lemon marmalade blossom.

Cannas and hedychiums make large specimens in tubs which can be lifted into a cool greenhouse or conservatory at the end of the summer to prolong the display.

Succulents in this terracotta pot are a suitable choice for a hot, dry location or where watering may be infrequent.

Both genera are often at their peak as the autumn days close in and frosts threaten. In fact, cannas can flower through the winter with a little heat, making them useful 'inside-outside' plants. Both are greedy plants and need large containers.

Plants to grow as specimens
Abutilon (most of the taller cultivars of all species)
Anisodontea capensis
Begonia fuchsioides
Bougainvillea cultivars
Brugmansia species and cultivars (grow as standard or small tree)
Canna cultivars
Coprosma species and cultivars
Cordyline australis and cultivars
Ensete ventricosum
Hedychium species and cultivars
Lantana most cultivars (can be grown as standards)
Olea europaea
Pseudopanax lessonii 'Goldsplash'
Senna corymbosa
Solanum rantonnetii (can be grown as a standard)
Sparrmannia africana (prune hard each spring)

All of these plants will perform well outside in most British summers and will avoid some of the pests such as red spider mite and whitefly which are troublesome under glass but less so outside.

JUST POTS
An extension of this style is to grow a whole range of tender perennials – specimens, succulents, pelargoniums and ordinary patio plants such as argyranthemums and petunias – in individual pots and then to arrange them in theatrical groups.

The creative and imaginative gardener has the chance to change his or her 'set' at intervals throughout the summer to produce an ever-changing eye-catching scene. As each star turn is over, another scene stealer can be shifted upstage to draw the attention. Possibilities are limitless and scene changes endless. Colour, style, texture and shape can be mixed and matched throughout the season. The excitement of experimentation at this level is that it will often produce successes that can be reproduced year after year – and if it doesn't work, the scene can be changed instantly, unlike border plantings where errors of judgement live with the gardener for at least a season.

Brugmansia, tulbaghia and clipped box in pots arranged for instant effect in an important garden location.

HANGING BASKETS
Using tender perennials in baskets can give the possibility of a more unusual display than the familiar multi-coloured mix of petunia, lobelia, impatiens, fuchsia and pelargoniums. Baskets made of tender perennials also require comparatively fewer plants than one would need if using seed-raised annuals. For example, one plant of the perennial *Lobelia richardsonii* will give as much flower as three or four seed-raised lobelia and flower for a longer season.

Many different plants can be used in hanging baskets. Generally they will be those that are prostrate or trailing or at the very least are compact in habit, but larger baskets will also take one or more upright plants to fill in the centres.

All the normal principles of design apply just as much to baskets as any other display – far too many baskets are made with a complete miscellany of unmatched plants and colours. Attention to colour and foliage interest is as important here as in a border. Alternatively, very effective balls of one colour can be created using

A bright mix of flowering and foliage plants fills this hanging basket for a colourful summer display.

several plants of just one type such as verbena, Surfinia petunias, diascia or balcony geraniums (ivy-leaved pelargoniums). There are numerous other possibilities with which to experiment.

Basket A – pinks and purples
Convolvulus sabatius dark form
Heliotropium 'Princess Marina'
Plectranthus oertendahlii
Tradescantia pallida 'Purpurea'
Verbena Tapien® Pink

Basket B – yellows and blues
Bidens ferulifolia
Lysimachia 'Outback Sunset'
Lobelia richardsonii
Scaevola aemula 'Blue Fan'
Solenopsis axillaris

Basket C – reds and whites
Coleus 'Wisley Tapestry'

Lotus berthelotii
Sutera cordata 'Snowflake' (better known as *Bacopa* 'Snowflake')
Tropaeolum majus 'Hermine Grashoff'
Verbena 'Lawrence Johnston'

Basket D – foliage only
Artemisia stelleriana
Coleus 'Picturatum' ('Rob Roy')
Coprosma × *kirkii* 'Kirkii Variegata'
Helichrysum petiolare 'Goring Silver'
Pelargonium tomentosum

Basket E – silver and white
Artemisia stelleriana
Lotus berthelotii
Plectranthus forsteri 'Marginatus'
Tradescantia 'Bridesmaid'
Verbena peruviana 'Alba'

Cultural points
A good hanging basket is dependent not only on a wise choice of plants but on the techniques used in planting and subsequent care. Ideally, hanging baskets should be made up in late spring under glass so that the plants can become well established before the basket is placed in its final position in early summer.

Fig. 2 A partially completed basket showing lining with plants tucked between the wires and the main plants angled towards the sides before filling with compost.

A restrained composition, primarily consisting of foliage in various shades of green with a few touches of white and yellow to provide highlights.

Always choose the biggest basket possible for the location and never use one less than 35 cm (14 in) in diameter. The basket must be lined in some way. The traditional liner is sphagnum moss, but this is now less acceptable for environmental reasons. As an alternative there are fibre liners of different types available, some coloured green to look like moss. Black plastic can also be used and it has the advantage of leaving a maximum space within the basket for compost and of retaining water well, although it must be punctured for drainage. Although initially unsightly, it is soon covered by plants.

A good potting compost should be used, to which can be added a slow-release fertilizer to give steady nutrition and water-retaining granules to reduce the need for regular watering. An initial layer of compost is placed in the basket to bring the level up to about halfway. At this stage small trailing plants such as *Lobelia richardsonii*, *Brachyscome*, *Plectranthus*, *Helichrysum* and *Verbena* can be threaded between the wires, though with tender perennials this extra layer is less important than with seed-raised bedding, which does not fill out so well. The basket is then filled with compost, packed around the lower layer of plants.

The main display in the top will comprise five or more plants, packed in fairly closely around the sides. Some gardeners like to add a taller bushy plant in the centre of the basket whereas others prefer to leave the middle open, dishing the surface to help with watering. After planting the basket should be well watered.

During the season regular watering is essential. The frequency will vary considerably, depending on the season, the plants, the position and the compost. In a heatwave this may be as often as twice a day, but on average once a day should be enough or every two days in the case of baskets with a water reservoir. Feeding is also essential, particularly if no additional fertilizer was added to the compost. There are many plants in a small volume of compost and they will rapidly starve if they are not given additional feed.

As the season progresses it will be necessary to deadhead some plants and trim back any that threaten to swamp their weaker neighbours. A good well-nurtured basket should give a ball of colour from early summer to mid-autumn.

Plants for hanging baskets

Abutilon megapotamicum 'Variegatum'
Acalypha hispida 'Hispaniola'
Aptenia cordifolia 'Variegata'
Argyranthemum 'Petite Pink'
A. 'Whiteknights'
Asteriscus maritimus
Bidens ferulifolia
Brachyscome multifida cultivars
Coleus 'Lord Falmouth'
C. 'Picturatum'
Convolvulus sabatius
Cuphea caeciliae
C. ignea
Diascia 'Blackthorn Apricot'
D. 'Lilac Mist'
D. 'Ruby Field' and many others
Felicia amelloides 'Read's White'
F. a. variegated
F. amoena
Helichrysum petiolare 'Goring Silver'
H. p. 'Limelight'
H. p. 'Roundabout'
Heliotropium 'Princess Marina'
Lantana montevidensis
L. m. 'White Lightning'
Lotus berthelotii
L. maculata
Lysimachia congestiflora
L. c. 'Outback Sunset'
Nemesia caerulea and cultivars
N. denticulata
Parochetus africana
Pelargonium – ivy-leaved types
P. tomentosum
Petunia 'Surfinia' and 'Million Bells'
Plectranthus forsteri 'Marginatus'
P. oertendahlii
Plecostachys serpyllifolia
  (syn. *Helichrysum microphyllum*)
Scaevola aemula 'Blue Fan'
Solenopsis axillaris
Streptocarpus saxorum
Sutera cordata 'Snowflake'
Tradescantia 'Bridesmaid'
Tropaeolum majus 'Hermine Grashoff'
Verbena – most cultivars, but not *V. corymbosa*
  'Gravetye', *V.* 'Homestead Purple' or *V. rigida*

7 Plants for the Conservatory

'The way to enjoy summer in England is to have it glazed in a comfortable room.' Horace Walpole.

The concept of a conservatory as an extension to the house really developed in the 19th century, when the abolition of the glass tax, the development of cast-iron technology and the introduction of efficient heating systems all occurred within a few years. At the same time there was a vast influx of new plants introduced by the Victorian plant hunters. It became fashionable to build a conservatory where new and exotic plants could be enjoyed without leaving the comfort of the house, and it was sometimes known as 'the winter garden' because plants continued to grow and flower throughout the winter under protected conditions. By Edwardian times furniture was also very much part of the conservatory, enabling it to be used for relaxation and informal meals. Nowadays conservatories often serve both purposes, providing an additional but leafy room.

Brugmansias have a long season of display in a conservatory, where their huge flowers and strong scent can be appreciated.

Today few people can afford to heat conservatories to a temperature suitable for tropical exotics and it is here that tender perennials can be of great value, thriving in a cool but frost-free environment. Given conditions around 10°C (50°F), many tender perennials continue to grow and often flower throughout the year.

Conservatory conditions can be very conducive to steady, even growth in tender perennials. Under such conditions they will make far more mature specimens than can ever be achieved in the garden, where plants are often propagated annually and destroyed at the end of the season. Even if left in the open in mild gardens, cold weather will often cause them to die back.

FLOWERING PLANTS

In a conservatory, abutilons and brugmansias will reach the proportions of small trees and their exotic bell-like flowers can be best appreciated at eye level or above. Trying to find and appreciate pendant flowers among damp foliage at knee level out of doors can be somewhat disappointing! Fuchsias can grown on for many years, making large specimens that can be trained up walls or pillars. One species that grows particularly well in a conservatory is *Fuchsia boliviana*, which makes a small tree with attractive peeling bark. The flowers are long and graceful and there is a white form, *F. b.* var. *alba*, with long white flowers flushed deep pink at the tips of the petals.

Flowering under conservatory conditions will often be earlier and more prolonged than with younger pot-grown specimens. Cannas will continue to grow quite happily throughout the year and will often produce blooms all winter. Rather than allowing them to die down, the old stems are merely removed as they become untidy, which allows new ones to replace them. The lovely *Canna iridiflora* sometimes fails to flower in the garden as its display is quite late, but under conservatory conditions its sugar-pink flowers can be appreciated throughout the autumn. A number of the gingers, such as *Hedychium coronarium*, are slightly too tender for regular growing outside and also flower rather late, but in a conservatory they will bloom to perfection, changing the usual earthy greenhouse smell to that of an exotic perfumed bower.

Argyranthemums are easy plants to grow in a conservatory, where they will make bold specimens.

Argyranthemums generally flower freely but a few cultivars are known as short-day plants because they produce their flowers in the shorter days of autumn, winter and spring. Cultivars such as *A.* 'Mary Wootton' and *A.* 'Mrs F. Sander' come in this category and provide good conservatory displays in the winter months.

A number of tender perennials are really climbing or scrambling plants, seen at their best when grown on trellises and allowed to become mature plants. One such plant is the pale blue *Plumbago auriculata*, which does not need a great deal of heat to overwinter and then provides an excellent summer display. There is a white form of the same plant, *P. a.* var. *alba*, which is just as easy and a pink species, *P. indica*, which needs a warmer environment. Then there is *Solanum rantonnetii*, a rich blue member of the potato family, *Sollya heterophylla*, *Pandorea jasminoides*, *Lapageria rosea*, *Rhodochiton atrosanguineus*, *Cestrum elegans*, the vivid orange *Senecio confusus* and many of the passifloras. All make excellent conservatory plants.

There are also good tender perennials for basket cultivation in conservatories. The compact *Acalypha hispaniolae* is really too tender to give a regular display outside in the summer but gives an exotic show of red cat's tails under glass. Among the coleus there are three procumbent cultivars that make excellent baskets of foliage: *C.* 'Lord Falmouth', *C.* 'Picturatum' and *C.* 'Blackheart', a small black-leaved cultivar that is probably *C. rehneltianus*. With all coleus, the flowers must be pinched out to encourage a luxuriant ball of foliage. *Lotus berthelotii* makes lovely cascading silver foliage in its first season and if grown on to a second in a conservatory will reward patience with a waterfall of red flowers.

FOLIAGE PLANTS

As well as flowering plants, there are a number of good foliage plants that will look attractive all the year round without needing as much heat as many houseplants require. The coprosmas from New Zealand include some interesting evergreens. The compact and almost hardy *C.* 'Beatson's Gold' is covered with tiny gold-centred leaves, while *C. kirkii* 'Kirkii Variegata' is silver and white and more upright. It will make a small weeping standard if trained. The spiky cordylines need no more than frost protection to maintain their striking foliage. The beautiful creamy *C. australis* 'Albertii' is too tender to be left outside but does very well in a conservatory. *C. a.* 'Purple Tower', *C. a.* 'Sundance' and any of the cultivars with 'Torbay' in the name are well worth a place in the conservatory. Then there are coloured-leaved pelargoniums, iresines, *Grevillea robusta* and pseudopanax.

DESIGNING AND EQUIPPING

When designing a conservatory where the main purpose is the growing of plants, great care should be given to providing the right conditions. Good light, especially for winter growing, is essential; blinds or shading can be added to keep out excess summer sun. Windows or ventilators should be adequate to provide a good air flow in the summer and if the conservatory is to be left untended regularly it is worth considering automated ventilators.

A source of heat is essential. For a conservatory connected to the home it may be possible to extend the domestic central heating supply, but remember it must be given a separate circuit and set of controls so that heat is supplied throughout the night when most domestic systems cut out. For small conservatories where a minimal temperature lift is required, an electric fan heater is cheap to purchase, but running costs can be very expensive. Simple direct-fired gas heaters which require no flue are made specifically for greenhouses and will run on mains or bottled gas. They are utilitarian in appearance and must be installed by a professional gas-fitter, but they are not expensive to purchase or run and are generally

potted specimens

potted specimens

chairs and table

plants in borders

plants in

1

2

3

4

5

6

7

8

9

10

11

12

13

13

13

14

25

26

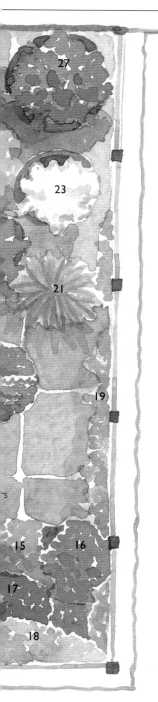

Hedychium gardnerianum will grow to perfection under glass, offering dramatic foliage and richly scented flowers.

very reliable. Thermostatic control of some sort is highly desirable, if not essential, with any form of heating.

GROWING MEDIA

For any sizeable conservatory display, beds of soil either at ground level or raised in brick structures will provide the most conducive root-run. Climbers and other permanent tender shrubs will be able to grow to a reasonable size and maturity in such an area. The depth should be 30 cm (12 in) or preferably 45 cm (18 in) and the base should be broken up for good drainage. Fill the beds with a loam-based compost such as John Innes Potting Compost No. 3 or improve an existing soil with peat, grit and a base fertilizer.

Alternatively, grow conservatory plants in large pots or tubs. Although growth may be more restricted, there is a greater amount of flexibility and in particular plants can be moved outside in the summer for patio display or to avoid excessive build-up of pests and diseases. When growing in containers it is vital to use a good potting compost. To reduce costs, a layer of good well-rotted garden compost can often be used in the base of large tubs, topping up with the sterile potting compost. Another advantage of growing in containers is that the compost can be varied according to the plant. Succulents such as agave will prefer a very open gritty mix compared to cannas, which revel in a more peaty mix.

CONSERVATORY MANAGEMENT

Routine care of plants in a conservatory, as in a greenhouse, is quite critical, although not difficult. A day or so of neglect in either winter or summer can result in total disaster. In summer regular watering and ventilation to prevent excessively high temperatures is essential.

Bougainvilleas grow well in a cool conservatory and are available in a whole host of colours.

In winter watering needs are much reduced and plants may survive for several days or even weeks without needing watering, but reliable control of the heating to provide a steady temperature is vital. Many plants will tolerate quite low temperatures if dryish and acclimatized to those temperatures. However, plants do not like fluctuating temperatures that dip dramatically on cold nights and then shoot up on sunny winter mornings.

Plant list

Almost any tender perennial could be grown in a conservatory, but the following list includes those tender perennials that are particularly suitable. Most will be quite happy at a temperature of around 8–10°C (45–50°F).

Abutilon – all the large-flowered hybrids	small trees	flower and foliage
Anisodontea capensis	shrub	flower
Argyranthemum – all cultivars	shrubs	flower
Begonia fuchsioides	shrub	flower
Bougainvillea cultivars	shrubs	flower
Bouvardia longiflora and *B. ternifolia*	shrub	flower and scent
Brugmansia – all cultivars	small trees	flower
Canna – all cultivars	tuberous	flower and foliage
Cestrum elegans	woody climber	flowers
Coprosma – species and cultivars	shrubs	foliage
Cuphea species	Sub-shrubs	flower
Ensete ventricosum	not woody but makes a large foliage plant	foliage
Euryops pectinatus and *E. chrysanthemoides*	shrubs	flower and foliage
Fuchsia – many types	shrubs	flower
Grevillea robusta	small tree	foliage
Hedychium – many types	tuberous	scent and flower
Heliotropium	shrubs	good for scent
Iresine – all cultivars	shrubs	propagate often to keep young
Lantana in variety	shrubs	grow in pots and move out
Lotus berthelotii	trailer good for permanent baskets	flower and foliage
Mimulus – shrubby types	shrubs	flower
Nerium oleander cultivars	shrubs	flower
Pandorea jasminoides	woody climber	flower
Pelargonium cultivars	shrubs	flower, foliage and scented leaves
Plumbago auriculata and *P. a.* var. *alba*	climber	flower
Polygala myrtifolia	shrub	flower
Senna corymbosa	shrub	flower
Solanum rantonnetii	shrub/climber	flower
Sollya heterophylla	climbers	flower
Streptosolen jamesonii and yellow form	shrub	flower
Tibouchina urvilleana	shrub	flower

8 The Mediterranean Garden

The picture is of a sun-drenched terrace dripping with bougainvillea or a mixture of acacias, olives and citrus set against a backdrop of umbrella pines. Inevitably this idyllic picture is seen under cloudless skies with shimmering blue water in the distance. It is therefore exceedingly difficult to re-create in a typical British summer, but it is worth a try! It should be emphasized that this chapter refers to Mediterranean style, the sort of garden that would be found in the south of France, Italy or Spain, as opposed to the Mediterranean climate, which is found in various areas of the world.

In style, a Mediterranean garden may be anything between formal and informal. The former might have a parterre with clipped box, formal avenues of pencil-thin

With its mild climate, the garden at Tresco Abbey can grow many tender subjects such as these palms with their Mediterranean feel.

cypress and architectural fountains whereas the latter would have rambling paths, rocky outcrops and gnarled olives dripping with swags of exotic climbers. Either picture can be re-created to some degree in other areas than the Mediterranean. Planting schemes are often open and airy, quite the opposite of the jungle effect. There is also the classic maquis vegetation of cistus, rosemary, phlomis, lavender, myrtle and arbutus, many of which are of course quite frost-hardy. Seaside locations often offer the best prospects of creating this type of garden.

Although there are other books that deal with Mediterranean gardens in much greater depth, it would be wrong not to include them here as so many tender perennials fit perfectly into this style and in a milder climate can be considered as permanent garden subjects.

THE MILDER GARDEN

To create a realistic Mediterranean garden, a mild climate is really needed. However, in almost any area it is possible to create conditions that are more favourable for tender plants and thereby increase the range of plants available to us. The main factors that threaten tender plants are cold, wind and wet soils. Wherever we garden, these may be modified in some measure.

Most of us move house relatively few times in a lifetime but for the keen gardener the garden attached to the house can be the point that clinches the deal. A sheltered garden, warm brick walls providing winter protection and a south-facing elevation are all valuable factors. City gardens are always a few degrees warmer than their country cousins and so are seaside gardens, although the latter may suffer from problems of wind and salt spray. Any small area, whether it be just a part of a garden, a whole garden or anywhere the climate differs from the general area, is said to have a microclimate, which may be warmer or colder than its surroundings. Recognizing and understanding such microclimates is of great value to the grower of any tender plants.

PROVIDING SHELTER

There are many things that can be done to help provide suitable conditions for tender perennials or to ease them through the winter months. Good shelter is the most

A sheltered corner such as this permits the successful planting of tender species.

basic essential. Some of the choicest gardens where tender plants thrive were once bleak windswept areas until shelter was provided. Such places as Abbotsbury in Dorset, Tresco Abbey in the Scilly Isles and Inverewe in Scotland all have shelter belts of tough tree and shrub species that moderate the wind and protect from the severest winter frosts. Any medium-sized or large garden can benefit from a shelter belt planted to protect it from the worst of the prevailing winds. In siting any shelter belt, it is important not to create a frost pocket by planting across a slope and preventing cold air from draining away in winter.

Depending on the size of the garden and the space available, two or three rows of trees and shrubs is usually enough. A row of a tree species such as *Pinus nigra* ssp. *laricio* backed by something shrubby such as *Hippophae rhamnoides* will in time provide both high- and low-level

protection. Plants need not be planted in formal rows, nor need there be just two species used; a mixed planting providing wind protection and a feature in itself can be planned. In the early years and on very exposed sites it is often useful to provide artificial shelter using plastic mesh, woven wattle hurdles or fencing. Remember, though, that the principle of good protection is to use a material that is permeable and filters the wind rather than a barrier that blocks it and causes turbulence.

WARM WALLS

Walls of any sort provide protection, but the most desirable are old mellow brick walls that not only provide a lovely setting for tender exotics but absorb the sun's rays and act as a natural storage heater on cold winter nights, raising the nearby temperature by a few degrees. Such protection will often be sufficient to grow tender wall shrubs and climbers that would otherwise not survive.

Building brick walls to provide homes for tender plants can be a very expensive exercise. Very often walls are there but may not be suitable for plants because there is no soil at the base. Although cutting out concrete or

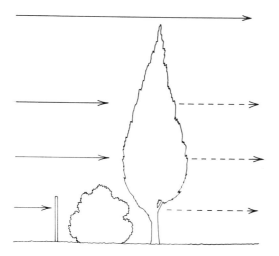

Fig. 3 A three-stage windbreak utilizing a fabric or fence, shrub layer and trees which together filter the wind.

Clianthus puniceus is only ever really successful when planted with the protection of a warm wall.

tarmacadam may seem a formidable exercise, such plant pockets will often provide a whole new range of sheltered homes. This is always preferable to trying to grow plants in large tubs, which not only need continuous summer watering but will be particularly exposed to frost in winter.

The walls of a house theoretically give the whole range of aspects – north, south, east and west – but this may not be the case in all situations. The warmest walls will be the south and west and will be suitable for tender climbers and wall shrubs. Abutilons, acacias, ceanothus, clianthus, *Berberidopsis corallina*, *Clematis armandii*, *Sophora tetraptera*, *Callistemon pallidus* and many others will appreciate such a cosy spot. However, the east wall will often provide a rain shadow and have a very dry sheltered spot at the base. This will be particularly suitable for plants that may not be too tall but require a dryer winter root-run. Gazanias, diascias, verbenas, euryops, *Convolvulus sabatius*, osteospermums and even argyranthemums may all overwinter in such sites.

THE PLANTS

Most Mediterranean-style gardens have a preponderance of evergreen trees and shrubs. The strongly vertical Italian cypress, *Cupressus sempervirens* 'Stricta', is really too tender for most temperate climates but there are other narrow conifers that can be substituted. The three commonly used pines, *Pinus wallichiana*, *P. pinea* and *P. pinaster*, are all frost-hardy trees. *Myrtus communis*, *Elaeagnus glabra*, *Griselinia littoralis*, the various osmanthus, pittosporums, olearias and yuccas will all tolerate a fair amount of

The New Zealand garden at Mount Edgecumbe in Devon with its startling geyser.

Many hardy plants with dramatic foliage such as this yucca help to give an exotic, Mediterranean air to a garden.

frost and can be used to provide a shrubby framework.

Many of the plants from the Mediterranean regions of the world have aromatic foliage, for example rosemary, phlomis, lavender, lippia and of course box. Grey-foliage plants fit well into this style, as do many plants from New Zealand. However, as you plan this style of garden remember that your climate may not be mild unless you have a very favoured location and so you must take more care over your choice of plants than the true Mediterranean gardener needs to do.

From the many wattles, *Acacia dealbata* and *A. baileyana* are fairly hardy, giving delicate silver foliage as well as the familiar yellow bobbly flowers. Many of the eucalypts are hardy but will give a Mediterranean feel. *E. gunnii*, *E. niphophila* and *E. perriniana* should all be reliable and are readily available.

Lagerstroema indica makes a splendid small tree but is barely hardy unless the summers are hot enough to ripen the wood. It is best grown as a potted specimen and given winter protection. *Nerium oleander* is also best grown in a tub and put out each summer as would be the olive, except in specially sheltered sites. Among the lavenders, there are many unusual species and *Lavandula denticulata* is well worth growing for its finely toothed grey foliage, but must be given the typical half-hardy treatment.

Polygala myrtifolia flowers almost continuously and is worth the gamble in a sheltered garden, although it will probably succumb to most winters. Likewise the daisy-flowered euryops such as *E. chrysanthemoides* and *E. pectinatus* will survive only some winters but are so easily replaced that their loss is of little consequence.

Osteospermums, gazanias and the tall nicotianas such as *Nicotiana sylvestris* and *N. glauca* can be added on an annual basis, with pelargoniums and cannas for colour.

TAKING A GAMBLE

Many of these plants are of borderline hardiness and cautious gardeners will not wish to gamble on planting them in most temperate situations. Nevertheless, optimistic gardeners may wish to try to grow these challenging genera. One such gardener works by the maxim 'Never concede that a plant is tender until it has died on you three times!' This lady has a garden near Manchester, in England's industrial north, where she grows many plants traditionally thought of as tender. Her success is based on common sense, plus an open-minded willingness to gamble with plants.

First she reads up all about a plant's country of origin and its requirements for soil and climate. She then tries to match these with the available spaces in her garden and give the plant as much of its natural needs as possible. In winter plants are cosseted, especially when young. Mulches are vital to insulate the root systems. Panes of glass or plastic sheets are used to protect young wall plants, and cloches guard freestanding plants. Taller plants are 'thatched' with branches of conifer tied firmly at the top and others are protected with four bamboo canes used to support old woolly sweaters. Her techniques may not be conventional but the results prove the effectiveness of simple protection for tender plants. For those of a more conventional nature, straw, horticultural fleece and other less avant-garde materials could be used. Companion planting with tougher species around tender ones can also provide that all-essential extra protection.

The precise nature of the winter protection needed will depend on the plant itself, its growth and flowering pattern. Those that grow fast and flower on new wood

will only require rootstock mulching as they can grow again the next season. Others will need the main branch framework protecting and those that flower only on the tips of old wood will need every shoot insulating.

Such insulation is a traditional technique that has reached great heights in countries such as Japan, where elaborate thatched structures constructed out of bamboo and straw are not only excellent insulation but attractive structures in their own right. One fashionable plant is *Cycas revoluta*, the sago palm, which is successfully overwintered in many gardens protected by a *wari-maki* (straw binding). The shape and construction of these shelters is an ephemeral art form in itself and a part of the Japanese winter garden.

A few plants can be used as their own protection. *Cordyline australis* can have its leaves firmly bound together to form a narrow pointed shape. This helps to keep the cold away from the growing point and the youngest leaves, which usually suffer in cold weather. *Gunnera manicata*, the enormous rhubarb-like waterside plant, is often protected by cutting down the leathery leaves in the autumn and laying them over the crown.

Many tender plants die of cold wet roots rather than actual frost. Good soil preparation is essential, breaking through any hard pan that will impede drainage. The addition of good sharp grit is beneficial in all clay or loam-based soils. Where soils are heavy and wet, it can help to construct a raised bed with a carefully prepared gritty soil mixture, but beware of increasing frost exposure by such raised beds.

It should be added that some plants that would normally be considered as hardy may not be so when very young. The vigorous growth associated with juvenility will often not be sufficiently ripened to be fully frost-hardy. One of my borderline 'gambles' has been *Abutilon vitifolium* var. *album*, planted against a warm wall and protected in the first two winters. It has well repaid the extra trouble but eventually a cold winter will be fatal.

There are no rules for the choice of plants for a milder garden. It is very much a matter of personal choice, coupled with gardening skills and a generous dose of luck. If you like a plant and think that there is a chance that you might have the right conditions for it, give it a go! The list of plants that follows is a brief selection of those shrubs and perennials that can be tried in a sheltered garden. They do not feature in the main plant A–Z as generally they do not easily adapt to the normal culture as a tender perennial or to conservatory culture.

ABUTILON
Malvaceae

See the main entry on page 22. Here are just a few species and cultivars that should be hardy in sheltered sites on a warm wall.

A. megapotamicum A native of Brazil which, although it is not quite hardy, will usually survive outside given a position on a sheltered wall. Flowers are like crinkly red balloons with yellow skirts. It has small green leaves. 2 m (6½ ft) ★★★★ There is a sturdy compact selection called **'Wakehurst'** and a variegated form, *A. m.* **'Variegatum'** which is less hardy than the true species. Both are 1.5 m (5 ft).

A. × suntense A hybrid between *A. vitifolium* and a lesser-known species, *A. ochsenii*. It is very vigorous and hardier than either of its parents, with violet-blue flowers copiously produced. 2.4 m (8 ft) ★★★★ There are various improved cultivars such as **'Jermyns'** ♔.

A. vitifolium Makes an enormous wall shrub in a sheltered site. It is erect of habit and needs merely a few ties to hold it back against its supporting wall or trellis. Flowers are large pale shimmering purplish-blue saucers produced in abundance in late spring and early summer. 4 m (12 ft) ★★★★ There is a cultivar called **'Veronica Tennant'** ♔ with large pale lavender flowers and two white forms, **var. *album*** and **'Tennant's White'** ♔. Both whites are slightly less hardy but well worth the gamble. The cultivars are all 3 m (10 ft).

ACCA
Myrtaceae

A. sellowiana Virtually hardy, although it comes from subtropical South America. Evergreen bush with white-backed, red-petalled flowers with long red stamens. There is a lovely creamy white-variegated form that is not so hardy. 2.4 m (8 ft) ★★★★

ACNISTUS SEE DUNALIA

ASTELIA
Asteliaceae/Liliaceae

A. chathamica Clump-forming perennial grown for its splendid arching silvery leaves with pure white undersides. Long-stalked spikes of yellowish-green flowers are produced in mid and late spring, but it is mainly grown for its foliage. It comes from New Zealand and should be hardy in sheltered spots in most areas. 1.2 m (4 ft) ★★★★ ♔

BESCHORNERIA
Agavaceae

B. yuccoides This exotic-looking succulent is virtually hardy in a sheltered site. It grows in a rosette habit, producing attractive sword-shaped grey-green leaves. The flowering spike is quite dramatic – the stems are reddish, while the flowers are greenish bells with striking red bracts. The whole structure reaches to 1.5 m (5 ft) high and a mature plant with several flowering spikes is a notable sight. ★★★ ♔

CALLISTEMON
Myrtaceae

There are 25 species in this genus of plants which are generally known as the bottlebrushes because of their typical flower pattern. They are evergreen trees and

shrubs from Australia and vary from tender to hardy. Most are propagated from semi-ripe tip cuttings.

***C. citrinus* 'Splendens'** Broad leaves, pinkish silky young shoots and crimson flowers. Just hardy in mild areas. 2–3 m (6½–10 ft) ★★★ ♈

C. pallidus Narrow lance-shaped leaves and greenish-yellow flowers. 2–3 m (6½–10 ft) ★★★

CHAMAEROPS
Arecaceae/Palmae

C. humilis The only species in this genus. Sometimes called the dwarf fan palm, it comes from the west Mediterranean. It has a bushy, suckering habit of growth

Dicksonia antarctica, the tree fern, is a great deal hardier than most people suppose.

and produces big, floppy, fan-shaped pinnate leaves. Grow in a sheltered spot outside or try as a cool conservatory plant. It will tolerate very light frosts. 2–3 m (6½–10 ft) ★★★ ♈

DICKSONIA
Catheaceae/Dicksoniaceae

A genus of tree ferns originating from eastern Australia.

D. antarctica The big woolly-looking trunk is actually an erect rhizome from which the enormous fronds are produced at the top. These may be up to 3 m (10 ft) in length. This luxuriant-looking but slow-growing plant epitomizes the exotic garden and can be seen in many sheltered frost-free gardens. Sadly it is not hardy but with a few precautions it can be persuaded to survive and sometimes thrive in many areas.

This plant is protected by the CITES agreement and may only be imported under licence from native locations. Recent collections from Tasmania seem to be hardier than stock from other sources. Young plants with no trunk should be kept in pots and plunged out for the summer months, then brought under frost-free glass for the winter.

These plants thrive in a well-drained acid compost with a high proportion of peat or peat substitute. During the winter, the compost should not become waterlogged. If conditions are dry, the trunk should be watered occasionally, just below the leaf crown. Newly imported plants may come as bare trunks with no roots but these are quickly produced after potting up.

Once the plant has a trunk it can be planted out in the garden, although the bigger the trunk the greater the chance of survival, so there should be no rush to plant permanently. During subsequent winters, some protection must be provided in all but the mildest of gardens. At the very least, the trunk must be protected with insulating material such as polystyrene, fibreglass wool or straw and straw packed around the crown. Cold weather will probably kill the fronds but these will rapidly be replaced the following spring. More sophisticated structures made from straw bales with a polythene cover may be possible and will protect the fronds from frost. The cover must be removed in mild weather for a change of air and to allow rain to keep the plants moist. Under such conditions plants have been known to survive when the outside temperature has dropped as low as −15°C (5°F). Larger, taller plants seem to survive excessively low temperatures better than small ones. 6 m (20 ft) ★★★ ♈

Dunalia australis, more commonly known by its old name of *Acnistus australis*, is capable of making a bush of considerable size if it is given a sheltered location.

DUNALIA
Solanaceae
D. australis (syn. *Acnistus australis*) Although it is frequently listed as being frost-tender, this exotic-looking shrub can be amazingly hardy if it is given a little local shelter. Eventually it makes a huge sprawling bush which throughout early summer is covered with masses of hanging bells. The best forms are blue but if it is grown from seed it will produce plants in every shade from white through to sky blue. It also roots easily from cuttings, so a good form can be easily perpetuated. 2½–3 m (6–10 ft) ★★★

ERYTHRINA
Leguminosae
From a large genus of over 100 species, relatively few are commonly grown.
E. crista-galli Almost hardy and will thrive outside in a favoured spot, but should be protected over winter with a thick mulch. Leaves are leathery and pinnate, topped by spikes of deep red pea-like flowers. 1.2 m (4 ft) ★★★★ ♛

GERANIUM
Geraniaceae
A vast genus from which are selected just a couple of the Atlantic Island geraniums. Both are almost hardy in sheltered locations on a well-drained site. They are short-lived herbaceous plants and are grown from seed. As they are taprooted, they must be transplanted while young.
G. maderense Foliage is cut as finely as a fern with contrasting brownish stalks. It makes an enormous mound covered with magenta pink dark-eyed flowers, hazed over by the prominent glandular hairs. Flowering is continuous throughout the summer. 1.5 m (5 ft) ★★★ ♛
G. palmatum This is similar although more compact. Flowers are purplish-pink with crimson centres. 90 cm (3 ft) ★★★★ ♛

GREVILLEA
Proteaceae
Relatively few species from this large genus are grown in the UK, although potentially there are many good garden plants that should survive in a sheltered location. Alternatively, grow in a cool conservatory or plant in large tubs and stand out for the summer. Many have fine needle-like foliage resembling rosemary.
G. 'Canberra Gem' Hybrid between *G. juniperina* and the less hardy *G. rosmarinifolia*, raised in the 1960s in Canberra. It has proved to be vigorous and amazingly hardy given a dry sheltered position, tolerating temperatures as low as −10°C (14°F). Flowering often commences in late winter and will continue for several months with a profusion of curious, waxy, deep pink flowers. 1.8 m (6 ft) ★★★★ ♛
G. juniperina f. sulphurea Despite its cumbersome name this is one of the most popular Australian shrubs, with delicate bright-green, needle-like leaves and tufts of yellow shrimp-like flowers. 1.5 m (5 ft) ★★★★
G. rosmarinifolia Another needle-foliaged type with rich pink flowers and greyish-green leaves. Almost hardy in most situations. 1.2 m (4 ft) ★★★★ ♛

LAVANDULA
Labiatae/Lamiaceae
This genus widely known and cultivated for its traditional hardy species contains some interesting and unusual tender members from the Canary Isles, the Mediterranean and parts of Africa, Asia and India. There are many subspecies and nomenclature is complicated. All will like dry, well-drained, hot and sunny sites to grow and thrive.

They do not take kindly to being moved, so unless they can be grown in sheltered frost-free sites they are better grown in large pots.

L. canariensis Leaves are pinnate or bipinnate and green. Flower stalks are long and slender, bearing violet flowers with prominent bracts. 1 m (3¼ ft) ★★★

L. dentata A spreading bushy shrub with scalloped dark green leaves. In late summer it produces long stalks with dense spikes of slightly fragrant purple-blue flowers. 1 m (3¼ ft) ★★★

L. multifida This one comes from the Iberian Peninsula, Italy, Sicily, Egypt and North Africa. Leaves are grey-green and softly pubescent, pinnate or bipinnate. Flowers are on a tall branching spike of a deep violet-purple with grey tomentose bracts. 60 cm (2 ft) ★★★

L. pinnata. The whole plant is hoary white and the broadly lobed foliage resembles the bedding plant known as *Cineraria maritima.* It is native to Madeira and the Canary Isles. 1 m (3¼ ft) ★★★

L. viridis Native to Spain, Portugal and Madeira and has green stems and leaves that smell of lemons when crushed. Flowers are white with greenish-white bracts. 45 cm (18 in) ★★★

Musa basjoo, the hardiest of the bananas, produces huge green leaves and suckers freely.

MUSA
Musaceae

M. basjoo This suckering perennial is the nearest to a hardy banana. It comes from Japan and will tolerate a little frost, although for the best results it is wise to protect the false stem overwinter with insulating bindings. If top growth is killed, it will usually regrow from the rootstock. The huge green leaves can extend to 3 m (10 ft). It produces creamy-yellow flowers but the subsequent fruit is unpalatable. 4 m (12 ft) ★★★

MUTISIA
Asteraceae/Compositae

A genus of daisy-flowered shrubs and climbers from South America. All are of borderline hardiness, so grow them in sheltered locations. They are rather like climbing argyranthemums in appearance and although spectacular they can be temperamental. Propagate from seed, cuttings or layers. As woodlanders, they are very happy growing through other shrubs and small trees.

M. decurrens Narrow leaves and bright orange flowers. 3 m (10 ft) ★★★★

M. ilicifolia Bright green holly-like leaves and pale pink flowers. 3 m (10 ft) ★★★★

M. oligodon Sharply toothed dark green leaves and long-stalked, pink daisy flowers 1.5m (5 ft) ★★★★

OLEARIA
Asteraceae/Compositae

O. phlogopappa Compact shrub with small grey-green leaves. Masses of daisy-like flowers in spring and early summer. Virtually hardy in sheltered locations. 2 m (6½ ft) ★★★★ **'Comber's Blue'** and **'Comber's Pink'** are good cultivars.

O. ramulosa Arching shrub with tiny linear leaves and small starry daisy flowers. Very delicate in appearance. Coming from Australia, it is not surprisingly frost tender. 1.5 m (5 ft) ★★

PHORMIUM
Agavaceae/Phormiaceae

Genus with two species of evergreen perennials bearing dramatic sword-shaped leaves. Both species originate from New Zealand and are moderately hardy, but the cultivars with fancy-coloured leaves are less so. The best specimens are achieved by settling them into a sheltered site in full sun. They can also be grown as specimens in large containers and can then be taken under cold glass for winter protection. All are exotic in appearance and associate well with many tender perennials. Some will eventually flower with elongated spikes of dull yellow or red flowers. The main display is the foliage.

P. cookianum Linear yellowish-green leaves. Tough but less interesting than cultivars. 1.5 m (5 ft) ★★★★ ♛

P. c. ssp. *hookeri* 'Cream Delight' Broad bands of creamy yellow. 1.5 m (5 ft) ★★★★ ♛

P. c. 'Sundowner' Bronze-green with dark rose-pink margins. 1.5 m (5 ft) ★★★★ ♛

P. tenax Huge, rigid, lance-like, dark green leaves up to 3m (10 ft). The flowering spike may grow to 4 m (12 ft). Plain but very striking appearance when mature and well grown. Fairly hardy. ★★★★ ♛

P. t. 'Dazzler' Rich bronze leaves overlaid with red, orange and pink stripes. Very exotic-looking but rather tender. 1 m (3¼ ft) ★★★

P. t. 'Purpureum' Slightly less vigorous than the species but a rich ruby purple and almost as tough. 2.4 m (8 ft) ★★★★ ♛

P. 'Yellow Wave' Leaves striped yellow and mid-green. 1.8 m (6 ft) ★★★ ♛

PITTOSPORUM
Pittosporaceae

A genus of over 200 species of evergreen shrubs and trees, mainly from Australasia. They need a well-drained, sheltered site in full sun or partial shade. They are useful specimens for large planters and will remain attractive for several years.

P. tenuifolium Large bush or eventually a small tree with small, glossy, crinkly leaves. Black stems and reddish-black honey-scented flowers in late spring. Good background plant for an exotic display. 4 m (12 ft) + ★★★★ ♛

P. t. 'Abbotsbury Gold' Yellow leaves with green margins. 3 m (10 ft) ★★★★

P. t. 'Irene Paterson' Leaves mottled and speckled with green and white. Amazingly tough for a variegated form. 1.5 m (5 ft) ★★★★ ♛

P. t. 'Tom Thumb' Rich bronze-purple leaves on a compact plant. 1 m (3¼ ft) ★★★★ ♛

TRACHYCARPUS
Arecaceae/Palmae

T. fortunei The Chusan palm is one of the few reliably hardy palms and is included within this book because of its exotic appearance, which mixes so well with many tender perennials. It is a single-stemmed evergreen with

From the many palms available, *Trachycarpus fortunei* is the hardiest for outdoor planting.

fan-shaped dark green leaves. It bears yellow flowers and blue-black fruit from female plants. Up to 20 m (70 ft) but slow-growing and quite manageable. ★★★★ ♛

TENDER BULBS

There are many bulbs, corms and tubers which are marginally tender and fit in with the general subject of this book. They tend to come from areas such as parts of South Africa, Mexico and eastern Asia with dry winters and wet summers, so naturally they grow and flower in the summer. Those that are not tough enough to survive underground over winter need to be lifted after flowering in the autumn and stored in frost-free conditions. When left in situ they should be mulched deeply to protect the roots. In most cases all parts of the plant that appear above the ground will be frost-tender.

Because British winters are not only cold but wet, it is important to ensure that the soil is well-drained and improved with grit before planting. Many bulbs grow well in containers and can be started under glass and used for conservatory display. If moved outside in summer, they can easily be returned to warmer conditions for the winter. All should be planted in groups for a bold effect. Mixtures from some mail order firms can be disappointing in that they do not easily overwinter but they are often cheap to purchase and might be considered as temporary additions to an exotic border.

Canna This rhizomatous plant is dealt with in detail on page 40.

Eucomis bicolor Huge strap-shaped leaves are produced throughout summer, heralding the tall racemes of purple-edged pale green flowers that appear in late summer. The flowering stem is topped with a tuft of foliage, giving it the common name pineapple lily. Can be left out but mulch well. 45 cm (18 in) ★★★★

E. comosa Leaves have undersides spotted with purple. Flower spike is straight and poker-like with masses of tiny white, dark-eyed flowers. 75 cm (2½ ft) ★★★★

Galtonia candicans This one comes from South Africa. In late summer the slender flowering spike is produced, bearing dozens of small white hanging bells. It is wisest to lift in autumn but you can mulch well and take a gamble. 1 m (3¼ ft) ★★★★★

G. viridiflora Pale green flowers. 1 m (3¼ ft) ★★★★ ♔

Gladiolus The genus is widely known for the large brash cut-flower and exhibition types that are regularly grown. There are however several much more classy species and small-flowered hybrids such as **'Amanda Mahy'**, **'Nymph'** and **'Prins Claus'** that are well worth growing. Most should be lifted at the end of the summer and stored overwinter.

G. callianthus Loose open spikes of strongly scented pure white flowers with purple-black markings in throat. 90 cm (3 ft) ★★★ ♔

G. cardinalis Tall spike of bright red funnel-shaped flowers with a white splash on each petal. 75 cm (2½ ft) ★★★

G. communis ssp. *byzantinus* Long spikes of magenta funnel-shaped flowers. Tough and hardy. Can be left outside. 1 m (3¼ ft) ★★★★★ ♔

G. papilio Arching stems bearing almost bell-shaped flowers of yellowish green with heavy purple blotching. 75 cm (2½ ft) ★★★★

G. 'The Bride' A delicate hybrid with small spikes of white flowers marked with yellow. Fairly hardy. 60 cm (2 ft) ★★★ ♔

G. tristis Very narrow leaves. Long wiry spikes of open funnel-shaped flowers in creamy white. Sweetly scented in the evening. 1.2 m (4 ft) ★★★

Hedychium This rhizomatous genus is covered in detail on page 71.

Hymenocallis × *festalis* The common name of spider lily neatly describes the white long-petalled flowers with prominent stamens. Best grown in conservatory. 75 cm (2½ ft) ★

H. narcissiflora Flowers white and strongly scented. This one is hardier and can be planted out if lifted for the winter. 30 cm (12 in) ★★

Ixia The corn lilies from South Africa are usually offered as mixtures of hybrids which are rainbow-coloured. They need very warm sunny conditions or cultivation in a container. Some species and cultivars may be found in specialist nurseries.

I. 'Mabel' Deep pink flowers. 45 cm (18 in) ★★★

I. viridiflora This has eerie bluish-green flowers with maroon centres. 45 cm (18 in) ★★★

Nerine Coming from Southern Africa, they are mainly tender and best grown under cool glass. Their culture is rather specialist and there are many cultivars which produce a spectacular firework-like display in mid-autumn. ★★★ to ★★★★★

Polianthes tuberosa Very popular in the 19th century for their waxy white flowers and sweet scent, they are less commonly grown now. Grow in pots or lift and store. The species is rarely grown, but 'The Pearl' is a good double cultivar. 1.2 m (4 ft) ★ ♔

Sparaxis tricolor Appropriately called the harlequin flower – flowers are available in orange, red, purple and white, each with black red or yellow central markings. 30 cm (12 in). Other species are available from specialists ★★★

Tigridia pavonia Tender bulbs from Mexico, available in orange, red, yellow or white, often with an elaborately marked centre. 30 cm (12 in) ★★

Watsonia Cormous perennials from South Africa and Madagascar. Many species, although relatively few are commonly cultivated. Showy spikes of red, orange, pink or white flowers. Grow in pots in a cool conservatory or if grown outside must be lifted before frosts.

W. 'Stanford Scarlet' Slender spikes of rich orange orange-red tubular flowers with spreading petals. 90 cm (3 ft) ★★★

Watsonia 'Stanford Scarlet' growing by the pond at Coleton Fishacre in Devon.

Part Four Propagation & Cultivation

9 Propagation of Tender Perennials

Tender perennials are generally easy to propagate and will respond quite well under basic conditions. Most are propagated from cuttings, which is the method that will be considered in depth. A good sterile rooting medium, careful preparation and a warm humid atmosphere are the basic requirements; high levels of skill are not required. Although a limited quantity of plants can be grown on a warm sunny windowsill, anything other than small numbers of easy plants will need the use of a heated greenhouse or conservatory.

THE BASIC EQUIPMENT

A frost-free greenhouse, conservatory or polythene tunnel provides the basic environment essential for propagating, growing and overwintering tender perennials. Information on heating systems can be found on page 147.

Ideally, cuttings should be rooted in an electric propagator with thermostatically controlled bottom heat or a mist unit. For the serious gardener a good propagator or mist unit should be considered an investment. Results from a mist unit are certainly fast and reliable, enabling more batches of plants to be produced, while heat from some source always helps to prevent the rotting of cuttings that can occur when conditions are cold, damp and dull.

Although sophisticated propagation equipment is desirable, you can achieve good results with the careful use of polythene bags over pots or trays of cuttings. Alternatively, a plastic dome propagator that fits neatly over a seed tray is only a small expense. With either of these simple devices you will need to take care to avoid excessive build-up of condensation within the system.

PREPARING CUTTINGS

Collect plant material for cuttings carefully, using a knife or secateurs, and selecting short, stocky shoots 7.5–10 cm (3–4 in) long. These should be without flowers wherever possible and be good representative specimens of the plant. Always select from plants with flowers of good size and colour or with good foliage; it is particularly important to select shoots with good leaf colour and patterns when propagating variegated plants. Avoid any plants showing symptoms of pests or diseases, but if it is essential to propagate from infected plants, dip the cuttings thoroughly in a suitable pesticide before rooting. Ideally, material should be collected early in the day when the water content is high and immediately placed in a plastic bag to avoid wilting. Cuttings that do wilt for whatever reason can often be 'crisped' by rinsing with cool water and leaving in a polythene bag overnight.

The actual preparation of the cuttings should be done with a clean, sharp knife. If you find sharpening and using a traditional propagator's knife difficult, try using a craft knife with disposable blades, but remember to cut onto a wood block or similar surface with this sort of knife as the blades are razor-like. You can also use secateurs, provided they are very sharp. Whatever tools you use, avoid crushing or fraying the cutting.

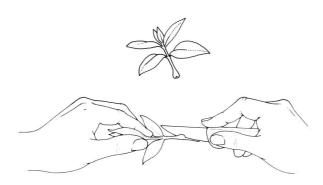

Fig. 4 a) Preparing a softwood cutting, using a sharp knife to remove lower leaves and trim below a node.

b) Twenty cuttings can be inserted in a half seed tray, which should be carefully labelled.

Fig. 5 Pots (especially the short half-pots) are very suitable for rooting small quantities of cuttings.

Trim the cutting to just below a node, giving an overall size of about 5–7.5 cm (2–3 in), then remove the lower leaves cleanly to give sufficient bare stem to insert in the compost. As a general rule, stocky growth with large leaves such as abutilons should be prepared as small cuttings with few leaves and wiry plants with small leaves such as diascias or nemesia can be prepared longer, retaining several leaves. If you are propagating a species with exceptionally large leaves, such as brugmansia, trim the leaves in half to reduce water loss.

LABELLING

Labelling is a vitally important aspect for all plant propagation, particularly where there are a number of similar plants; a collection of penstemons without labels, for example, will become totally indistinguishable during the winter months. Further propagation or sensible planting cannot take place until they flower and identification is again possible. A useful technique is to write the labels before propagation and then slip the relevant label in the bag when the material is collected. Use a pencil or a special indelible plant label marker, never ball-point pen. Adding the date when the cuttings are taken is a useful additional piece of information. The label then follows the cuttings through the various stages to maturity.

ROOTING MEDIA AND CONTAINERS

A mixture of peat and sharp sand in equal proportions or peat and fine grade bark are both successful mixtures for rooting cuttings. Species that require a slightly drier rooting medium may benefit from a mixture of equal parts of peat, bark and perlite. For those who prefer not to use peat for environmental reasons, this may be replaced quite successfully with coir, although the watering requires greater care. Bark should be 'propagation grade', which is a fine, well-composted material. Plants that are difficult to root may benefit from a very well-drained open mix, which can be made with equal parts of bark, peat and perlite. A slow-release fertilizer such as Osmacote can be added to all such mixes, although this is not essential.

If you do not wish to mix your own rooting media, a proprietary multi-purpose compost will suffice. Whatever the media, it should be sterile and moist to avoid dehydrating a delicate new cutting. (Dry peat will literally suck the moisture out of a cutting.) This means that if you are using peat from a dried compressed bale it must be left to soak for a few hours first.

Cuttings can be rooted in pots or trays, depending on quantities. A full-size seed tray will take 35–48 cuttings and the useful half size 20–24. For smaller quantities use pots or, for economy, half pots, which require less compost. Place three cuttings in a 9 cm (3¾ in) pot, five in a 10 cm (4 in) pot and so on – the numbers need not be exact. There is no advantage in placing cuttings tight up against the sides of plastic pots as was the traditional practice with clay pots; position them at least 1 cm (½ in) from the edge. Small peat pots, peat pellets or unit modules can be useful, especially for rooting the larger cuttings such as brugmansia or abutilon which need a little more space. Good results can also be achieved with rockwool blocks.

Fill pots or trays with a rooting medium lightly, tapping the containers on the bench to consolidate the compost gently without destroying natural aeration and drainage. Never firm compost for rooting. Most cuttings should be rigid enough to insert without the use of a dibber; the exceptions are a few of the very frail types such as diascias that have stems no thicker than a piece of thread. Insert the cutting to no more than 2.5 cm (1 in) deep and firm very gently with your fingers, just enough to hold the cutting upright. Finish the job by watering in well, using a watering can with a fine rose, and placing the cuttings in whatever propagating facilities are available.

Hormone rooting powders are not really necessary for most tender perennials, although they can be used to encourage rooting where conditions are less than ideal, or when you are propagating out of the normal seasons.

Regal pelargoniums are normally grown as conservatory plants but are well worth trying outside in a sheltered spot.

Most rooting powders also contain a fungicide. With poor rooting conditions or after a wet summer when growths are very soft, watering in the prepared cuttings with a solution of fungicide is an added safeguard.

AFTERCARE

During the rooting procedure, which usually takes between two and three weeks, watch for decaying leaves or rotting cuttings and remove immediately to avoid the spread of disease. Polythene bags should be turned and plastic propagators wiped out at daily intervals. Normally such sealed environments do not dry out easily, but should the rooting media appear dry, water thoroughly with clean tap water. Never be tempted to use water from a rainwater barrel or tank in a greenhouse – any values it may have in being rainwater are far outweighed by the likelihood of it containing disease.

Cuttings can be tested for rooting by gently pulling. Those that offer resistance are likely to have rooted; those that come out have not! These can be carefully reinserted to allow rooting to continue. This seemingly drastic action does not seem to harm the cuttings as long as it is done gently.

Before potting, rooted cuttings should be 'weaned' to acclimatize them to the usual greenhouse conditions by increasing ventilation in the propagator or removing cuttings from a mist unit. If there are any signs of wilting, damp the cuttings lightly using a fine rose on a watering can. Newly rooted cuttings should be shaded from bright sun using old newspaper, milky polythene or fleece for a few days. If cuttings are likely to stay in the rooting units for more than a few days after rooting, they should be fed with a weak liquid feed as most rooting media have no nutrients.

PROPAGATING SEASONS

The two most useful seasons for propagating tender perennials are autumn and spring, though technically they can be propagated at almost any time of the year when there are actively growing shoots that can be prepared as cuttings. Autumn propagation is a necessity for many plants in order to provide young stock that can be overwintered in a greenhouse ready for the next season, while spring propagation gives a second chance to take cuttings from those plants overwintered. The latter is particularly useful for propagating large batches that would take up too much space under glass during the winter months.

It is logical to consider the autumn batch first, as this is the season when you must propagate tender perennials or lift them and bring them under cover before the autumn frosts threaten to destroy them. Late summer through to early autumn is a target time, when there should be plenty of suitable shoots on plants out in the garden. A wet summer will have produced soft, lush growths that will need careful handling to avoid wilting. Conversely, a hot, dry summer will result in good, stocky, well-ripened shoots, although there may be difficulty with some species in finding growths without flowers.

Another batch can be taken in early to mid-spring, either from last year's potted-up plants or from the plants grown from autumn cuttings. Not only is it surprising that the autumn batch will have produced enough growth to be stock plants themselves by the spring, but these late cuttings will root fast and produce good plants by early summer. Tender perennials are fast-growing, rewarding plants.

TIMING

Because of their amazing speed of growth, the production period for tender perennials is quite short. There is nevertheless some variation in their growth patterns and some fine tuning is needed to bring the many types of plants to peak condition, ready for planting out in early summer. Propagating too early can mean plants that become leggy or starved before it is time to plant them out, so don't be in too much of a hurry.

Local conditions such as temperature and composts used may give some variation, but the following table puts some of the commonly grown plants roughly in the order necessary for propagating.

Autumn propagation

Most autumn cuttings will be grown to provide specimens for display the next season, so they need the longer growing period. They will generally be grown fairly warm, around 10–12°C (50–54°F) over winter, moving on to large pots (see page 172). Small plants can also be produced from spring cuttings.

Abutilon cultivars
Anisodontea capensis
Argyranthemum for standards

An alternative growing regime

Gardeners with a limited budget and very basic growing conditions may like to try this alternative growing regime perfected by a keen amateur grower. Take cuttings in late summer, planting several to a pot in a home-made compost of equal parts of garden compost, moist peat and sand. Water the pots well, place them in the greenhouse and cover them with milky polythene until the cuttings are rooted. In winter heat the greenhouse sufficiently to keep it frost free and keep the plants almost dry.

In mid-spring, as the light and natural warmth increase, pot up the rooted cuttings singly into 9 or 10 cm (3½ or 4 in) pots, again in garden compost with added base fertilizer. Remove the tops to encourage bushy growth. As the plants grow, space them out and harden them off in preparation for planting out at the end of spring. You will need to perfect such a regime to obtain predictable results as garden compost can be a very variable material.

Brugmansia cultivars
Heliotropium for standards
Lantana cultivars
Plumbago auriculata and *P. a.* var. *alba*
Streptosolen jamesonii and yellow form
Pelargonium for standards

In addition there will be those of many genera that can be propagated to provide stock plants for spring cuttings.

Winter/spring propagation

Most of these will provide the bulk of your displays. A large number of small, strongly growing plants will provide the best show.

Late winter
Begonia fuchsioides
Centaurea gymnocarpa
Euryops chrysanthemoides
E. pectinatus
Iresine herbstii and cultivars
Mimulus – shrubby types
Pelargonium cultivars
Penstemon cultivars

Early spring
Argyranthemum cultivars

Calceolaria integrifolia and cultivars
Convolvulus sabatius
Cosmos atrosanguineus
Cuphea species and cultivars
Fuchsia species and cultivars
Gazania cultivars
Heliotropium cultivars
Osteospermum cultivars
Salvia species and cultivars
Rhodanthemum gayanum

Mid-spring
Arctotis cultivars
Bidens aurea and *B. ferulifolia*
Bracteantha 'Dargan Hill Monarch' and 'Skynet'
Dahlia cultivars
Diascia species and cultivars
Felicia species and cultivars
Helichrysum species and cultivars
Nemesia cultivars
Plectranthus
Sutera (*Bacopa*)
Tropaeolum cultivars
Verbena cultivars

A few of the hardier types such as penstemon, diascia and osteospermum can be propagated in the autumn and grown with the barest frost protection. Such plants will stay stocky and compact and can, because of their toughness, be planted out a little earlier in mid to late spring than the softer, spring-raised plants and more tender types.

PROPAGATION BY DIVISION

There are just a few tender perennials that need to be propagated by division. This is a very simple method of propagation that is commonly used for hardy herbaceous perennials. In this case the technique is similar but as the plants are not fully hardy the practice is usually carried out in a greenhouse either in the autumn or more commonly the spring. Autumn divisions often sulk and rot so spring is by far the preferable season, ideally just before growth starts in earnest.

There are several lobelias that are on the borderline of hardiness, such as *Lobelia* 'Queen Victoria', with dark red leaves and scarlet flowers. It makes a leafy clump, growing well in damp conditions. To be sure of its survival it should be dug up before winter and kept in a frost-free greenhouse until early spring, when it can be divided. Pull the clump apart by hand, or if necessary cut it with a knife, to make sections with three to five small shoots on each. Each new division should be potted in a 9 or 10 cm (3½ or 4 in) pot directly into a potting compost and watered in. No special propagating conditions are required, but a careful watch on watering and avoidance of bright sun for a few days will help establishment.

A choice little member of the onion family known as *Tulbaghia*, normally seen in the variegated form *T. violacea* 'Silver Lace', is also divided in a similar way. Handle the fragile stems gently and after potting place in a warm spot in the greenhouse for a couple of weeks to help them re-root. *Commelina* is also easily divided.

Arundo donax 'Variegata', that woody giant member of the grass family, is also traditionally divided. It does not

Fig. 6 Before repotting, herbaceous species can be divided by using a sharp knife or by gently pulling the shoots apart.

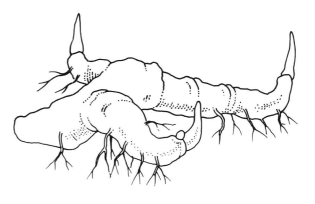

Fig. 7 Canna rhizome showing three growing points. This could be divided into three separate plants or potted entire to make one large clump.

make many offsets so only a few new ones can be separated each year. As its rootstock is amazingly tough, it may be necessary to use a serrated kitchen knife or secateurs to separate the divisions. The woody stems must be shortened to about 20 cm (8 in) before potting in a 12 or 15 cm (5 or 6 in) pot. New shoots will usually come from beneath the soil, although sometimes they appear from the leaf axils of the remaining stem. An alternative method is described on page 36.

GROWING FROM SEED

There are a number of tender perennials that can be propagated from seed. However, as most named cultivars of plants do not breed true, seed propagation can only be used for growing true species or mixed batches of certain plants.

Among these are the nicotianas, such as the lovely white *Nicotiana sylvestris* and the curious green *N. langsdorffii*. These are actually perennial and will, given mild winters, survive from year to year, though they grow so easily from seed that it is easier to raise them afresh each spring and treat as annuals. Seed can sometimes be difficult to obtain, so once you have them it is wise to collect and keep a few pinches of seed each year.

Several members of the banana family make striking specimens to grow among tender perennials and can be easily grown from seed. The easiest and most readily available is *Ensete ventricosum*. The seed needs soaking in warm water for 24 hours before sowing. A small dish of water placed in a propagator or airing cupboard or on a radiator will probably suffice, with an ideal temperature of 18–20°C (64–68°F). Germination only takes place at high temperatures, in excess of 21°C (70°F), and not all seeds germinate. The speed of growth of the plants that do germinate, though, is impressive and the end result dramatic.

Other tender perennials to grow from seed

Acca sellowiana (formerly *Feijoa sellowiana*)
Agastache species
Agave species
Alonsoa 'Firestone Jewels Mixed'
Bidens 'Golden Goddess'
Brugmansia suaveolens
Canna species and mixtures
Cordyline australis
Cuphea species
Eccremocarpus scaber
Datura inoxia
D. metel 'La Fleur Lilas'

a) Nick the hard coat of canna seeds with a small file or hacksaw blade.

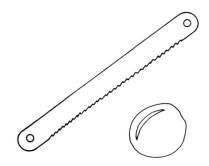

b) Soak them in warm water for 48 hours.

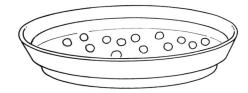

c) Plant them individually in small pots to avoid root disturbance when they are germinated.

Fig. 8 Growing canna from seed.

Dunalia australis (formerly *Acnistus australis*)
Ipomoea lobata (formerly *Mina lobata*)
Lampranthus mixed
Lobelia Fan Series
Passiflora species
Penstemon species and mixtures
Phygelius × *rectus* 'African Queen'
Plumbago auriculata
Rhodochiton atrosanguineus
Solanum laciniatum.

10 Growing On & General Care

Whether they are propagated by cuttings, division or seed, the basic procedures for the growing on of tender perennials are roughly the same. Likewise the majority of tender perennials, regardless of genera, will tolerate very similar growing conditions and techniques – yet another reason why they can be described as easy and rewarding.

POTTING COMPOSTS

Thirty years ago, when I first started my career in horticulture, I worked at a seaside parks department, growing a very traditional range of pot and bedding plants including many of the old coloured-leaved geraniums, cannas, palms, ferns and abutilons. Compost was prepared from locally collected materials – loam from trimmings from the grass verges, leafmould from the park leaves and sand from the beach, allowed to weather to leach out its salt. To this we added a fearsome mix of blood, fish and bone. Despite the profusion of weed seedlings, which had to be removed from every pot and tray by hand, plants grew strong and healthy.

Today the range of composts available to the gardener is ever-widening. Traditional loam- or soil-based composts are still available, most of which are based on the John Innes mixtures; these are recipes, not brand names, and there are both good and bad suppliers. The John Innes mixes are very good for long-term plantings in tubs and planters and for conservatory plantings, as they retain a good open structure and hold their nutrient levels steady. They are not so good for short-term plant production. Many growers of exhibition coleus regard John Innes composts as essential for good leaf colour.

Loamless composts are those that do not have any soil within the mix. For many years these were all based on peat, sometimes with added sand, bark or other materials. All the nutrients are added as chemical fertilizers, together with lime to adjust the acidity. Tender perennials grow well within these composts and good young plants can be produced within a very few weeks. All peat composts tend to remain too wet for stock and specimen plants that are overwintered. A compost made with a coarse-grade peat or with added sand is preferable for larger pots and those plants to be retained beyond a single season. Cannas and hedychiums do particularly well in peat-based composts.

In recent years, with growing concern about the use of peat, various non-peat mixes based on coir, bark, wood and recycled waste have been produced. Results using

Rhodochiton atrosanguineus is a tender perennial climber which is easily grown from seed and flowers in its first season.

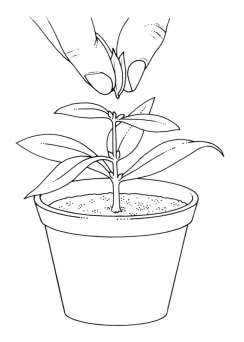

Fig. 9 Pinching out the growing tip of a young tender perennial to encourage sideshoots.

these composts are variable and it is best to carry out a small-scale trial before relying on a new product. In general, they are free-draining and need frequent watering as well as regular feeding.

POTTING UP

When cuttings are thoroughly rooted and acclimatized, potting can take place using the chosen compost. For autumn-rooted cuttings avoid high levels of nutrition, which can give soft, lush growth. A 'general purpose compost' is more likely to have a low nitrogen level than a 'potting compost'. Remember with loamless composts not to over-firm, but merely to consolidate lightly and finish by tapping the pots on the bench. Most cuttings should be potted into 7.5 cm (3 in) or 9 cm (3½ in) pots, which should be thoroughly clean. Water in well and place the pots on the greenhouse bench in a position that will receive good winter light.

GROWING ON

Two to three weeks after potting, most tender perennials should be pinched to encourage sideshoots and create

OVERWINTERING TEMPERATURES

Almost hardy

These require frost protection only; many may come through the winter outside in a mild year. An unheated greenhouse will often give sufficient protection.

Calceolaria
Canna – dormant tubers
Centaurea gymnocarpa
Chrysanthemopsis gayanum
Convolvulus sabatius
Dendranthema pacificum
Diascia
Lobelia 'Queen Victoria'
Osteospermum
Penstemon
Phygelius
Zauschneria

Half hardy

These need minimum temperatures of 5–10°C (41–50°F)

Abutilons – survive but not grow
Anisodontea
Arctotis
Argyranthenmum
Bidens
Bracteantha
Canna – growing plants
Cuphea
Euryops
Felicia
Fuchsia
Gazania
Helichrysum
Heliotropium – survive only
Lantana – becomes dormant
Lotus
Mimulus – stock plants
Nemesia

Pelargonium
Plumbago
Salvia
Tropaeolum
Verbena

Tender

These plants require a minimum temperature of 12–15°C (54–59°F).

Abutilon – young plants and
    A. 'Savitzii' at all stages
Brugmansia
Canna – actively growing
Coleus
Heliotropium – to thrive
Iresine
Lantana – young plants
Mimulus – young plants
Scaevola
Streptocarpus

a bushy plant. This involves removing just the tip of the growing shoots with either your fingers or a sharp knife (Fig. 9). Plants that have been allowed to grow leggy may have a larger amount removed, but take care as not all types respond well to hard trimming. Repeat the pinching procedure throughout the winter and spring months as soon as sideshoots achieve a length of approximately 5 cm (2 in) or have two or three leaves with axilliary buds which will break into further shoots.

The need for pinching such as this makes many tender perennials unpopular with commercial nurserymen, although growth regulants are sometimes used to give dwarf plants with a branched habit. By comparison many modern seed-raised bedding plants are naturally compact and it is not difficult to see how some of these older types lost favour for a while.

When they are first potted, plants can be stood close together with the pots touching. Nurseryman call this 'pot thick' and it enables many plants to be accommodated in a small space, so minimizing heating costs. As the plants grow they must be spaced to allow adequate room for development without crowding. Ideally, no plant should touch its neighbour but in reality there is rarely enough space in a greenhouse to be quite so generous.

WINTER TEMPERATURES

Most tender perennials do not require high temperature levels, but heating should be adequate to provide frost protection under all winter conditions. Where heating is a bare minimum, it is an advantage to root cuttings early in the autumn to get well-established plants before the onset of cold weather. During particularly cold periods plants should be kept somewhat drier than normal, as a dry plant is more tolerant of cold than a wet one.

Sufficient heat to give a night-time minimum of 7–10°C (45–50°F) will keep most plants growing slowly and help to avoid some of the problems associated with low temperature such as botrytis and root rots. However, although such simple generalizations are useful, the keen gardener will soon find that plants have more specific requirements and that some are tougher than others. The table on the previous page identifies some of the common groups and their ideal heat requirements.

OVERWINTER CARE

Over the winter months, good greenhouse hygiene is as essential with tender perennials as any other group of plants. Remove all dead or dying leaves from plants before

Young tender perennials growing under glass in the spring months in a commercial greenhouse.

infection starts. Keep benches and particularly the spaces under them clean and free from debris that could harbour pests and diseases.

Whenever weather conditions allow, greenhouses should have the ventilators opened to allow a change of air. On very cold or wet days in winter this may not be possible at all, although ideally the ventilators should be opened at least a crack every day, even for just an hour or so at the mildest part of the day. This will help with plant growth as well as deterring disease.

As many tender perennials come from parts of the world with higher light levels than those of the British winter, it can be beneficial to use supplementary artificial light from autumn through to spring to increase the intensity of light and the day length. Always buy specialist lighting equipment that is both suitable for plants and safe to be used in the damp greenhouse environment. Most 'growlights' are based on sodium, mercury vapour or metal halide lamps. To gain maximum use, a time-switch is a useful accessory. Great care should be taken in fixing the light at the correct distance from the plants as too much light can cause distorted growth and scorch.

POTTING ON

Although it is possible with careful feeding to keep autumn-rooted plants in the same small pots through until planting time the following summer, in most cases it is advantageous to pot on to a larger-sized pot; 10–12.5 cm (4–5 in) pots will be adequate for this stage. Potting on should not normally take place until light levels improve some time in late winter and some new growth becomes evident. By this time plants should

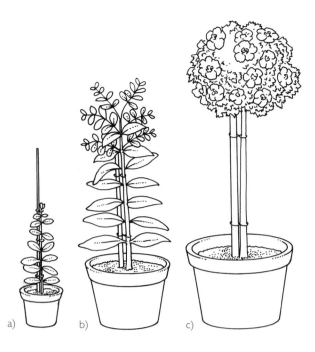

Fig. 10 a) A young plant being trained as a standard with its leader tied to a cane. b) The tip is pinched at an appropriate height to encourage sideshoots. c) The fully grown standard with stem leaves removed.

have thoroughly colonized the rooting space within the first pot with good active white roots. A John Innes No. 2 compost can be used or a loamless compost with a slow-release fertilizer added, although this is not essential. A final potting on to 15–20 cm (6–8 in) pots will be needed for large specimens or standards, using John Innes No. 3 or a loamless compost with a slow-release fertilizer.

These sheep seen in France were grown from *Helichrysum petiolare* trained over a wire framework.

FEEDING

It should be remembered that all loamless composts have very limited feed incorporated within them and additional nutrition, either as a liquid feed or as a slow-release fertilizer, must be used according to the manufacturer's recommendations. Give a balanced feed through the winter months; a high-nitrogen feed will produce lush soft growth and a distinct lack of flowers and should be avoided in most circumstances. By late spring and early summer, when flowering growth is required, give a high-potash feed such as those recommended for tomatoes.

In summer feeding twice a week is the average. In the winter once a week is adequate for growing plants, although those that are dormant at very low temperatures will not need feeding at all. Some growers prefer to feed with every watering, using a very dilute feed, on the basis that it causes more regular growth. A diluter that automatically meters the feed is needed for such a regime and once a week pure water should be

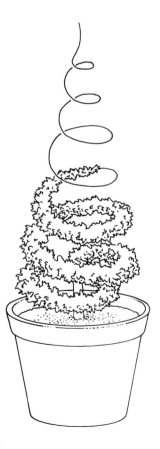

Fig. 11 *Helichrysum petiolare* can be trained into many shapes, such as this formal spiral.

used to leach out any excess build-up of salts in the compost.

TRAINING AS A STANDARD

Any plants such as pelargonium, heliotrope or argyranthemum which are destined to become standards should not be pinched but should have their leading shoot tied to a short split cane. In this situation it can help to break the normal rules and keep these plants close together. They will then stretch up to the light and achieve a good long stem in a shorter period of time. Frequent tying and turning will be necessary to ensure that the 'leg' remains straight.

Plants for standards should be potted on to 15 cm (6 in) pots as soon as the roots fill the initial pots. The process of producing the leg continues with tying in and trimming (Fig. 10). Do not remove the leaves on the main stem as these feed the plant and encourage growth. Eventually most standards will need to be potted on to a larger pot, around 20 cm (8 in), and have a taller cane of about 75 cm (2½ ft) added.

Once the leg has grown to about 10 cm (4 in) beyond the desired stem height, remove the tip. Allow the topmost five or six sideshoots to grow out to form the head of the standard. As they grow, pinch them regularly to encourage a good bushy head – a well-grown standard should look like a ball on a stick. Only when the head is fully grown should the leaves on the leg be removed to give a clear stem.

LIVING SCULPTURES

Helichrysum petiolare is a versatile plant and one of the easiest to train into various shapes. The simplest is the pillar, which is achieved basically by training a young plant up a cane. The plant needs to be pinched out initially to encourage sideshoots at the base or the pillar will be thin at the bottom. A good strong growth is then tied in to the cane as a new 'leader' and other sideshoots pinched quite hard to two or three leaves.

As the plant grows, it must be potted on until it reaches a 20 cm (8 in) pot and a 1.2 m (4 ft) cane. Such a silver pillar can be planted out as a centrepiece of a planter or flower bed. Some pinching or trimming must continue throughout the season or the sideshoots will soon grow out to shaggy bushes.

By using a spiral wire framework with a central supporting cane, you can create a spiral shape in exactly the same way (Fig. 11). You can either clip it tightly to the frame or allow it to grow into the centre, giving a more solid twist of silver. If you wish to be adventurous, you can grow all sorts of shapes by using wire netting frameworks; for animals and other more complex shapes, a number of plants may be needed. You will obviously have to take great care when transferring the final structure to its summer display area and planting it out.

PESTS AND DISEASES

With such a wide range of plants included within the overall grouping of tender perennials, there is correspondingly a wide range of pathogens that may affect plants at various stages. In general, more problems occur while plants are under glass rather than when they are outside in the garden. Plants that spend the whole year under glass or within conservatories will suffer particularly and require constant pest control. For this reason, many people opt to move plants outside for the summer to reduce pest attack.

There are many ways of controlling pests and diseases. Traditionally the use of chemicals was regarded as the main weapon, but in recent years a whole host of biological controls has become available. A range of specific predators or parasites can be introduced to a greenhouse to provide a measure of control, although they do not usually totally decimate a pest – in fact, destroying the pest altogether would also prevent the continued existence of the biological control. The aim must be to achieve a happy balance with predator and pest, and this will mean accepting a minimal level of damage.

Additionally, there are a whole host of cultural techniques that you can use to deter pests. This simply means that by altering the way you grow a plant you can deter pest attack. Many growers like to use a combination of biological control together with cultural techniques and a minimal use of low-toxicity chemicals to control pathogens. Such a technique is known as integrated control and is environmentally acceptable.

Pests

Aphids

These sap-suckers include greenflies and blackflies, both of which can decimate plants, excreting honeydew that in turn results in sooty mould. Many aphids also spread viruses, so their control is essential. They are found on a very wide range of plants.

Using regular sprays of soft soap is one method of control. More drastic chemical control is possible using a wide range of products including malathion, pyrethrins, heptenophos and, particularly, pirimicarb. Systemic insecticides such as those containing heptenophos that reside in the plant are also very effective because they control future generations as they hatch and commence feeding. A range of predators and parasites are available for gardeners who prefer to use biological controls rather than chemicals.

Leaf miner

This pest lives within the leaves, making small white or brown bubbles and tunnels as it feeds. Argyranthemums and related plants in the Compositae family are particularly prone to attack.

Control must be by a systemic insecticide such as heptenophos in order to get to the pest within the leaves. Small outbreaks can be controlled by squashing the pest with a fingernail.

Mealy bug

This occasional pest covers itself with a sticky waterproof coating resembling cotton wool. The individual pests are found in crevices on stems and leaves of a whole range of plants. Coleus, plants grown permanently in conservatories and succulents are particularly affected.

Chemical controls are possible, including regular sprays of soft soap. In particular methylated spirits applied with a small paintbrush to individual troublespots is very effective, albeit time-consuming. A predatory ladybird called *Cryptolaemus montrouzieri* is quite effective against long-term infestations.

Red spider mite

This pest can have a devastating effect and it can be very difficult to control. It lives on the underside of leaves, sucking out the cell sap, causing the leaves to become progressively yellow and then brown. It is microscopic in size, looking like a fine dusting of pepper. With bad infestations, the mites create webs as they travel to new leaves. Cannas, brugmansias, lobelias, diascias, dahlias and hedychiums suffer particularly, but many other plants may be affected.

Red spider mite is deterred by increasing greenhouse humidity, which is achieved by regular damping down. A predatory mite called *Phytoseilus persimilis* can be used under glass during the summer months. Chemical control of this pest is not easy but soft soap gives some control, as do pirimiphos-methyl and bifenthrin.

However, several regular sprays will be required to reduce the populations significantly.

Sciarid fly

This pest is particularly troublesome with plants grown in composts with a high peat level. The adults are small black flies that can be seen flying around the plants, particularly when they are disturbed. The larval stage is a tiny white grub no more than 2–3 mm (⅒ in) in length which lives in the compost and eats plant roots. It can easily go unnoticed until the plant wilts due to a total lack of roots. A bad attack can be ruinous.

There is a biological control available consisting of an eelworm which parasitizes it. Alternatively, drenches of malathion made up to 50 per cent of the normal strength and applied to the compost will control the larva. Soft soap sprays help to reduce the adult population.

Slugs

Many plants are attacked by slugs, both under glass and outside. In particular, cannas should be protected from slugs when they are first emerging in the spring as slugs will nibble the rolled leaves, causing immense damage which is apparent as soon as the leaf unfurls. The effect, not unlike a child's paper-folding and tearing, can be both interesting and annoying!

Traditional slug pellets containing metaldehyde or methiocarb can be used. Numerous non-chemical controls are available, generally based on the trap principle, together with a biological control in the form of a parasitic eelworm specific to slugs.

Vine weevil

This pest has become increasingly prevalent in recent years. It is extremely difficult to eradicate and can easily be imported to a garden within pots of new plants. The adult, which causes relatively little harm, is a small dusty brown beetle-like creature that crawls around on the ground and the lower leaves of plants. The larvae tunnel under the soil and feed on plant roots with devastating effect. Usually there is little indication of the presence of this pest until a plant fails to thrive and eventually collapses and dies. Examination will then show that all the roots have been eaten by fat white grubs. In the summer, plants may grow fast enough for replacement roots to be produced at sufficient rate to keep the plant alive and so the pest may go undetected for many weeks.

Control is difficult and so prevention is an important aspect of control. New plants should always have their root systems examined for signs of the weevil. Any tunnellings should be investigated and if necessary the root system completely washed off and the plant repotted in clean compost. Insecticidal drenches are possible but the most effective chemicals are only available to the commercial grower. A parasitic eelworm is available as a biological control.

Whitefly

These tiny white insects are probably the most troublesome of all greenhouse pests and attack a wide range of plants. Among the tender perennials, verbenas, abutilons, lantanas and melianthus are particularly badly affected. All of these plants are best moved outside for the summer if major infestations are to be avoided. Whitefly breed at a prodigious rate and any chemical control must rely on frequent sprays, around every four days to try to break the life cycles.

The simplest sprays are based on soft soap and are totally safe in use, although they are not always very effective in greenhouses. More powerful chemical controls are available, such as permethrin, malathion, pirimiphosmethyl and heptenophos, which is systemic and gives longer-lasting protection from pest attack.

Biological control is by a small parasitic wasp called *Encarsia formosa* and is relatively effective under glass in summer. It must be introduced to the greenhouse or conservatory in two or three stages in mid-spring and its effectiveness carefully monitored. It cannot be used in the winter unless temperatures are constantly above 18°C (64°F), which is unlikely with tender perennials.

Diseases

Botrytis

Often called by the descriptive term grey mould, this is probably the only major disease that attacks a wide range of tender perennials under glass. During the winter months when light is low and plants are struggling to grow there will often be many leaves dropped and a certain amount of die-back on some plants. The atmosphere is often damp and colder than ideal and under such conditions botrytis often starts. Starting on dead leaves, it easily spreads to live material, causing rotting and die-back.

Good plant hygiene is the most important cultural control, making sure that all dead leaves are removed from the plants and not left lying around. Good greenhouse ventilation is essential whenever weather conditions allow to keep the atmosphere as dry as possible. From late autumn to late winter it is also worth applying a routine fungicidal spray, using a product such as carbendazim. This acts as a preventative measure and should be repeated every two weeks.

Powdery mildew

Verbenas suffer occasionally from powdery mildew. This shows as a white mealy covering on the upper surface of leaves, which rapidly spreads. Plants that are kept too dry are particularly susceptible, although it actually spreads from plant to plant in a damp atmosphere.

Control is helped by keeping the root systems adequately watered and preventing the build-up of humidity under glass by good ventilation. Chemical control is by carbendazim or bupirimate.

HARDENING OFF

As with all plants produced under greenhouse conditions, it is necessary to harden off tender perennials in the final weeks before planting out in the garden. Such a process will start in mid to late spring, ready for planting out when all danger of frost is past. This will involve slowly decreasing the temperature in the greenhouse and allowing additional ventilation in the day and possibly at night too. Alternatively, plants can be moved to a cooler environment such as a cold frame, unheated greenhouse or polythene tunnel. Where only small quantities of plants are involved, these can be stood outside on warm sunny days and taken back under glass at night, especially when frost threatens. Eventually, during late spring, the plants should be fully acclimatized to outdoor conditions ready for planting.

PLANTING SEASONS

By their very nature, tender perennials should not be planted out until all danger of frost is past. This will usually be in late spring or early summer, according to the locality, the season and the microclimate of each individual garden. Local knowledge will help the gardener to calculate just when it is safe to plant out tender plants.

Cold soils and air conditions will slow down the establishment of such plants, so there is no advantage to early

Coleus 'Lord Falmouth' is a compact cultivar which is excellent for bedding or for growing in a hanging basket.

planting if weather conditions are not conducive. In a cold season it is always preferable to keep plants in pots and under some protection for an extra week or so rather than planting them out early.

Occasionally, a late frost may be forecast after tender perennials have been planted. In this situation it can be useful to cover plantings with a light protection of horticultural fleece overnight. If this is unavailable, polythene, fabric such as muslin or even newspaper and empty pots will provide sufficient protection. If a late frost occurs unexpectedly, the damage can be minimized by spraying the plants lightly with water before the sun reaches the frosted leaves. The water causes slow thawing and minimizes scorch. Such a technique will only work with a very light frost, but it is worth trying.

Some of the tougher tender perennials will tolerate light frost provided they have been well hardened. Such plants as penstemons, diascias, and osteospermums can therefore be planted a little earlier than very tender species such as canna, dahlia, heliotrope and coleus, which will not tolerate even a touch of frost.

BORDER PREPARATION

The sites for growing tender perennials are very varied, including both formal flower beds and positions among permanent plantings of shrubs, roses and herbaceous plants. In general, tender perennials, like most plants, enjoy a well-prepared soil. This will mean digging or loosening the soil to a depth of about 20–30cm (8–12 in) and incorporating garden compost or some other source of organic matter. A base dressing of a balanced general fertilizer will also be beneficial; with the rapid speed of growth of most tender perennials there is a need for a fairly rich soil to support such growth, although too much nitrogen should be avoided or there will be an excess of foliage at the expense of flowers. When preparing to plant among shrubs or other permanent plantings, take care to avoid damaging existing roots. Some compost and base fertilizer should be lightly forked in. A few plants, for example osteospermums, like a poorer soil or they will make large, lush, leafy plants that do not flower and subsequently do not overwinter if left in place.

Most tender perennials like a well-drained soil and this is particularly important for those plants that are intended to overwinter outside. Incorporate a good dressing of sharp grit at the preparation stage and make sure that there is no soil compaction to prevent good drainage.

PLANTING OUT

In any planting scheme, it helps to lay out the plants in their pots to check spacing and the general balance of the constituents before actually planting them in the soil. This is particularly important with large schemes. Plants from large pots are usually planted first, using a spade. The smaller type sold as a border spade is a very comfortable tool to use for this. The smaller plants are then planted with a trowel. Firm planting is the norm and unless rain is imminent plants should always be watered in gently but thoroughly.

Compact species such as felicia, nemesia, cuphea and verbena are generally planted quite close at around 23–30 cm (9–12 in) apart, with the taller and shrubby types such as argyranthemum, salvia and phygelius 38–45 cm (15–18 in) apart. Generally, tender perennials cover more space than seed-raised bedding plants, so fewer plants are needed to cover the ground. Most trowels are approximately 23–30 cm (9–12 in) long and this is a useful guide for planting at the front of the border. Never plant closer than a trowel's length to grass edges.

SUMMER CARE

Tender perennials do not need excessive care during the summer. Weeding to reduce competition is essential, as it would be in any planting. Watering will help to promote growth in dry seasons, although many tender perennials will tolerate dry conditions once established and a few such as gazanias, arctotis and osteospermums will give the best displays when dryish. Some of the greedy feeders such as cannas, dahlias, fuchsias and pelargoniums respond well to liquid feeding. Such a feed should have a high potash content to encourage flower rather than leaf at this stage.

A few tender perennials, for example abutilons, need staking, as will any plant that is grown as a standard or pillar. Be sure to provide a good stout cane or light stake on planting or damage can ensue if windy conditions prevail.

Dead-heading is a desirable but tedious exercise. It both tidies up a display and also encourages further flowering in species that readily set seed. With some small-flowered types, this can be very laborious and it may be quicker and easier to trim over the whole plant with shears or secateurs. A light feed and adequate water will usually cause the plant to flush into fresh new growth and repeated flower. Nemesias, diascias, verbenas and even argyranthemums will respond well to this treatment.

Young cordylines can be lifted at the end of each season, but in time they will become too big for this and can be left outside.

The roots of dahlias must be lifted at the end of each season and stored in frost-free conditions.

Sometimes tender perennials flower so copiously that it can be difficult to find suitable propagation material. If you require large quantities of autumn cuttings for propagation purposes, trim a few plants over in late summer to encourage a flush of fresh shoots suitable for taking as cuttings in early autumn. This is not normally necessary if only small quantities are required.

END-OF-SEASON CARE
Generally little else is required for a good display of tender perennials that will continue to grow and flower until the frost. If you wish to overwinter stock or specimen plants rather than just rooted cuttings, take those plants under cover before the risk of the first frosts. Lift them carefully, trim them back if they are too big and pot them in a suitable pot with a good potting compost. After watering in, stand them in a shady position for a few days until the plant recovers from the check of moving. Before taking them back under glass it is also important to examine them for any pests or diseases and spray if necessary. Such plants will be of

value as stock for spring cuttings or as specimens for future years.

Plants to overwinter
The following list is of plants that are likely to be planted out for summer display and are worth growing on to a second year.

Arundo donax 'Variegata'
Canna – cut down tops and dig up rhizomes to overwinter
Cordyline australis and cultivars
Cosmos atrosanguineus – dig up tubers
Dahlia cultivars – dig up tubers for overwintering
Ensete ventricosum
Fuchsia cultivars especially standards
Hedychium – cut down tops and dig up roots for overwintering
Melianthus major
Pelargonium – standards
Plumbago auriculata.

Appendix 1 *Where to See Tender Perennials*

With the increasing popularity of tender perennials in recent years, there will be few notable gardens that do not include at least a few in chosen spots for particular effects. The gardens listed below have a particularly wide range of these plants or display them especially well. By the very nature of tender perennials, their displays are only likely to be worth visiting during the summer months. For checking times, *The Yellow Book* can be purchased in many booksellers in the UK. The National Trust can be contacted through PO Box 39, Bromley, Kent BR1 3XL.

THE GARDENS

Abbotsbury Sub-Tropical Gardens
The low rainfall and shelter gives an ideal location for growing the many tender plants for which this 8 hectare (20 acre) garden is noted. Some of the original 19th-century introductions such as palms and tree ferns are of formidable size. Open mid-March to mid-October. On the B3157, 15 km (9 miles) west of Weymouth, Dorset.

Bristol Zoological Gardens
This unexpected horticultural oasis is a small gem of traditional horticulture with many time-honoured garden features. The formal bedding which is still carried out on a grand scale includes many tender perennials grown to excellence: standard lantanas and *Centaurea gymnocarpa*, old-fashioned heliotropes, cannas, verbenas, geraniums, abutilons, salvias, iresines and many more. There is usually a subtropical border and the cannas are often interplanted with gladiolus, a 19th-century trick that gives the impression of early canna flowers. There are also urns, baskets and planters. Downs Road, Clifton, Bristol.

Coleton Fishacre
Here is all that one could expect of a West Country garden, lying in a sheltered valley that runs down to the sea near Salcombe. Once the home of the D'Oyley Cartes, it is now owned by the National Trust. Tender plants can be found throughout its 8 hectares (20 acres), but there are particular concentrations in the rill garden and the terraces near the house. The four beds surrounding a Jekyll-style stone-edged rill are packed with tender perennials – cannas, argyranthemums, diascias, felicias and many more. The walls are clad with *Callistemon*, *Leptospermum lanigerum*, *Vestia foetida*, *Hibbertia aspera* and many others. The terraces near the house also display many good tender perennials including deep maroon penstemons, spiky beschornerias, grevilleas, corresa and hakeas. For opening refer to the National Trust handbook. 5 km (3 miles) from Kingswear, near Dartmouth, Devon.

Glanleam Subtropical Gardens
As Europe's most westerly garden, this is not surprisingly the mildest in Ireland. These 15 hectares (38 acres) date from the 1830s and are filled with southern hemisphere plants. The *Dicksonia antarctica* have reached rain-forest proportions. Many of the tender plantings here are permanent and amazingly mature. Open all the year round from 11am to 7pm. It is situated on the north-east edge of Valentia Island, off the coast of Co. Kerry, Eire.

Great Dixter
When in 1993 Christopher Lloyd ripped out the roses from the traditional 1911 rose garden designed by Lutyens, there was a howl of protest from traditionalists and particularly so because he replanted it in an exotic style with tender perennials. However, this doyen of gardening literature was not deterred and has achieved a notable composition of exotic luxuriance.

Bold foliage is a key theme within the design, with big blocks of *Canna musifolia*, *Ricinus communis* 'Carmencita', *Musa basjoo*, an almost hardy banana, and spiky-leaved yuccas. Each part of the garden is planted with carefully orchestrated groups such as the salmon-flowered *Canna* 'Louis Cayeux' together with the grey and rose wands of *Phormium* 'Sundowner'. The virulent yellow stripes of *Canna* 'Striata' are contrasted with the dark red flowers and bronze foliage of *Dahlia* 'Bishop of Llandaff'.

As well as foliage there is a wealth of flowering plants, with annuals such as stately white towers of *Nicotiana sylvestris*, the exotic tomato-red trumpets of *Brugmansia sanguinea* and, through all, the threads of mauve *Verbena bonariensis*. *Ailanthus altissima* and *Paulownia tomentosa* are stooled annually, resulting in vigorous regrowth and enormous leaves at an acceptable level. Open most afternoons from April to October. Near to Northiam, 19 km (12 miles) north of Hastings, Sussex.

Kew Gardens

One would expect a botanic garden to have a wide range of plants but it is often forgotten that Kew specializes in species rather than garden cultivars. However, it is in the annual bedding displays that there is an exception to this policy and in the many beds along the Broad Walk and other areas are often found an amazing range of well-labelled tender perennials. The vast formal area in front of the Palm House also has similar formal displays. Many of the plants that Kew uses are unusual, although not normally rare, and it would not be surprising to find vegetables and herbs mixed in with annuals and tender perennials in such schemes. Open daily. Kew Green, Richmond, just south of Kew Bridge, Surrey.

Le Jardin Exotique de Roscoff

Located within a few minutes of the ferry terminal at Roscoff, Brittany, this garden can easily be missed unless you are looking for it. The 1.5 hectare (3¾ acre) garden is owned by a group of keen amateurs and is open at some time most of the year. The wide range of exotic and tender plants include genera from South Africa, New Zealand, Tasmania, Australia, South America, the Canaries and Madeira.

Lamorran House

This garden is owned by Mr Dudley-Cooke, who has created 1.6 hectares (4 acres) of hillside gardens with views out to St Anthony's Head. Palms, cycads, agaves and many other tender exotics fill this garden. For opening times see *The Yellow Book*. Upper Castle Road, St Mawes, Cornwall.

La Mortola

An historic garden which was laid out in the 19th century and nearly disappeared into oblivion until it was rescued and restored in recent years. Situated on a rocky promontory stretching out into the Mediterranean, just across the Italian border from France, it has a perfect mild climate. Tender plants from Australia, Mexico, South Africa, Madeira, Bolivia and Argentina thrive side by side.

Marwood Hill

This 8 hectare (20 acre) garden has interest for gardeners with a wide range of tastes but in particular it includes a good collection of Australian and New Zealand plants as well as other tender shrubs and climbers. It holds the National Collection of *Tulbaghia*. Open throughout the year. 6.4 km (4 miles) north of Barnstaple in the village of Marwood, Devon.

Overbecks

Another gem of a plant fanatic's garden, owned by the National Trust. The setting overlooking the Salcombe estuary is in itself almost Mediterranean. The sheltered microclimate supports a wide range of plants of border-line hardiness, including many that we would normally think of as tender but survive and even thrive outside at Overbecks. As well as the many garden plantings, there is a well-stocked conservatory with pelargoniums, brugmansias and abutilons. For opening times see the National Trust handbook. 2.4 km (1½ miles) south-west of Salcombe, Devon.

Powis Castle

Powis Castle in Wales would not generally be classed as an exotic garden but it contains an excellent 'tropical' border as well as a fine display of tender perennials in classical containers. The border is sited along one of the wide terraces at the base of the castle and has been planted in a tropical style for many years. A permanent framework is provided by yuccas, phormiums, olearias, stooled paulownia, *Canna iridiflora* treated as a permanent resident and the lovely climber *Mutisia ilicifolia* with its pink daisy flowers. To this is added an annual planting of osteospermums, argyranthemums, salvias and brugmansia.

Across the balustrades and in the niches of the castle and its terraces are numerous huge pots filled each year with a mix of old favourites such as *Pelargonium* 'The Boar', *Fuchsia* 'Thalia' and *Helichysum petiolare* or adventurous combinations such as the funereal *Salvia guaranitica*, scarlet *Tropaeolum majus* 'Hermine Grashoff' and the silvery trails of *Lotus maculatus*. For opening times see the National Trust handbook. 1.6 km (1 mile) south of Welshpool in Powys.

Rosemoor

This RHS garden located in rural Devon also features tender perennials. The main displays here are in four long borders alongside the main terrace in front of the entrance building. They are grown among permanent plantings of tender shrubs, roses and herbaceous plants. Plants are grouped in good large drifts and well labelled. Although a West Country garden, Rosemoor is set in a frost pocket, so apart from the displays mentioned there are few permanent tender plants in this garden. Some can be found in the sheltered areas around the house and nearby gardens. Open throughout the year. On B3320, 1.6 km (1 mile) south-east of Great Torrington, Devon.

RHS Gardens Wisley

A lovely garden that includes tender perennials in many of its displays throughout the garden. The summer garden particularly includes many argyranthemums, verbenas, felicias, penstemons, arctotis and many more in a classical mixed planting with shrubs, roses and hardy herbaceous plants.

Near to the old laboratory building there is usually an impressive traditional carpet bed with alternantheras, echevarias, coleus, agaves and others. Near to the glasshouse range can often be found a long subtropical border featuring a host of well-grown cannas and other exotics. Various small demonstration beds in this area often include tender perennials in displays that change each year.

In recent years, the RHS has trialled a number of tender perennials and the results of these trials have sorted out many problems of nomenclature as well as earmarking the best plants for garden use by means of the AGM system. Penstemons, argyranthemums, salvias and gazanias have featured in recent years. Within the glasshouse range will also be found many of the conservatory plants mentioned in this book, as well as a superb collection of well-grown coleus (*Solenostemon*). The plant centre at Wisley often displays a good range of tender perennials for sale. Open daily throughout the year. Just off the A3, 11 km (7 miles) from Guildford, near Woking, Surrey.

Ventnor Botanic Gardens

The mild maritime climate of this 9 hectare (22 acre) garden encourages the growth of an amazing range of tender plants. The garden has been almost totally restored since the 1987 storm which almost destroyed it. The Mediterranean Terrace, the South African and Australian Banks, the Victorian Sub-Tropical Palm Garden, the New Zealand Garden and the Walled Garden all contain many interesting tender plants. There is also an impressive Temperate House with a wide range of plants from the southern hemisphere and some of the Oceanic Islands. There are mouth-watering collections of phormium, salvia, hebe, argyranthemum, euryops, olearia, osteospermum, tender geraniums and the National Collection of Pseudopanax. Open daily. Undercliffe Drive, Ventnor, Isle of Wight.

NATIONAL COLLECTIONS

Although the National Collections are approved and listed by the National Council for the Conservation of Plants and Gardens (NCCPG), they mostly represent personal collections made by individuals, organizations and sometimes commercial nurseries. Here will usually be found some of the finest individual plant collections within the country and also the greatest accumulation of knowledge on those particular plants.

They are all open to the public on occasions and for opening arrangements the reader should consult *The National Collections Directory*, which is published annually. There are sometimes plants for sale at these gardens and nurseries that cannot be obtained anywhere else. The National Council for the Conservation of Plants and Gardens is based at The Pines, Wisley, Woking, Surrey GU23 6QP.

Abutilon

N. Rigden, Somerset College of Agriculture and Horticulture, Cannington, Bridgwater, Somerset TA5 2LS (2 species and 22 cultivars)
N. Sayers, 105 Nutley Crescent, Goring-by-Sea, W. Sussex BN12 4LB (3 species, 16 cultivars)

Argyranthemum

N. Rigden, Somerset College of Agriculture and Horticulture, Cannington, Bridgwater, Somerset TA5 2LS (8 species and 23 cultivars)

Canna

Ian Cooke, Brockings, North Petherwin, Launceston, Cornwall PL15 8LW (12 species and 85 cultivars)

Citrus

T. E. Read, Reads Nursery, Hales Hall, Loddon, Norfolk NR14 6QW (74 species and cultivars)

Coleus (Solenostemon)

Ian Cooke, Brockings, North Petherwin, Launceston, Cornwall PL15 8LW (70 cultivars)

Coprosma

G. Hutchins, County Park Nursery, Hornchurch, Essex RM11 3BU (26 species, 50 cultivars)

Dahlia

D. L. Brown, Cornish Dahlias (Rosewarne), 34 Cosawes Park, Perranarworthal, Truro, Cornwall, TR14 0AB (1500 cultivars and species)

Diascia

W. Boulby, Church View Cottage, Barmby Moor, York (16 species and 64 cultivars)

Grevillea

Shirley Clemo, Pine Lodge Gardens, Cuddra, St Austell, Cornwall PL25 3RQ (7 species and 8 cultivars)

Hedychium

Ken and Lyn Spencer-Mills, Hoopers Holding, 45 High Street, Hinton St George, Crewkerne, Somerset TA17 8SE (24 species and 19 cultivars)

Osteospermum

N. Rigden, Somerset College of Agriculture and Horticulture, Cannington, Bridgwater, Somerset TA5 2LS (2 species and 21 cultivars)

Mr and Mrs Simpson, Moor House, Brereton Heath Lane, Somerford, Congleton, Cheshire, CW12 4SZ (2 species and 38 cultivars)

Pelargonium

Fibrex Nurseries, Honeybourne Road, Pebworth, Stratford-upon-Avon, Warwicks CV37 8XT (145 species and 1677 cultivars)

Penstemon

Kingston Maurward Gardens, Kingston Maurward, Dorchester, Dorset DT2 8PY (45 cultivars)

Clive and Cathy Gandley, Highwood House, Culm Davy, Hemyock, Cullompton, Devon EX15 3UU (87 species and 118 cultivars)

Pershore College of Horticulture, Pershore, Worcs WR10 3JP (130 species and cultivars)

Mr and Mrs Pitman, Mews Cottage, 34 Easton St, Portland, Dorset DT5 1BT (155 species and cultivars)

The National Trust, Rowallane Garden, Saintfield, Ballynahinch, Co Down, NI, BT24 7LH (54 large-flowered hybrids)

Phormium

The National Trust, Mount Stewart Garden, Grey Abbey, Newtownards, Co. Down, NI, BT22 2AD (2 species and 27 forms)

Phygelius

Neil Lucas, Knoll Gardens, Hampreston, Wimborne, Dorset BH21 7ND (2 species and 12 cultivars)

Salvia

Kingston Maurward Gardens, Kingston Maurward, Dorchester, Dorset DT2 8PY (90 species and cultivars)

Mr and Mrs B. D. Yeo, Pleasant View Nursery, Two Mile Oak, Denbury, Newton Abbot, Devon TQ12 6DG (200 species and cultivars)

Appendix 11 *Where to Buy Tender Perennials*

NURSERIES

Relatively few nurseries specialize in tender perennials, although a great many stock a limited range as additions to their main specialisms. This can make obtaining plants difficult.

In the UK, the well-established publication *The Plant Finder* lists thousands of plants and the nurseries that grow them. Those searching for a specific plant can often find it via this publication and a few phone calls. For really rare plants it may be necessary to add your name to a waiting list.

Many, although not all, specialist nurseries offer a mail order service. This may have restrictions such as mini-mum orders or certain despatch seasons that do not always match when one would wish to buy tender perennials.

At a less specialist level, tender perennials are most widely available during the late spring and early and mid-summer period. Garden centres will stock a basic range and sometimes some unusual types may be found, espe-cially some novelties that are appearing for the first time. In recent years more and more plants are available as part-grown plugs which can, with basic protection, be grown on to maturity. Generally they are very economical and rapidly make good plants without the hassle of propa-gation. Visits to markets, car boot sales and traditional nurseries may also be productive.

Conservatory plants will either be found among ten-der perennials or in specialist displays of plants for conservatories. Full-grown display specimens can be very expensive, so it is worth checking out prices and plant sizes carefully.

For the serious plant collector, flower shows and rare plant fairs are a must. It is here that many specialist nurseries will be showing and selling and may have the small quantities of unusual plants that are often not listed in catalogues. Don't be late – serious plant-hunters get up early!

UK

Brian and Heather Hiley, 25 Little Woodcote Estate, Wallington, Surrey SM5 4AU – Tender perennials and hardy plants, good ranges of penstemon, salvia and grasses. Attractive demonstration area and small garden.

Brockings Exotics, North Petherwin, Launceston PL15 8LW – Specialists in tender perennials, many argyranthemums, abutilons, osteospermum and others, together with the National Collections of Canna and named Coleus (Solenostemon).

Burncoose and South Down Nurseries, Gwennap, Redruth, Cornwall TR16 6BJ – Extensive range of plants including many tender perennials and a 12 hectare (30 acre) garden.

Cannington College Plant Centre, Cannington, Bridgwater, Somerset TA5 2LS – Specialities linked with the college's plant collections: abutilon, argyranthemum, ceanothus, osteospermum, salvia, felicia, diascia and euryops. Some display gardens.

Drysdale Garden Exotics, Bowerwood Road, Fordingbridge, Hampshire SP6 1BN – Fairly wide range of mainly hardy plants but chosen for exotic effect. Many bamboos from the National Collection.

Duchy of Cornwall Nursery, Cott Road, Lostwithiel, Cornwall PL22 0BW – Amazing range of shrubs, trees and tender plants all grown in the nursery. Good for Mediterranean and exotic shrubs rather than 'patio plants'. Good ranges of cordyline, phormium and conservatory plants.

The Palm Centre, 563 Upper Richmond Road West, London SW14 7ED – Palms, cycads, hardy and tender exotics.

Hardy Exotics, Gilly Lane, Whitecross, Penzance, Cornwall TR20 8BZ –Trees and shrubs to create tropical and desert effects. Both hardy plants and tender perennials for gardens, patios and conservatories.

Hayloft Plants, Cooks Hill, Wick, Pershore, Worcestershire WR10 3PA – Mail-order firm specializing in tender perennials and basket plants. Fair range supplied as plugs of various sizes.

Hopley's Plants Ltd, High Street, Much Hadham, Hertfordshire SG10 6BU – Wide range of unusual plants with many tender perennials. Large garden showing much of plant range grown to maturity.

Lower Ickenfield Farm Nurseries, Meadle, Princes Risborough, Aylesbury, Bucks HP17 9TX – Wide range of basket and patio plants including many argyranthemums. No mail order.

Special Plants, Laurels Farm, Upper Wraxall, Chippenham, Wilts SN14 7AG – Wide range of tender perennials and conservatory plants, including many new South African introductions.

Ray and Val Hubbard, Hill House, Landscove, South Devon – Treasure trove of tender perennials and hardy plants, many types of fuchsia, argyranthemum, garden and conservatory plants. No mail order. 1.2 hectare (3 acre) garden once owned by Edward Hyams and described as it was in his time in his classic book *An Englishman's Garden*.

Reads of Norfolk, Hales Hall, Loddon, Norfolk NR14 6QW – This traditional nursery specializes in conservatory plants, citrus, vines and various hardy plants. Enormous range, many bougainvilleas, passifloras, neriums, lantanas and abutilons.

Chessington Nurseries, Leatherhead Road, Chessington, Surrey KT9 2NG – Specialist in conservatory and plants for the terrace. Passiflora, citrus, bougainvillea, brugmansias and many others.

Architectural Plants, Cooks Farm, Nuthurst, Horsham, West Sussex RH13 6LH – A fascinating nursery full of plants with dramatic foliage or interesting shapes, mainly hardy but all very exotic-looking. Some tender plants such as the purple-leaved form of *Ensete ventricosum*, gingers, cannas and spiky plants.

USA

Logee's Greenhouses, 141 North Street, Danielson, Connecticut T06239 – Tropical and subtropical shrubs, vines, tender perennials, begonias and geraniums.

Color Farm, 2710 Thornhill Road, Auburndale, Florida 33823 – Specialist coleus nursery.

Horn Canna Farm Route One, Carnegie, Oklahoma – Specialist canna nursery.

TyTy Plantation Bulb Co Box 159, TyTy, Georgia 31795 – Specialist canna nursery.

Kelly's Plant World, 10266 E. Princeton, Sanger, CA 93657 – Specialist canna nursery.

France

Pierre Turc et Fils, Les Richelets, 49630, Maze, France – Specialist canna nursery.

New Zealand

Podgora Gardens, Shoemaker Road, PO Box 46, Waipu, North Island, New Zealand – Specialist canna nursery.

SPECIALIST SEED FIRMS

Chiltern Seeds, Bortree Stile, Ulverston, Cumbria LA12 7PB – Wide range of seeds, many unusual, and a proportion of 'Mediterranean' seeds.

Thompson & Morgan, London Road, Ipswich, Suffolk IP2 0BA – A very wide selection of seeds from all over the world.

The Botanical Society of South Africa, Kirstenbosch Botanical Garden, Private Bag X7, Claremont 7735, CP, South Africa – Seeds of many unusual trees, succulents and 'Mediterranean' plants.

SOCIETIES

Half Hardy Group

This is a specialist group within the Hardy Plant Society that brings together a wide-ranging group whose interests embrace any plant on the borderline of hardiness. Their publication *Borderlines* is produced twice a year and there are events and garden and nursery visits arranged from time to time. The organizers can be contacted through the Hardy Plant Society, based at Little Orchard, Great Comberton, Pershore, Worcs WR10 3DP, UK

Mediterranean Garden Society, Sparoza, PO 14, Peania, 19002, Greece.

The Australasian Plant Society

Specializes in plants from Australia and New Zealand. Offers a substantial twice-yearly newsletter, *Pentachondra*, and a fascinating seed list. Secretary: Jeff Irons, 'Stonecourt', 74 Brimstage Road, Heswall, Wirral, Cheshire L60 1XQ, UK

International Heliconia Society

Devoted to the appreciation of the genus *Heliconia* and other related plants such as Musaceae, Strelitziaceae, Cannaceae, Costaceae, Zingiberaceae and Marantaceae. Flamingo Gardens, 3750 Flamingo Road, Fort Lauderdale, Florida 33330, USA.

IMPORTING PLANTS

Sooner or later the keen gardener may wish to import plants from abroad, either as a result of a spontaneous purchase on holiday or through a particular plant search that has culminated at a foreign nursery. Purchasing is easy but ensuring that plants make their way through customs, legally and without delay, can be a major problem.

Since 1993 it has been legal to transport plants between the various countries of the European Union (EU) as long as they have been grown in the EU. Travellers returning from non-EU countries within the Euro-Mediterranean area may bring back a maximum of five plants, 2 kg (4¼ lb) of bulbs, corms or tubers and five packets of seed. Such concessions are based on the plants being free from visible pests and diseases, being for domestic use and being carried in personal baggage.

A few plants such as chrysanthemums, potatoes, pelargoniums and grasses have restrictions. Remember that some wild plants may be rare and covered by the CITES agreement (Convention on International Trade in Endangered Species.) Examples of such plants are cyclamen, orchids and cacti. In general travellers should not dig up attractive native plants.

Importing plants from one country to another outside the EU can be very difficult and will require a phytosanitary certificate which indicates that the plants are free from pests and diseases on arrival. Plants may be inspected in the country of origin and on arrival in the country of importation. The process is complicated and there are many pitfalls, not the least of which can be delays, which mean that when plants eventually arrive they may no longer be viable. Some foreign nurseries are willing to do all the necessary procedures but the cost can be prohibitive for a small order of plants.

Anyone seriously wishing to bring plants back home after a holiday or to import from a foreign nursery would do well to prepare thoroughly in advance. In the UK, the Plant Health Division of the MAFF can be contacted at: Plant Health Division, Ministry of Agriculture, Fisheries and Food, Foss House, 1/2 Peasholme Green, Kings Pool, York YO1 2PX. There are a number of local Plant Health and Seeds Inspectorates which can be located under the MAFF in local directories.

Large pale salmon flowers and a compact form make *Canna* 'Gnom' a popular choice with gardeners.

Appendix III *Origins of Tender Perennials*

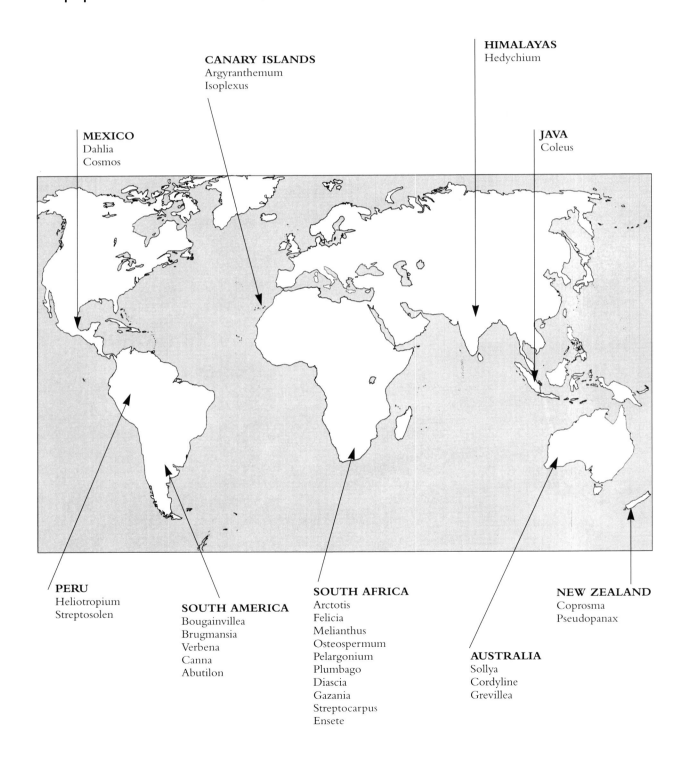

HIMALAYAS
Hedychium

CANARY ISLANDS
Argyranthemum
Isoplexus

JAVA
Coleus

MEXICO
Dahlia
Cosmos

PERU
Heliotropium
Streptosolen

SOUTH AMERICA
Bougainvillea
Brugmansia
Verbena
Canna
Abutilon

SOUTH AFRICA
Arctotis
Felicia
Melianthus
Osteospermum
Pelargonium
Plumbago
Diascia
Gazania
Streptocarpus
Ensete

NEW ZEALAND
Coprosma
Pseudopanax

AUSTRALIA
Sollya
Cordyline
Grevillea

Index